# THERE BEFORE US

# THERE BEFORE US

*Religion, Literature, and Culture*
*from Emerson to Wendell Berry*

*Edited by*

Roger Lundin

WILLIAM B. EERDMANS PUBLISHING COMPANY

GRAND RAPIDS, MICHIGAN / CAMBRIDGE, U.K.

Wm. B. Eerdmans Publishing Co.

2140 Oak Industrial Drive N.E., Grand Rapids, Michigan 49505 /

P.O. Box 163, Cambridge CB3 9PU U.K.

www.eerdmans.com

Printed in the United States of America

12 11 10 09 08 07      7 6 5 4 3 2 1

**Library of Congress Cataloging-in-Publication Data**

There before us: religion, literature, and culture from Emerson to Wendell Berry /
   edited by Roger Lundin.
      p.      cm.
   ISBN 978-0-8028-2963-4 (pbk.: alk. paper)
   1. Religion in literature.   2. American literature — 19th century — History
and criticism.   3. American literature — 20th century — History and criticism.
   4. Religion and literature — United States — History.   I. Lundin, Roger.

PS166.T47 2007
810.9′382 — dc22

                                                          2006013770

The editor and publisher gratefully acknowledge permission to reprint material from the
following sources:

"'Rare and Delectable Places': Thoreau's Imagination of Sacred Space at Walden" by John
Gatta is reprinted from MAKING NATURE SACRED by John Gotta, © 2004 by Oxford
University Press, Inc. Used by permission.

Selected poems by Emily Dickinson are reprinted by permission of the publishers and the
Trustees of Amherst College from THE POEMS OF EMILY DICKINSON: READING
EDITION, edited by Ralph W. Franklin, Cambridge, Mass.: The Belknap Press of Harvard
University Press. Copyright © 1998, 1999 by the President and Fellows of Harvard College.
Copyright © 1951, 1955, 1979, 1983, by the President and Fellows of Harvard College.

# Contents

Contents

# Acknowledgments

L IKE ALL of the work of the American Literature and Religion Project, this book would not have been possible without a generous
grant from the Pew Christian Scholars Program at the University of Notre Dame. Each of us who has been involved in this project over the past
five years owes special thanks to Nathan Hatch, Michael Hamilton, and
Kurt Berends for their skillful leadership of the overall program and their
unstinting support of our particular labors.

Our project was co-sponsored by the Erasmus Institute at Notre
Dame. In 1999 James Turner, the Institute's founder, provided funding
for the working group that eventually led to formation of the American
Literature and Religion Seminar. I thank Jim and his successor Robert
Sullivan for their initial encouragement as well as for their ongoing sup-
port of our work.

I am grateful to Wheaton College for a sabbatical leave that enabled
me to complete my work on this volume and for the college's generous
support of my travel and research needs.

Finally, I want to thank several people who are not represented in
these pages but who nonetheless contributed vitally to the work of the
seminar. Matt Lundin offered splendid assistance with the planning of
our initial symposium and provided able editorial help with this manuscript. And as ongoing members of the seminar, James Dougherty, Brian
Ingraffia, and Ralph Wood made excellent contributions to our discussions of these essays and related works on our project theme.

# Contributors

**Katherine Clay Bassard** is associate professor of English at Virginia Commonwealth University. She is the author of *Spiritual Interrogations: Culture, Gender, and Community in Early African American Women's Writing* (Princeton).

**Lawrence Buell** is the Powell M. Cabot Professor of American Literature at Harvard University. He is the author of numerous studies of the literature of the United States, including *New England Literary Culture: From Revolution through Renaissance* (Cambridge), *The Environmental Imagination: Thoreau, Nature Writing, and the Formation of American Culture* (Harvard), and *Emerson* (Harvard).

**Harold K. Bush, Jr.**, is associate professor of English at Saint Louis University. He is the author of *American Declarations: Rebellion and Repentance in American Cultural History* (Illinois).

**Michael Colacurcio** is Distinguished Professor of English at UCLA. He has written extensively on the literature of New England, and his works include *The Province of Piety: Moral History in Hawthorne's Early Tales* (Harvard), *Doctrine and Difference: Essays in the Literature of New England* (Routledge), and *Godly Letters: The Literature of the American Puritans* (Notre Dame).

**Andrew Delbanco** is the Julian Clarence Levi Professor in the Humanities at Columbia University. He is a frequent contributor to *The New York*

*Review of Books* and *The New Republic* and is the author of *The Death of Satan: How Americans Have Lost the Sense of Evil* (Farrar, Straus, and Giroux), *The Real American Dream: A Meditation on Hope* (Harvard), and *Melville: His World and Work* (Knopf).

**John Gatta** taught for three decades at the University of Connecticut and is currently associate dean of the college at Sewanee: The University of the South. He is the author of *American Madonna: Images of the Divine Woman in Literary Culture* (Oxford) and *Making Nature Sacred: Literature, Religion, and Environment in America from the Puritans to the Present* (Oxford).

**Roger Lundin** is the Blanchard Professor of English at Wheaton College. From 2000-2005, he served as the Director of the American Literature and Religion Project. He has written several books on the intersection of theology, literature, and culture, including *Emily Dickinson and the Art of Belief* (Eerdmans) and *From Nature to Experience: The American Search for Cultural Authority* (Rowman and Littlefield).

**Gail McDonald** is senior lecturer in English at the University of Southampton. She is the author of *Learning to Be Modern: Pound, Eliot, and the American University* (Oxford) and *American Literature and Culture 1900-1961: An Introduction* (Blackwell).

**Barbara Packer** is professor of English at UCLA. She has written widely on the literature of nineteenth-century New England and is the author of *Emerson's Fall: A New Interpretation of the Major Essays* (Continuum).

**M. D. Walhout** is professor of English at Seattle Pacific University. He is the co-editor of *Literature and the Renewal of the Public Sphere* (St. Martin's).

# Introduction

*Roger Lundin*

N EAR THE CLOSE of Alfred Kazin's distinguished six-decade career as a literary critic, the novelist Robert Stone went to hear his fellow countryman speak about the state of literature in their native land. The venue was the Harbourfront Literary Festival in Toronto, Canada, and the lecture focused on the book that proved to be the critic's last, *God and the American Writer.* The subject of the talk was "American writers and their uneasy relations with the numinous," and according to Stone, Kazin's performance that day was animated by his longstanding passion for "the God-infused, post-Calvinist literature of America."[1]

Yet not everyone in his Toronto audience shared Kazin's passion for this topic. As the critic concluded his remarks, a listener seated behind Stone "remarked to his companion, with bitter humor, 'Why do they have this thing about themselves and God?'" The novelist reports that "at that point the Holy Spirit descended upon me and I was moved to reply," but he hesitated, thought twice about where he was, and kept his polite silence.

This was Toronto, after all. In this city where everything is "clean," "everything works," "crime is discouraged," and "the subway routes are comprehensible," how could he, Robert Stone, an *American,* begin to explain his nation's obsession with "the power of Almighty God" or its ter-

---

1. Robert Stone, "American Apostle," *The New York Review of Books* 45 (26 Mar. 1998), http://www.nybooks.com/articles/906.html.

rifying sense of its own failure? Take a look at the United States from a Canadian vantage point, Stone says, and "it's impossible not to wonder: Where did we go wrong?"

Yet at the same time, the novelist mused, was it possible that this Canadian man somehow did "not know, after all, that the Lord had led Americans, alone among the world's peoples, out of bondage" for the purpose of redeeming the whole world? Did this man not realize that to humble "these fawners, parading with baubles, heathen honors, and jeweled crosses" in Toronto and elsewhere, "we [the people of America] had been raised up, appointed a City on a Hill, a light unto the nations?"

"Probably not," Stone concludes. After all, no doubt this man from the North "had come of age during the Vietnam War. All the rest" — all that business about God, human destiny, and the City upon a Hill — "would probably have been news to him. He might even, in invincible ignorance of the Word, have rejected it."

If in response to the novelist's gibes, the Canadian skeptic were to plead innocent on the grounds of cultural distance, what is to account for the ongoing mystification of many of Stone's contemporaries about this "thing" that writers in the United States have had for so long about "themselves and God?" How are we to explain the fact that so many academic observers of the literature of the United States have, in effect, expatriated themselves from one of their culture's most vibrant and fascinating provinces?

## The Invisible Domain Before Us

A decade ago, the late Jenny Franchot called religion the "invisible domain" of the study of literature in the United States: "We are rich in studies that foreground gender, race, and to a lesser extent, ethnicity and class. But where is religion? Why so invisible?" The invisibility of religion in American literary studies, she lamented, has produced "a singularly biased scholarship." Because intellectuals rarely regard as significant something they themselves neither practice nor profess, the neglect of the serious study of religion in American literary criticism "may reflect how unimportant religion is in the lives of literary scholars." Such narrowness of focus may be an inevitable component of contemporary intellectual life in general, but according to Franchot, it is "especially ruinous" in the particular study of American culture, "since America has been and continues to be manifestly religious in complex and intriguing ways. And not only America but American literature." As a consequence of this neglect, the study of that literature's enduring struggle with the "invisibles" has itself become an "invisible domain."[2]

*There Before Us* seeks to bring the activities of that domain to light. The authors of these essays have all been participants in the American Literature and Religion Seminar, an ongoing project sponsored by the Pew Charitable Trusts and co-sponsored by the Erasmus Institute at the University of Notre Dame. For the past five years, the seminar has explored the interplay of religion and literature in the United States from the time of Emerson to the present. It has trained its sights primarily, though not exclusively, on the influence of Judaism and Christianity on that literature. The reason for this focus has to do with cultural history more than anything else; over the period covered here (from the 1830s to the present), virtually all of the major writers of the United States proved to be products of Jewish and Christian culture, and their works show the enduring impact of their religious traditions, even in those instances where the authors shed any specific commitments to these historic faiths.

The scholars who have participated in the American Literature and Religion Seminar have themselves come from a variety of faith traditions within Judaism and Christianity. The following essays employ a richly varied set of interpretive practices, and they assume in some cases widely different stances towards the substance of religious belief. Yet at the same

---

2. Jenny Franchot, "Invisible Domain: Religion and American Literary Studies," *American Literature* 67 (1995): 834, 839. Franchot provides a concise account of the theoretical background to this neglect of religion: "Literary theory has further tended to marginalize interest in institutionalized religion and the more private regions of the 'interior life' as naïve unless those regions are subordinated to the domain of linguistic representation or to the critiques of Marx, Nietzsche, Freud, and Foucault. In the wake of these thinkers, religion (like aesthetic form more generally) has become that which inhibits, transmutes, or enables political change but is hardly ever an achievement whose priorities take precedence over the social." "Invisible Domain," p. 834.

time, what these authors share without question is a marked commitment to the serious study of the role of religion in American literature.[3]

That commitment manifests itself in a manner that I might best describe by referring to the passage of poetry that has lent this book its title. It is from a Richard Wilbur poem, "Lying." This lyric ranges widely across a number of topics but focuses particularly upon questions that have to do with language and its capacity both to tell the truth and to forward a lie. According to the poem, the act of lying can take many forms, including that of imagining scenarios that do not or cannot exist. The speaker of the poem notes that "in the strict sense," we do not invent anything, "merely bearing witness / To what each morning brings again to light." Much of what we see, from "gold crosses" to "turbine-vents," astonishes us, but most remarkable of all is the fact that

> All those things
> Are there before us; there before we look
> Or fail to look; there to be seen or not
> By us . . . .[4]

To the student of American culture, this is true of religious belief and experience as well. They are "there before us" — behind us in our cultural past and all about us in our cultural space. And whether we are pleased or bedeviled by this fact, throughout the course of U.S. history, deeply felt and sometimes devastatingly held religious beliefs and practices have long been "there before we look or fail to look." In light of this reality, wisdom, or at least prudence, would seem to call for a degree of humility from those who study American literature. Yet humility is not the same thing as servility, and to acknowledge the crucial role of reli-

---

3. Over the past several decades, the question of the place of religion in American literature has played itself out against the background of an ongoing academic debate over the claim that there exists such a thing as a distinctly *American* culture. Although that debate is not the focus of this book, several essays, particularly those by Michael Colacurcio and Lawrence Buell, address some of its central concerns. For a sharply defined introduction to the current debate, see Alan Wolfe, "The Difference Between Criticism and Hatred: Anti-American Studies," *The New Republic,* 10 Feb. 2003, pp. 25-32, and Michael Bérubé, "The Loyalties of American Studies," *American Quarterly* 56 (2004): 223-33.

4. Richard Wilbur, *New and Collected Poems* (New York: Harcourt, 1988), p. 9.

gion in American culture is not in any way to suggest that its practices or professions are beyond critique. Indeed, although the authors in this book treat their subjects with respect, they also cast a critical eye on many of the theoretical implications and theological claims of the writers and works they discuss. And in developing their arguments, the essayists draw upon a wide array of contemporary theoretical resources — from African American poetics to environmental criticism, from the hermeneutics of suspicion to the new historicism.

## From Emerson to Eliot, and Beyond

*There Before Us* takes as its starting point Emerson's "The American Scholar," which called in 1837 for the creation of a national culture free of "the learning of other lands" and "other men's transcripts of their readings" of the divine.[5] In championing a view of religion as the experience of inwardness cut off from any specific theological commitments, Emerson had sought to establish a new foundation for American literature and made its relationship to religion suddenly and significantly more complex. The book follows a trail that leads from Emerson's generation to the Modernist writers who came almost a century later and who fulfilled his mandate even as they struggled to find their way through some of the religious impasses the Emersonian tradition had reached.

Emerson told a Harvard Divinity School audience in 1838, "That which shows God in me, fortifies me. That which shows God out of me, makes me a wart and a wen."[6] For him this divine self-fortification called for a sublime indifference towards orthodox treatments of the scriptures and sacraments of the Christian tradition. As the opening chapters of this book argue, however, such "indifference" hardly indicated a lack of interest in religious practice or personal spirituality on the part of Emerson or Henry David Thoreau. They and many others in their cultural cohort were intensely curious about the religions of Asia and the Indian

---

5. Ralph Waldo Emerson, *Essays and Lectures*, ed. Joel Porte (New York: Library of America, 1983), pp. 53, 58.

6. Emerson, *Essays*, p. 81.

subcontinent; they also remained invested in the symbols of the Christian faith and were moved by the passions of its most ardent adherents. In his later years, Emerson became, in Barbara Packer's words, a "seeking pilgrim," and, according to John Gatta, "Thoreau sustained a lifelong belief in the spiritual significations of nature."

Packer's "Signing Off: Religious Indifference in America" deftly sets the context for the essays to follow, as she documents the rise of religious indifference in antebellum New England. That indifference is foreshadowed in Emerson's valedictory sermon, "The Lord's Supper," preached in 1832. Setting aside the historical, critical, and theological arguments he has marshaled against the continued administration of the sacrament, Emerson concludes, "That is the end of my opposition, that I am not interested in it." While it is focused on the Transcendentalists, Packer's chapter more broadly charts the emergence of indifference as a crucial category of religious experience in the nineteenth century, particularly for the social movements, including abolitionism, that riveted the attention and animated the discourse of antebellum America. "What the struggle against the Fugitive Slave Law, and against slavery itself, restored to Emerson," she writes, "was not belief in a divine principle, for that he had never lost, but a sense that he could once again claim to belong to a community of believers." If Emerson and some of his contemporaries could no longer enjoy epistemological certainty, they had at least discovered in their outrage at slavery a source of moral clarity.

Thoreau believed he had discovered such a place of clarity — a genuine "sacred space" — in the cabin he inhabited and the woods he haunted at Walden Pond. According to Gatta, Walden represented to Thoreau more than "just an attractive place to live cheaply and freely. As the focal point of Thoreau's romantic naturalism, it was also the locus of his worship and spiritual discovery." In his exploration of *Walden's* treatment of sacred space, Gatta is especially interested in Thoreau's syncretistic appropriation of historic Christianity. He finds Thoreau to be a complex religious thinker who read nature as a sacred text but did so in the light cast by nineteenth-century science and biblical criticism. The author of *Walden* refused to employ the argument from design, as Protestant apologetics had done for two centuries, and did not grant the Bible a privileged place in the hierarchy of religious authority. Instead, he turned to his interaction with nature for the spiritual resources and authority he sought. According to Gatta, "naturalistic science" replaced the church and the biblical record for Thoreau, and "rather than the company of visible saints, the visible facts of creation became his chief source of revelation and spiritual authority beyond the human soul."

A number who came after Emerson and Thoreau found they could neither rest in the indifference the Transcendentalists had embraced nor draw sustenance from the fresh spiritual resources they had tapped. In his essay, Michael Colacurcio focuses on Herman Melville's complex response to the religious upheavals of his day by analyzing the treatment of evil in Melville's fiction. Colacurcio focuses special attention on those points in Melville's work at which the "problem of universal defect comes face to face with the question of human obligation." The questions of "defect" and "obligation" raised the issue of politics in the American republic, but Colacurcio suspects Melville may have believed more than anything that "it was the politics of the *universe* that most needed investigating." The crux of Colacurcio's argument is that though the problem of evil may be a byproduct of theism, for American writers it hardly disappears with the eclipse of God.

In Colacurcio's reading of the short stories, Melville agrees with Karl Marx that only the illusion of immortality prevented the poor and oppressed from "rising up against an injustice not altogether the result of divine incompetence or inattention." Yet Melville pulled back from the more radical implications of his exhausted theology, and he remains for Colacurcio a divided, enigmatic religious thinker. To the end, the novelist harbored a great suspicion of all who seek to impress their own version of the divine order upon the universe, but he also trusted, in Colacurcio's words, that God would not destroy him for "pursuing without cynicism the moral evidences that call into question our best metaphysical proofs." Though this diffident confidence hardly represented the "definite belief" that his friend Nathaniel Hawthorne said Melville craved, it was nonetheless "a position that left ample room for faith, should it ever be given."

Emily Dickinson came closer than Melville to an outright affirmation of such faith, but like him, she remained hesitant and uncertain about belief throughout her life. My chapter on Dickinson takes its title from one of her famous letters, in which she told an acquaintance, "on subjects of which we know nothing, or should I say *Beings* — . . . we both believe, and disbelieve a hundred times an Hour, which keeps Believing nimble."[7] I use evidence from Dickinson's letters and poems to investigate her incessant struggle with God and the question of belief and ask why scholars have so readily overlooked her passion for these subjects. My concern is to situate her within the emerging culture of unbelief in the mid-nineteenth century America and to see how she anticipates twentieth-century theories about this culture and its consequences. I argue that in "her troubled explorations of the divided self" as well as in "her restless exploration of the new polarities of belief and unbelief, Dickinson traced the outlines of theoretical arguments" that were to emerge almost a century after her death. In my argument, the neo-Kantian philosophical background, James Turner's historical account of unbelief, and Paul Ricoeur's elaboration of "the conflict of interpretations" all provide resonant contexts for Dickinson's poetry and experience.

For many nineteenth-century writers in the African American tradition, Katherine Clay Bassard argues, Christian belief provided a source of power rather than an occasion for internal struggle. Bassard's chapter focuses upon the poetry and prose of Frances E. W. Harper, who found at the core of the Christian faith a "Christocentric view of human liberation" that sustained her as she sought to reconcile faith and politics, spiritual renewal and social change. Bassard's expansive essay analyzes the lethal conjunction of biblical hermeneutics and the sanctioning of chattel slavery in antebellum America. What she calls a "specifically racialized hermeneutic" had become so widespread by the early nineteenth century that it provided "a kind of subconscious marginalia to the reading of the Bible itself." To counter this pernicious hermeneutic before the Civil War and to challenge its continuing legacy in the decades after Emancipation, Harper developed her Christocentric view, which not only informed her appropriation of the Bible but also shaped her poetry.

Bassard's essay on Frances Harper brings us to the close of the nineteenth century and the opening of the twentieth, and the religious

---

7. Emily Dickinson, *The Letters of Emily Dickinson,* ed. Thomas H. Johnson and Theodora Ward (Cambridge: Belknap Press of Harvard University Press, 1958), 3:728.

frame of reference in the second half of *There Before Us* becomes less explicitly Christian and more broadly religious, as did American public culture in the years these chapters cover. Taken together, the final four chapters depict a cultural landscape that has been transformed by the realities of war and by the formidable twin forces of social change and intellectual discovery.

With his account of Mark Twain's conflicted response to the Civil War, Harold Bush guides us across that altered landscape. In the wake of that war, American culture entered a period "in which the object of faith" shifted gradually but distinctly away from the theistic God of the scriptures and creeds towards "an impersonal, nationalistic faith in America itself." Bush shows that this shift went hand in hand with the deification of Abraham Lincoln and the Union cause. Within weeks of Lincoln's assassination in April 1865, leading preachers and theologians in the North began "the construction of the Union as holy political entity, and the war as sacred national cleansing."

As a southerner who was merging into northern culture and who remained "highly conscious of his outsider status among gentrified Yankees," Twain had instincts that led him initially to resist this Northern reinterpretation of the war, but his interests eventually led him to embrace it. So it was that in the decades after 1865, he went from being a moderate supporter of the Southern cause to a staunch defender of Abraham Lincoln's view of the Union, the Civil War, and God. In 1907, near the end of his own life, Twain said that to be saved, the Union had required in 1861 precisely Lincoln's skills: "It needed a man of the border, where civil war meant the grapple of brother and brother and disunion a raw and gaping wound." Bush believes the author of *Huckleberry Finn* found in Lincoln a profoundly religious man whose reluctance to claim God's unambiguous approval either of the Union cause or the larger American experiment was only matched by his skepticism about human nature. "It is plausible to claim that this emergent modern agnostic temperament," Bush concludes, "may be what Twain meant" when he called Lincoln a "man of the border."

Through the writings of William and Henry James, M. D. Walhout's essay on "The Liberal Saint" examines the liberal individualist tradition that began to consolidate its hold upon the public culture of the United

States in the decades after the war. Walhout is sympathetic to this tradition but also critical of some of the key categories it has brought to the discussion of human agency and the moral life. In his assessment, a central problem for liberal political philosophy is that it has shown a primary concern for general "maxims having to do with rights or utility" but has neglected the question of personal character. Only in the face of powerful contemporary challenges, have liberal political philosophers begun to ask, "What type of character, what virtues, does liberalism presuppose or require?"

Walhout believes that the literature of the United States at the turn of the century provides one of the most satisfying answers to that question. Developing a line of enquiry found in the work of Timothy Jackson, a contemporary Christian ethicist, he suggests the "category of the 'liberal saint'" and finds such a figure emerging in William James's *The Varieties of Religious Experience* and in Henry James's *The Wings of the Dove*. Both of these works are situated between Christian conceptions of personality and an emerging secular order in which categories borrowed from the Christian past are pressed into the service of the political present. Like a number of other cultural observers in their day, the James brothers believed that a secular revival of Christian saintliness was needed to counter what William called "the worship of material luxury and wealth, which constitutes so large a portion of the 'spirit' of our age." In their explorations of saintliness, however, the Jameses discovered tragic dimensions that may not sit well with the "democratic perfectionism" of liberal social theory. Yet at the same time, according to Walhout, tragedy "certainly accords with the experience of liberal society, whose saints, from Abraham Lincoln to Martin Luther King, Jr., tend to be marked by tragedy. Liberalism needs its saints," he concludes, for they "remind us of the moral limits of society even as they point beyond them."

In Gail McDonald's essay, we move from William and Henry James at the turn of the century into the heart of literary modernism. McDonald is concerned more with the social significance of religious experience than with its internal dynamics, and her subject is the "Social Gospel," that American amalgam of theological and political liberalism which reached its peak of influence in the opening decades of the twentieth century. McDonald takes issue with the "standard narratives of modernity," which have customarily treated religious belief as something that was either "lost" or rendered irrelevant in the decades after Darwin. She speaks instead of "the varieties of faith that writers in the modern period experienced or sought or wrote about."

For many, the Social Gospel proved to be a central category of that faith. It grew out of American Progressivism and represented an effort to challenge the harmful effects of rampant urban and industrial development. McDonald focuses upon three Protestant writers who came to maturity in the first decade of the twentieth century: Ezra Pound, H. D., and T. S. Eliot. Each came from a liberal or progressive Christian tradition, and each came of age at the height of the Social Gospel's flourishing. Their responses to that movement varied dramatically — ranging from Pound's pagan efforts to promote the "gods" to Eliot's passionate embrace of orthodox Christianity. McDonald concludes her account by encouraging us to consider the effort of these writers with a measure of charity: "The effort to make God (or the gods) *new* is an effort to retain the category of divinity in human thought, to keep the sacred alive and meaningful, to posit a world not utterly divorced from heaven."

Lawrence Buell's wide-ranging essay on "Religion and the Environmental Imagination in American Literature" concludes the book. This chapter surveys the historical period covered by the other essayists and carries the discussion into the contemporary era, as Buell probes the boundary lines where religious belief and environmental concern have met from the time of Thoreau to the present. In addition to discussing the work of American creative writers, Buell also draws modern American literary history into the discussion. Both the mid twentieth-century enthusiasts of the American enterprise and contemporary revisionist detractors share a common reading of "the dream of U.S. national destiny as underwritten by a mystique of American nature."

More than anything else, Buell claims, it has been their immersion in this "mystique of nature" that has led the creative writers of the United States to have a "conspicuous animating spiritual concern" for the fate of the earth. "Backsliders and reprobates though they usually seem from an orthodox religious standpoint," poets, novelists, and essayists have displayed "styles of environmental imagination . . . often suffused and animated to a remarkable degree by a sense of the religious." Buell closes with the example of Emerson, the writer with whom this book began. "Emerson the minister becomes Emerson the poet," and by taking that turn toward an open religious and environmental quest, "early national writers showed better prophetic intuition than the churches did" in their confrontation with "the great questions of environmental value." To Buell, the passionate concern for such questions "in U.S. creative writing may be cause for hope. But just how much hope remains an open question."

It seems fitting to have *There Before Us* close by striking these twin notes of questioning and hope, for we live in a period when the conversation about the role of religion in American life is too often marked by suspicion and acrimony instead. The contributors to this book seek to change the tone of that conversation and have undertaken their work in the spirit championed by Kenneth Burke many years ago in *The Philosophy of Literary Form*. In that book Burke argued that we should see history as a "'dramatic' process, involving dialectical oppositions." To understand where the drama gets its materials, he suggests we think of learning as the art of joining a conversation that was going on long before anyone who is presently talking arrived on the scene. As an individual "you listen for a while" and finally "put in your oar. Someone answers; you answer him," and the conversation goes on. "The hour grows late, you must depart. And you do depart, with the discussion still vigorously in progress."[8]

Of the many things that Burke is attempting to describe with this rich analogy, one of the most important is the dialectic of tradition and innovation that has always been central to the question of identity, individual and cultural, in the United States. As each essay in *There Before Us* demonstrates in its own way, negotiating the tensions between the demands of the past and the possibilities of the future has been the task of America's religious traditions as well as of its authors and, indeed, of the nation itself. Despite the stereotypes to the contrary, religion has more often been a dynamic force than a static power in American life, and from the beginning both its most passionate adherents and its most trenchant

8. Kenneth Burke, *The Philosophy of Literary Form: Studies in Symbolic Action*, 3rd ed. (Berkeley: University of California Press, 1973), pp. 110-11.

critics have recognized the powerful mediating role it plays in a prolific and ever-changing culture.

However we judge its role in our past or conceive of its place in our future, we cannot deny that religion has always been a voluble partner in the conversation of this culture. In combining critical clarity with a spirit of interpretive charity, the authors in this book invite us to "put in our oars" and join the lively conversation that was, is, and always will be "there before us" in the drama of religion, literature, and the American experience.

# Signing Off: Religious Indifference in America

*Barbara Packer*

W HEN THE Marquis de Lafayette made his triumphant return visit to the United States in 1824-25, he reached New Haven on a Sunday. Wishing to show respect to Connecticut customs, he expressed a wish to attend divine service. His secretary Levasseur noted in his account of the tour that the people of Connecticut "are rigid observers of religious customs, but they have long since freed themselves from the persecuting spirit, which animated the founders of the colony." Their very tolerance, however, put Lafayette in an awkward position. Congregationalists and Episcopalians had both invited him to their churches. It would have been difficult to accept the offer of one church without appearing to neglect the other. Lafayette therefore attended each in turn: first the Congregational, then the Episcopal. "These sermons were listened to with an equal respect by all, and on coming out of church, the two ministers cordially shook hands, mutually congratulating each other on the happiness they had enjoyed of receiving among them the nation's guest."[1]

Levasseur's anecdote is a typical story in writings about the early Republic. A foreigner surveys the American religious scene and marvels at the combination of religious toleration with religious zeal. The citizens

---

1. Auguste Levasseur, *Lafayette in America in 1824 and 1825; or, Journal of a Voyage to the United States*, trans. John D. Godman, M.D. (Philadelphia, 1829), 1:32. Levasseur describes himself on the book's title page as "Secretary to General Lafayette during his journey."

are so pious that an invitation to church is their highest sign of respect, yet so little given to bigotry that they happily share Lafayette between them and shake hands at the conclusion of the second service. Had Americans really managed to tame the religious passions that had so often laid Europe waste without falling prey to religious skepticism?

Six years after Lafayette's visit, two young Frenchmen who were touring the country to inspect its prisons encountered the same toleration between sects that Lafayette's secretary had found so remarkable. When Alexis de Tocqueville and Gustave de Beaumont visited Sing Sing prison in May 1831 they learned that the divine service held for the prisoners each Sunday was conducted by ministers drawn from different Christian denominations in turn. They attended service at the prison and found that the prisoners seemed to have no objection to this practice of rotating ministers. "As a matter of fact," Beaumont wrote home to his mother, "nothing is commoner in the United States than this indifference toward the nature of religions, which doesn't however eliminate the religious fervor of each for the cult he has chosen. Actually, this extreme tolerance on the one hand for religions in general — on the other hand this considerable zeal of each individual for his own religion, is a phenomenon I can't yet explain to myself. I would gladly know how a lively and sincere faith can get on with such a perfect toleration; how one can have equal respect for religions whose dogmas differ; and finally what real influence on the moral conduct of the Americans can be exercised by their religious spirit."[2]

Everywhere they traveled, the young Frenchmen discovered that citizens of the new nation appeared to hold the same set of opinions concerning religion. Americans agreed, first of all, that religious faith was essential in a Republic. A trustee of the College of New Jersey, the Rev. James Richards, told them that he regarded "the maintenance of the religious spirit" as one of the country's "greatest political interests," since no nation could be moral if it was not religious. Yet Americans also insisted that the religious spirit so important to the preservation of the Republic was to be maintained without the state's help. The first amendment to the Constitution prohibited the Congress from establishing any religion as a

---

2. George Wilson Pierson, *Tocqueville in America* [originally published as *Tocqueville and Beaumont in America*] (1938; Baltimore: Johns Hopkins University Press, 1996), p. 106.

state religion, and popular sentiment seconded what the Constitution decreed. The clergy did not seek political power; many thought it improper for a minister even to vote.[3] Tocqueville was surprised to discover that the Catholic clergy were as enthusiastic about maintaining the separation between church and state as the Protestants were. In the first two volumes of *Democracy in America,* published in 1835, he reported that the Catholic priests he met in the United States believed "that the main reason for the quiet sway of religion over their country was the complete separation of church and state. I have no hesitation in stating that throughout my stay in America I met nobody, lay or cleric, who did not agree about that."[4]

Still, the questions that Beaumont had expressed in his letter from Sing Sing continued to trouble both men throughout their journey. No one could doubt that Americans were tolerant or that they considered religion important to the maintenance of personal virtue and social order. They impressed Tocqueville as a temperate people: industrious, cold in their personal relations, and pure in morals — particularly the women, whose air of unassailable virtue he found admirable but a little frightening. But the chilliness of Americans, who appeared as unmoved in their devotions as in their passions, made it hard to believe that the fire of faith really burned in hearts, which seemed truly ardent only in the pursuit of wealth. Had the toleration forced upon Americans by political necessity acted to quench the zeal of the true believer? Would the final fate of American tolerance be complete religious indifference? In a long letter to a friend, begun on 29 June 1831, Tocqueville confesses that he has begun to suspect that underneath the superficial reverence paid to religion in the United States there is "a great depth of doubt and indifference. . . . Faith is evidently inert."[5]

For his part, Beaumont found it impossible to believe that the bewildering number of religious sects could exist indefinitely; he thought that Americans' faith would sooner or later conclude in natural religion or lapse back into Catholicism. When he and Tocqueville reached Boston in

---

3. See, for instance, the record of their conversation with the New York Anglican minister Jonathan Mayhew Wainwright. Pierson, *Tocqueville in America,* pp. 137-38.

4. Alexis de Tocqueville, *Democracy in America,* trans. George Lawrence, ed. J. P. Mayer (Garden City, N.Y.: Anchor, 1969), p. 295.

5. Pierson, *Tocqueville in America,* p. 154.

October 1831 they were especially eager to question William Ellery Channing, the celebrated Unitarian preacher. Was Unitarianism, they asked him, in danger of so purifying Christianity from its grosser errors that it would eventually disappear into natural religion? They had put the same question to John Quincy Adams at a dinner party the night before, and he had agreed with Beaumont's guess that Unitarianism would end in natural religion. But Channing disagreed. He told his visitors that he did not fear that his faith would terminate in a renunciation of the supernatural. "The human spirit," he told them, "has need of a positive religion, and why should it ever abandon the Christian religion? Its proofs fear nothing from the most serious examination of reason."[6]

That serene faith in the Unitarian synthesis of faith and reason proved premature, O. B. Frothingham notes in *Boston Unitarianism*.[7] Frothingham insists that Channing was inspired by genuine piety: "At the bottom of his heart was a passion for pure religion, undefiled by rite or doctrine. It was the only passion he had, a real thirst for the living God."[8] But he pointed out that Channing's articles of faith were full of contradictions: "The creed itself would not have satisfied a severely critical mind. It appealed to nature and yet accepted the supernatural. It denied the deity of Christ and still called him the son of God. It ascribed moral attributes to persons, but termed him Savior, Redeemer, Mediator, lavishing on him every epithet of glory. It received the stories of the resurrection, the ascension, the raising of the dead, the multiplication of the loaves, miracles, prophecies, and yet applied reason to the story of the superhuman birth."[9] Still, Unitarian clergymen and laymen of Channing's generation sincerely believed that they had successfully combined reason with faith, the testimony of the senses with that of revealed religion; "Theirs was the honest conviction that development could go no further."[10]

Younger Unitarians, however, were already discovering leaks in the supposedly watertight shelter of their faith. The proofs of the Christian

6. Pierson, *Tocqueville in America*, p. 422.

7. Octavius Brooks Frothingham, *Boston Unitarianism, 1820-1850: A Study of the Life and Work of Nathaniel Langdon Frothingham* (New York, 1890).

8. Frothingham, *Boston Unitarianism*, p. 5.

9. Frothingham, *Boston Unitarianism*, pp. 41, 243.

10. Frothingham, *Boston Unitarianism*, p. 69.

religion that Channing deemed able to withstand the most serious examination of reason were beginning to look vulnerable. Hume's famous attack upon the credibility of miracle stories in the tenth chapter of the *Enquiry Concerning Human Understanding* had shaken one traditional proof of Jesus' divine mission, while the German biblical criticism that Unitarians had welcomed to their shores was now calling into question the authenticity and authority of the Gospels themselves. As James Turner has noted, "even partial acceptance of the higher criticism had radical implications, for its very method of historical criticism presumed that the evidences of Christianity were subject to the same historical processes as other historical truths."[11]

## Emerson and the Rise of Indifference

In 1826 Ralph Waldo Emerson, fresh from a course of study at Harvard's Divinity School and waiting to be approbated to preach, echoed the anxieties of his seniors about the evidences of their common religion. He worried that the assaults of the "German scholars" against the "foundations of external evidence" were threatening to give Christianity up to "the historical speculators & pleasant doubters." He feared that the faith "that has for ages kept a commanding check on the dangerous passions of men" will "roll away & let in the ghastly reality of things." Nothing but moral confusion can ensue. The glories and consolations of Christianity "must now pass away and become ridiculous . . . and every drunkard in his cups & every voluptuary in his brothel will loll out his tongue at the Resurrection from the dead; at the acts, the martyrdoms the unassailable virtues & the traditionary/legendary/greatness of Christianity. God forbid."[12]

11. James Turner, *Without God, Without Creed: The Origins of Unbelief in America* (Baltimore: Johns Hopkins University Press, 1985), p. 151. The story of how the higher criticism of the Bible was first embraced by liberal Christians in America and later distrusted by some of them has been told by Jerry Wayne Brown, *The Rise of Biblical Criticism in America, 1800-1870: The New England Scholars* (Middletown, Conn.: Wesleyan University Press, 1969).

12. *The Letters of Ralph Waldo Emerson*, ed. Ralph L. Rusk, vols. 1-6, and Eleanor M. Tilton, vols. 7-10 (New York: Columbia University Press, 1939-95), 7:141-42.

By 1831 Emerson had decided that the attempt to prove the truths of Christianity through external evidences was impossible. The only unshakeable proofs of faith are inner proofs. We are convinced that Jesus was divinely sent not because he performed miracles described in documents purported to be written by contemporary witnesses; we are convinced that Jesus performed miracles because we recognize his own words as divine. Emerson explained to his aunt Mary Moody Emerson, his mentor and muse: "religion in the mind is not credulity & in practice is not form. It is a life."[13] The Lord's Supper, once a central rite in Puritan churches and a coveted sign of church membership, had come to seem to Emerson a vestigial rite, the memory of a sacrament in a denomination that had given up rites and symbols, an act of veneration to a Person no longer thought to be divine. He believed that he could no longer continue to administer the Lord's Supper with "indifference & dislike."[14] He wrote a letter (now lost) to the Second Church in the summer of 1832 declaring his unhappiness with current modes of celebrating the rite. It was referred to a seven-man committee of church members who reluctantly concluded that they could not concur with him in his desire to make the rite merely commemorative, without real bread and wine.

Just at this point, the Second Church had to close for six weeks for repairs. Emerson had time to take a vacation in the White Mountains and consider his response to the church committee's refusal. He returned to Boston with opinions unchanged. On September 9, 1832, he preached the sermon that effectively ended his ministry. Sermon CLXII, "The Lord's Supper," takes its text from Romans 14:17: "The kingdom of God is not meat and drink; but righteousness and peace and joy in the holy ghost."[15]

13. Emerson, *Letters*, 7:7.

14. *The Journals and Miscellaneous Notebooks of Ralph Waldo Emerson*, ed. William H. Gilman et al. (Cambridge: Belknap Press of Harvard University Press, 1960-82), 4:30.

15. The "Textual Introduction" to vol. 1 of Emerson's *Complete Sermons* tells us that "Emerson never supplied titles for his sermons, but instead followed the ministerial practice of his day by identifying them for his own reference with Roman numerals, almost invariably centered at the top of the first page." *The Complete Sermons of Ralph Waldo Emerson*, ed. Albert von Frank (Columbia: University of Missouri Press, 1989-92), 1:33-34. Notes to Sermon CLXII reveal that shortly after he delivered it, Emerson "prepared a second manuscript, a revised fair copy, perhaps with a momentary intent to publish, but certainly for circulation among interested friends." In 1857 he sent this copy to Cyrus Bartol, who

It marshals evidence from Scripture, from Church history, and from textual criticism to prove that the institution of the Lord's Supper is at bottom a misunderstanding of the glowing, bold, and figurative language habitually used by Jesus. Emerson drew largely on Thomas Clarkson's *A Portraiture of Quakerism*[16] for Quaker arguments against the communion rite. He also asked his brother William (who had studied for a time with Eichhorn in Göttingen) to supply him with arguments drawn from the German higher critics.[17] Emerson asks us to imagine the supper in its historical context. "Jesus is a Jew sitting with his countrymen celebrating their national feast. . . . He did with his disciples exactly what every master of a family was doing at the same hour with his household."[18] Talmudists tell us that it was the custom for the head of the house to bless the bread and wine and distribute it to every one at the table. In passing the bread and wine to his disciples Jesus was following Jewish custom; in describing the bread and wine as his body and blood he was speaking in figurative language:

---

had requested it, and it became the source of the text published in Octavius Brooks Frothingham's *Transcendentalism in New England* (1876), as well as in the posthumous Riverside and Centenary editions of Emerson's works (Note to Sermon CLXII, *Complete Sermons*, 4:185), where it is entitled "The Lord's Supper." It was the only sermon published during his lifetime.

16. Wesley T. Mott, the editor of vol. 4 of Emerson's *Complete Sermons*, notes that Emerson's extensive use of Thomas Clarkson's *A Portraiture of Quakerism* (New York, 1806), was described in an article by Marie C. Turpie, "A Quaker Source for Emerson's Sermon on the Lord's Supper," *New England Quarterly* 17 (1944): 95-101. Mott notes that Emerson borrowed the first two volumes of Clarkson's book from the Boston Athenaeum and took them with him on his trip to the White Mountains. See *Complete Sermons*, 4:185.

17. Emerson's biographer Ralph L. Rusk notes that Emerson once asked William "to mark, in the works of Eichhorn or others, the passages that would tend to destroy a candid inquirer's belief in the divine authority of the New Testament." *The Life of Ralph Waldo Emerson* (New York: Columbia University Press, 1949), p. 52.

18. *Complete Sermons*, 4:187-88. In interpreting the Lord's Supper this way Emerson was well within the tradition of Unitarian biblical criticism. Brown quotes a sermon of Joseph Stevens Buckminster's explicating the Letter of Paul to Philemon according to historical principles. Buckminster wrote, "Instead of looking into every text, separated from its context, to find something which may bear upon a favorite system, we should be content to understand the apostles, as they meant to be understood by those to whom they wrote." See Brown, *Rise of Biblical Criticism*, p. 20.

> He always taught by parables and symbols. . . . Remember the readiness which he always showed to spiritualize every occurrence. He stooped and wrote on the sand. He admonished his disciples respecting the leaven of the Pharisees. He instructed the woman of Samaria respecting living water. He permitted himself to be anointed, declaring that it was for interment. He washed the feet of his disciples. These are admitted to be symbolical actions and expressions. Here in like manner he calls the bread his body and bids the disciples eat.

If we no longer believe it necessary to wash one another's feet — as Jesus told his disciples they should do — why are we still celebrating the Lord's Supper with bread and wine? If we say that foot washing is "a local custom unsuitable in western countries" and important only for the humility that it signifies, why should we not apply the same logic to the Supper? "The passover was local too and does not concern us." All that concerns us is the love that the communion rite symbolizes.[19]

At the end of his discourse Emerson offers an argument against the communion rite drawn not from scripture or history but from individual sensation — the "repulsion" many people feel when they are invited to take part in the Lord's Supper. There is an element of falseness that makes the rite painful; "We are not accustomed to express our thoughts or emotions by symbolical actions." Attempting to pay tribute to "Eastern" forms alien to our own habits of thought involves the spirit in insincerity fatal to its life: "It is of the greatest importance that whatever forms we use should be animated by our feelings; that our religion through all its acts should be living and operative." This objection bears more weight with him then any of the historical or scriptural arguments he has so far advanced. "It is my own objection. This mode of commemorating Christ is not suitable to me. That is reason enough why I should abandon it." He will substitute for it other practices that he is sure Christ would approve more: "For what could he wish to be commemorated for? Only that men should be filled with his spirit." Emerson has no objection to anyone else's administering the Lord's Supper; he simply wishes to be relived of administering the rite himself. "That is the end of my opposi-

19. Emerson, *Complete Sermons*, 4:188-89.

tion, that I am not interested in it," he said. With this quietly devastating remark he dismisses as irrelevant the opinions of the church committee and parishioners assembled to hear him.[20]

If Tocqueville and Beaumont had stayed in Boston a year longer they might have heard this sermon, which would have cast new light upon the career of religious indifference in America.[21] Emerson makes his boredom with the Lord's Supper his chief reason for wishing to alter the rite; he elevates distaste into a principle of criticism. Although he is careful to say in Sermon CLXII that his opinions are his alone, he makes clear in later texts that the indifference he feels toward many Christian rites and doctrines was very widely shared. In a lecture of January 1837 entitled "Religion," he warned that "established churches have become old and ossified under the accumulation of creeds and usages," with the result that the Soul of religion was stealing away, "leaving a corpse in their hands. A deep enthusiasm does not exist; an ardent fellowship for the furtherance of spiritual ends does not exist." Only the belief that "unbelief never lasts long" can keep men and women from despair.[22] In this he echoed the sentiments of his brother Charles, who had died in 1836 shortly before *Nature* was published. In 1837 Emerson filled a notebook with his brother's sentiments, quoted from his writings or from remembered conversations. In one of these he wrote as if Charles were still alive. "C[harles].C[hauncy].E[merson]. thinks there is no Christianity, & has not been for some ages," he wrote. Charles, however, had spoken from a greater faith, not a greater skepticism; he esteemed Christianity "the most wonderful thing in the history of the world,"[23] and thought it absent from current societies because they were not capable of attaining it:

> If Christianity were no more than a fine drama, how faithful it is to what is in Man. How it symbolizes all our history & the constitution

20. Emerson, *Complete Sermons*, 4:192, 194.

21. Emerson's sermon was delivered on September 9, 1832; Tocqueville and Beaumont left Boston for Connecticut on October 3, 1831. See Pierson, *Tocqueville in America*, p. 440.

22. *The Early Lectures of Ralph Waldo Emerson*, ed. Stephen E. Whicher and Robert E. Spiller (Cambridge: Belknap Press of Harvard University Press, 1959-72), 2:97.

23. Emerson, *Journals*, 5:266.

of our souls' height out of lowliness & victory out of sacrifice: here the crown of thorns & the cross; & there the transfiguration the Miracles the ascension.[24]

Charles did not believe that the Christian should attempt to *imitate* Christ, since "every man is a new creature & should propose to himself an original life," and since "all beings, except God, stand to us in the relation of Phenomena." Christ represents spiritual freedom, both his and ours; "Christ therefore ought not to be preached as having any claims on man — that is, of Lordship, but simply as the epiphany of the truest 'spirit,' which if we can love we may receive from God & go about our work of whatever sort rejoicing & free."[25] When a group of seniors from the Harvard Divinity School wrote to Emerson on 21 March 1838 to invite him to deliver "the customary discourse, on occasion of their entering upon the active Christian ministry" at their commencement ceremonies in July, he accepted at once.[26] He was leaving one form of ministry behind in asking to be relieved of his duties in East Lexington for the wider field of the lecture hall and published text; what better time to celebrate the piety of a Theism purged of all false reverence, which could regard everything besides God as phenomenal yet still pay tribute to Christ as the purest embodiment of spirit in human form? Emerson had hoped to edit a memorial volume of his brother's writings, but discovered as he went through Charles's journals and letters "the immense disparity between his power of conversation & his blotted paper." He remembered some witty sayings, as when Charles had said "he never spent anything on himself without thinking he deserved the praise of disinterested benevolence." But the genial influence of Charles's thought upon Emerson's was now ended. "Beside my direct debt to him of how many valued thoughts, — through what orbits of speculation have we not traveled to-

24. Emerson, *Journals*, 5:267.

25. Emerson, *Journals*, 5:265. Emerson identifies these sentences as extracts from an April 13, 1836, letter to Charles's fianceé Elizabeth Hoar. Charles died May 9, 1836.

26. Quoted by Conrad Wright, "Emerson, Barzillai Frost, and the Divinity School Address," in *The Liberal Christians* (Boston: Beacon, 1970), p. 51. The essay first appeared in the *Harvard Theological Review* 49 (1956): 19-43. The letter from the divinity school students is reprinted in Emerson, *Letters*, 2:147, n. 169.

gether, so that it would not be possible for either of us to say, This is my thought, this is yours."[27]

Emerson's most striking portrait of religious indifference is his 1838 Address to the Senior Class in Divinity College. So many studies of that famous address have focused on its theological content — its attack on biblical miracles, its use of strategies of interpretation borrowed from the German critics — that we need to remember how large a part sheer boredom and exasperation played in its genesis. During 1837 and 1838 Emerson had endured the preaching of a new Harvard Divinity School graduate, Barzillai Frost, who had come to Concord as assistant to the Rev. Ezra Ripley, Emerson's aged step-grandfather.[28] Frost's mechanical sermons, his raw, half-screaming bass voice, his deadly rationalism, drew from Emerson a pitying exclamation: "Ah! unhappy man that is called to stand in the pulpit & *not* give bread of life."[29] Frost was an exemplar of how not to preach, and Emerson turned his unhappy Sundays in the Concord church into a warning to the aspiring young ministerial candidates of the Divinity School:

> I once heard a preacher who sorely tempted me to say, I would go to church no more. Men go, I thought, where they are wont to do, else had no soul entered the temple in the afternoon. A snowstorm was falling around us. The snowstorm was real; the preacher merely spectral; and the eye felt the sad contrast in looking at him, and then out of the window behind him, into the beautiful meteor of the snow. He had lived in vain. He had no one word intimating that he had laughed or wept, was married or in love, had been commended, or cheated, or chagrined. If he had ever lived and acted, we were none the wiser for it. The capital secret of his profession, namely, to convert life into truth, he had not learned.[30]

He speaks here largely as a suffering member of the congregation, though in fact he had continued to supply the pulpit at East Lexington

27. Emerson, *Journals*, 5:151, 153.

28. The story of Emerson's growing discontent with the preaching of Barzillai Frost is told by Conrad Wright, "Emerson, Barzillai Frost."

29. Emerson, *Journals*, 7:12.

30. *The Collected Works of Ralph Waldo Emerson*, ed. Robert E. Spiller and Alfred R. Ferguson (Cambridge: Belknap Press of Harvard University Press, 1971-), 1:85-86.

until March 1838.[31] Elsewhere in the Divinity School Address he presents the decline of Christian religious faith as it is refracted through the social humiliations endured by the minister himself as he tries to kindle enthusiasm in his parishioners: "Would he ask contributions for the missions, foreign or domestic? Instantly his face is suffused with shame, to propose to his parish, that they should send money a hundred or a thousand miles, to furnish such poor fare as they have at home. . . . Will he invite them to the Lord's Supper? If no heart warm this rite, the hollow, dry, creaking formality is too plain, than that he can face a man of wit and energy, and put the invitation without terror. In the street, what has he to say to the bold village blasphemer? The village blasphemer sees fear in the face, form, and gait of the minister."[32] We notice that in this series of vignettes Emerson's minister endures deepening degrees of shame: from the congregants unwilling to give their missionary money; from the businessman or sea-captain whom he dares not invite to the Lord's Supper; and finally from the bold village blasphemer whose ridicule he cannot answer.

31. Wright notes ("Emerson, Barzillai Frost," pp. 27-28) that Emerson had been preaching at East Lexington for something like two years when he told the church committee there that he wished to put off his charge, even though the term of his engagement had not ended. A letter Emerson wrote to Lidian on February 19, 1838, announces that the meeting has taken place and that the consent of the committee has been secured, so long as he engaged to provide John Sullivan Dwight as a replacement. Rusk suggests in a note to this letter that "the final separation from the church, already perhaps inevitable, may nevertheless have been influenced in some degree by Carlyle's letter of December 8, 1837, which was a kind of official recognition of Emerson's status as a literary man." *Letters*, 1:113, n. 35. In that letter Carlyle praised "An Oration, Delivered before the Phi Beta Kappa Society at Cambridge, August 31, 1837," now known as "The American Scholar," which had been printed by James Monroe and Company of Boston in September 1837 as a 28-page pamphlet. See Joel Myerson, *Ralph Waldo Emerson: A Bibliography* (Pittsburgh: University of Pittsburgh Press, 1982), pp. 22-23. Emerson mailed copies to Harriet Martineau and to Carlyle. Carlyle did not receive his copy until January, but he had already read Martineau's copy, and sent his congratulations to Emerson along with his wife's opinion that "there had been nothing met with it since Schiller went silent." He added, "May God grant you strength, for you have a *fearful* work to do." *The Correspondence of Emerson and Carlyle*, ed. Joseph Slater (New York: Columbia University Press, 1964), pp. 173-74, 181.

32. Emerson, *Collected Works*, 1:87.

## Signing Off

It is time, Emerson argues, to acknowledge what all people know but few are willing to say: "I think no man can go with his thoughts about him, into one of our churches, without feeling that what hold the public worship had on men, is gone or going. It has lost its grasp on the affections of the good, and the fear of the bad. In the country, — neighborhoods, half parishes, are *signing off*, to use the local term."[33] To "sign off" was to declare before a local magistrate that you did not wish to be considered a member of the local Congregationalist parish or pay taxes toward its support. Thoreau describes the process in "Resistance to Civil Government": "Some years ago, the State met me in behalf of the church, and commanded me to pay a certain sum toward the support of a clergyman whose preaching my father attended, but never I myself." At the request of the town's selectmen he "condescended" to make some statement like the following in writing: "Know all men by these presents, that I, Henry Thoreau, do not wish to be regarded as a member of any incorporated society which I have not joined." He adds, "If I had known how to name them, I should then have signed off in detail from all the societies which I never signed on to, but I did not know where to find a complete list."[34] His feelings were widely shared. Robert Gross has recently pointed out that "with the separation of church and state in 1834, scores of Concord residents 'signed off' from all denominations, Unitarian, Trinitarian, and Universalist alike."[35]

Thoreau's flippancy about religion, here and in the "Sunday" chapter of *A Week on the Concord and Merrimack Rivers* (1849), suggests that Emerson had been right when he observed that tradition was losing all force with the young. In an 1840 lecture on "Religion" he asked: "With Judaea, what has the genuine life of Paris and New York to do? With Moses or Paul? It is seen and felt by all the young that the entire catechism and

---

33. Emerson, *Collected Works*, 1:88.

34. "Resistance to Civil Government," in *Reform Papers*, ed. Wendell Glick, *The Writings of Henry Thoreau* (Princeton: Princeton University Press, 1973), p. 79.

35. Robert Gross, "Faith in the Boardinghouse: New Views of Thoreau Family Religion," *Thoreau Society Bulletin* (Winter 2005): 4.

creed in which they were bred, may be forgotten with impunity."[36] It now seemed impossible to conceive of "any church, any liturgy, any rite" that would seem "quite genuine."[37] In the Divinity School Address he had confessed that "all attempts to project and establish a Cultus with new rites and forms" seemed to him vain. "Faith makes us, and not we it, and faith makes its own forms. All attempts to contrive a system, are as cold as the new worship introduced by the French to the goddess of Reason — today pasteboard and filigree, and ending tomorrow in madness and murder."[38] Another possibility — that of returning to a traditional religion, centralized and liturgical — seemed wholly retrograde, though in certain moments he could indulge in the luxury of nostalgia for sacramental religions. In 1843 Emerson went to hear mass in the Baltimore Cathedral and wrote Margaret Fuller a playful letter about his sensations there:

> It is so dignified to come where the priest is nothing, & the people nothing, and an idea for once excludes these impertinences. The chanting priest, the pictured walls, the lighted altar, the surpliced boys the swinging censer every whiff of which I inhaled, brought all Rome again to mind. . . . It is a dear old church, the Roman I mean, & today I detest the Unitarians and Martin Luther and all the Parliament of Barebones.[39]

36. Emerson, *Early Lectures*, 3:274.

37. Emerson, *Early Lectures*, 3:263. This quotation is from the lecture "Reforms," which precedes "Religion" in the series entitled "The Present Age."

38. Emerson, "An Address Delivered before the Senior Class in Divinity College" in *Collected Works*, 1:92.

39. Emerson, *Letters*, 3:116. He wrote a similar, though more sober, letter to his wife a few days later (January 8 and 9, 1843): "Today I heard high mass in the Cathedral here, & with great pleasure. It is well for my Protestantism that we have no Cathedral in Concord. Abby Adams & I should be confirmed in a fortnight. The Unitarian church forgets that men are poets. Even Mr. Frost himself does not bear it in mind." *Letters*, 1:117-18. Abby Larkin Adams was the adopted daughter of Abel and Abby Adams of Boston. Abel Adams had been a close friend and financial advisor of Emerson since his Second Church days. Abby Larkin Adams had recently shocked her "Aunt & Uncle" (as she called her adoptive parents) by expressing an interest in joining the Catholic Church. See Emerson's letter to his brother William, August 11, 1842. *Letters*, 3:78-79.

If Roman Catholicism offered a momentary vacation from Protestant egotism, Emerson did not for a moment believe that its gorgeous pageantry solved the problem of disbelief. However venerable the ceremonies of any church might be, they seemed to him incrustations when not resting on truth and animated by living faith.

His trip to England in 1847-48 only confirmed him in this opinion. In *English Traits* he wrote that the Church of England showed evidence of its origin in architecture that still glowed "with faith in immortality." In Anglo-Saxon England "the violence of the northern savages exasperated Christianity into power," and the religion that grew out of this clash never lost the force of the clash that had produced it.

> Heats and genial periods arrive in history, or, shall we say, plenitudes of Divine Presence, by which high tides are caused in the human spirit, and great virtues and talents appear, as in the eleventh, twelfth, thirteenth, and again in the sixteenth and seventeenth centuries.

The modern age is no longer the age of Wycliffes, Beckets, Latimers, and Mores, driven away by "silent revolutions in opinion" that no one can reverse. "The spirit that dwelt in this church has glided away to animate other activities; and they who come to the old shrines find apes and players rustling the old garments."[40] The modern English Church was a respectful caretaker of its inherited faith: "It keeps the old structures in repair, spends a world of money in music and building; and in buying Pugin, and architectural literature. It has a general good name for amenity and mildness. It is not in ordinary a persecuting church; it is not inquisitorial, not even inquisitive, is perfectly well-bred and can shut its eyes on all proper occasions. If you let it alone, it will let you alone."[41] The chapter on "Religion" in *English Traits* makes mid-century Anglicanism sound a good deal like the Boston Unitarianism he had described in the Divinity School Address: "The prayers and even the dogmas of our church, are like the zodiac of Denderah, and the astronomical monuments of the Hindoos, wholly insulated from anything now extant in the life and business of the people. They mark the height to which the waters

40. Emerson, *Collected Works*, 5:124, 122, 124.
41. Emerson, *Collected Works*, 5:126.

once rose."[42] Should the true spirit of religion then be looked for in the dissenting sects? Emerson thought not: "they are only perpetuations of some private man's dissent, and are to the Established Church as cabs are to a coach, cheaper and more convenient, but really the same thing."[43]

Back home in Concord, Henry David Thoreau (who had moved from his cabin at Walden to the Emerson house to serve as surrogate man-of-the-house while Emerson was abroad) was seeking publishers for his first book, *A Week on the Concord and Merrimack Rivers* (1849). Several publishers rejected it before Thoreau finally agreed to publish it at his own expense — a decision that would involve him in several years of debt, for the book did not sell, and he was finally invited to remove the unsold copies from the publisher's basement in a wheelbarrow. Many reviewers praised the beauty of its descriptive passages, though they observed that its wandering essays on character, friendship, philosophy, and the like might better have been published separately from the slender narrative of the river journey. Nevertheless, one reviewer noted that the book's effect upon him had been hard to account for: "It is invested with a strange, long-lingering charm, an indescribable fascination for which we can hardly account, except by saying that it springs from pure, naked truth. For with that the soul of all nature is in unison; to that the core of every heart is loyal, and responds, even when unconscious of it, with an instinctive pleasure." On the other hand, Thoreau's attacks on Christianity in the "Sunday" chapter of the book were as offensive as its descriptive passages were beautiful. Readers of the book, the reviewer warned, must be prepared to find its valuable thoughts in-

---

42. Emerson, *Collected Works*, 1:86-87. His dismay at the current state of the English church was heightened by his longstanding interest in the seventeenth-century Cambridge philosophers and divines whose works he had gotten to know at Harvard and continued to mine for inspiration throughout his career. Daniel Walker Howe points out that Emerson already praised Ralph Cudworth and his successors in the school of "ethical intuitionism" in his Harvard essay for the Bowdoin Prize: "The Present State of Ethical Philosophy" (it won second prize). In later years he continued to find kindred sentiments in Cudworth and other Cambridge Platonists. See Howe, "The Cambridge Platonists of Old England and the Cambridge Platonists of New England," in *American Unitarianism 1805-1865*, ed. Conrad Edick Wright (Boston: Massachusetts Historical Society and Northeastern University Press, 1989), pp. 87-119.

43. Emerson, *Collected Works*, 5:130.

terspersed "with inexcusable crudities, . . . with contempt for every thing commonly esteemed holy, with reflections that must shock every pious Christian."[44]

What had Thoreau said to create such dismay? He referred to Christianity as a "mythus" and casually shoveled Jesus and Buddha together as kindred sages, but one might have thought that these radical gestures had lost their power to shock after Emerson and Theodore Parker used them. Still, there was a difference. Emerson in the Divinity School Address and Parker in the South Boston sermon were still speaking as Christians eager to rescue congregations from wretched preaching or the Scriptures from mythological encrustations; they were clerical, passionate, and *serious*. But Thoreau approaches his subject with insouciance. He begins his discussion of religion in "Sunday" with a meditation on the durable appeal of fable, mentioning Bacchus and the Tyrrhenian mariners, Narcissus, Endymion, Mennon the son of morning, Phaeton, Pan, Prometheus, and the Sphinx. "This is an approach to that universal language which men have sought in vain. This fond reiteration of the oldest expression of truth by the latest posterity, content with slightly and religiously retouching the old material, is the most impressive proof of a common humanity."[45] A fable is "to the wise man an apothegm, and admits of his most generous interpretation."[46] Then he confesses, "The reading which I love best is the scriptures of the several nations, though it happens that I am better acquainted with those of the Hindoos, the Chinese, and the Persians, than of the Hebrews, which I have come to last."[47] He finds in the New Testament traces of that mythologizing impulse he admired in the Greeks and Egyptians:

---

44. A — R. [William Rounseville Alger], Review of *A Week on the Concord and Merrimack Rivers, Universalist Quarterly* 6 (October 1849): 422-23. Reprinted in Joel Myerson, ed., *Emerson and Thoreau: The Contemporary Reviews* (Cambridge: Cambridge University Press, 1992), pp. 348-49. Alger's indignation at Thoreau's mockery of Christian churches was widely shared among contemporary reviewers of *A Week on the Concord and Merrimack Rivers*.

45. Thoreau, *A Week on the Concord and Merrimack Rivers*, ed. Carl F. Hovde et al. (Princeton: Princeton University Press, 1980), p. 59.

46. Thoreau, *A Week*, p. 58.

47. Thoreau, *A Week*, pp. 71-72.

One memorable addition to the old mythology is due to this era, —
the Christian fable. With what pains, and tears, and blood these centuries have woven this and added it to the mythology of mankind! The
new Prometheus. With what miraculous consent, and patience, and
persistency has this mythus been stamped on the memory of the race!
It would seem as if it were in the progress of mythology to dethrone
Jehovah, and crown Christ in his stead.[48]

If Christ is the new Prometheus, then his gift to mankind must be the divinity they have bestowed upon him and themselves. Only a disinterested
spectator can understand this mythologizing. Hence "it is necessary not to
be Christian to appreciate the beauty and significance of the life of Christ."

Behind this mythological Christ, the product of centuries of human
need and distortion, lies the Jesus who speaks in the Gospels, and whose
candor is so arresting that Thoreau confesses that his readings of the
story have never gotten him as far as the crucifixion. In this, however, he
is almost alone. "It is remarkable that, notwithstanding the universal favor with which the New Testament is outwardly received, and even the
bigotry with which it is defended, there is no hospitality shown to, there
is no appreciation of, the order of truth with which it deals. I know of no
book which has so few readers."[49] What would a Yankee congregation
make of such commandments as these, if it ever paid attention to them?
"Seek first the kingdom of heaven." "Lay not up for yourselves treasures
on earth." "If thou wilt be perfect, go and sell that thou hast, and give to
the poor, and thou shalt have treasure in heaven." "For what is a man
profited, if he shall gain the whole world, and lose his own soul? Or what
shall a man give in exchange for his soul?"[50] Yet even Jesus, sublime as his
thoughts are, directs our hopes to another world instead of teaching us
how to live in this one. "There are various tough problems yet to solve,
and we must make shift to live, betwixt spirit and matter, such a human
life as we can."[51] Christianity, after all, "has hung its harp on the willows,
and cannot sing a song in a strange land. It has dreamed a sad dream, and

48. Thoreau, *A Week,* pp. 66-67.
49. Thoreau, *A Week,* p. 72.
50. Thoreau, *A Week,* p. 72.
51. Thoreau, *A Week,* pp. 73-74.

does not yet welcome the morning with joy."[52] What morning, exactly, is Thoreau expecting to dawn in 1849? His statement sounds like an echo of an earlier era, the mid-1830s, when he had briefly boarded with Orestes Brownson, founder of the Society for Christian Union and Progress.[53] Brownson's *New Views of Christianity, Society, and the Church* (1836) had proclaimed humanity's modern religious mission in a tone of supreme confidence: "We are to reconcile Spirit and matter; that is, we must realize the atonement. Nothing else remains for us to do. Stand still we cannot." The future then looked radiant: "He, who takes his position on the 'high table land' of Humanity, and beholds with a prophet's gaze his brothers, so long separated, coming together . . . may hear celestial voices chanting a sweeter strain than that which announced to Judea's shepherds the birth of the Redeemer."[54]

By 1849 the brave hopes for a religion of humanity had faded. Brownson, disillusioned with democracy and hungry for a certitude that Transcendentalism could not give him, had converted to Roman Catholicism and repudiated his former associates. Brook Farm had failed after a seven-year run. And the quest for some faith to replace a moribund Christianity had ended in frustration, at least if we can credit the description of American religiosity Emerson gives in "Worship" (1860):

52. Thoreau, *A Week*, p. 77.

53. In 1835 Brownson was serving as the Unitarian minister of Canton, Massachusetts. He was asked that summer to examine Thoreau, then in his sophomore year at Harvard, who wanted to teach in the Canton school. Of this meeting Arthur Schlesinger, Jr., writes, "Thoreau and Brownson spent a stimulating summer, reading German together and walking the shady banks of the cool Neponset River," a period that Thoreau later described as "the morning of a new *Lebenstag.*" *A Pilgrim's Progress: Orestes A. Brownson* (Boston: Little, 1966), p. 32. In early 1836 Thoreau took a leave from Harvard to teach in Canton, boarding with Brownson while the latter was writing *New Views of Christianity, Society, and the Church*, which Thoreau read with interest in 1837. See Linck C. Johnson, *Thoreau's Complex Weave: The Writing of 'A Week on the Concord and Merrimack Rivers'* (Charlottesville: University Press of Virginia, 1986), pp. 85, 87. The influence of Brownson's *New Views* on the Sunday chapter of *A Week* is strong. Thoreau's mocking demand that orthodox believers produce their "authority" for the doctrine of the Trinity recalls a similar passage in Brownson's work.

54. Brownson, *New Views of Christianity, Society, and the Church* (Boston, 1836), excerpted in Perry Miller, ed., *The Transcendentalists: An Anthology* (Cambridge: Harvard University Press, 1950), p. 123.

We live in a transition period, when the old faiths which comforted nations, and not only so, but made nations, seem to have spent their
force. I do not find the religions of men at this moment very creditable
to them, but either childish and insignificant, or unmanly and
effeminating. The fatal trait is the divorce between religion and morality. . . . In creeds never was such levity; witness the heathenisms in
Christianity, the periodic 'revivals,' the Millennium mathematics, the
peacock ritualism, the retrogression to Popery, the maundering of
Mormons, the squalor of Mesmerism, the deliration of rappings,
thumps in table-drawers, and black art. . . . Not knowing what to do,
we ape our ancestors; the churches stagger backwards to the mum-
meries of the dark ages.[55]

This declension, ludicrous as it is, results from historical forces no one
could have withstood.

By the irresistible maturing of the general mind, the Christian traditions have lost their hold. The dogma of the mystic offices of Christ
being dropped, and he standing on his genius as a moral teacher, 'tis
impossible to maintain the old emphasis of his personality; and it recedes, as all persons must, before the sublimity of the moral laws.[56]

Were sublime moral laws in themselves really capable of inspiring right
action? In "Fate" Emerson reminded his readers: "Perception is cold, and
goodness dies in wishes; as Voltaire said, 'tis the misfortune of worthy
people that they are cowards; 'un des plus grands malheurs des honnetes gens
c'est qu'ils sont des laches.'" To convert insight into energy of will requires
conversion — "the conversion of the man into his will, making him the
will, and the will him."[57] How is this conversion to be accomplished? History, Emerson had learned, sometimes makes resolute actors even of
timorous people.

His own conversion experience came, as it did for many of his generation, when a seventeen-year-old fugitive named Thomas Sims was cap-

55. Emerson, *Collected Works*, 6:111.
56. Emerson, *Collected Works*, 6:111.
57. Emerson, *Collected Works*, 6:16.

tured in Boston. A Boston magistrate, Judge Lemuel Shaw, acting according to the provisions of the 1850 Fugitive Slave Law, refused to release
Sims from jail and instead ordered him returned to the Georgia slave
owner who claimed him.

The Sims rendition affected Emerson as no previous incident had. To
see the wealth, power, and intellect of Boston massed against a poor
black boy who had risked death to gain freedom changed Emerson from
a measured sympathizer with antislavery causes to a believer in the necessity of abolition. That his hero Daniel Webster, now Secretary of
State and a firm supporter of the Fugitive Slave Law, had been in Boston
when the Sims capture occurred and had applauded the rendition only
made matters worse. Webster's defense of expediency over justice now
seemed to epitomize the corruption of an entire class. The names that
had once meant honor and learning to Emerson — "Mr Choate, Mr
Webster, & Mr Foote, Mr Clay, & Mr Everett" — now signified something else:

> Their names are tarnished: what we have tried to call great, is little;
> and the merely ethnographic fact remains that an immense external
> prosperity is possible, with pure cowardice & hollowness in all the
> conspicuous official men. I cannot read longer with any comfort the
> local good news[,] even "Education in Massachusetts."[58]

That politicians vacillated was only to be expected; what hurt more was
the tameness of the intellectual classes. "It is not to be disguised that all
our contemporaries[,] scholars as well as merchants[,] feel the great Despair, are mere Whigs, & believe in nothing. Repent ye, for the Kingdom
of heaven is at hand."[59]

Unbelief as Emerson is here defining it has nothing to do with assent
to doctrines of the Christian churches, or with universal religion, or even
with the tenets of impersonal Theism. Willingness to enforce, or approve of, the Fugitive Slave Law was now the sole test of belief, and the
Episcopalian clergyman who in conversation blandly praised Webster revealed himself as a limb of the devil. But the powers of darkness, formi-

58. Emerson, *Journals and Miscellaneous Notebooks,* 11:346.
59. Emerson, *Journals and Miscellaneous Notebooks,* 11:375.

dable though they seemed in 1851, had enemies even more powerful than themselves. The Fugitive Slave Law "is contrary to the sense of Duty; and therefore all human beings, in proportion to their power of thought & their moral sensibility, are, as soon as they are born, the natural enemies of this statute."[60] Indeed, it contravenes the laws of nature, as Webster would discover when it cost him his reputation. "For it is <as> certain <as> that water will boil at 212° or stones fall, or sap rise, that he will be cast & ruined. He fights with an adversary not subject to casualties." And he added his favorite line from the *Marseillaise:* "Tout est soldat pour vous combattre[.]"[61]

What the struggle against the Fugitive Slave Law, and against slavery itself, restored to Emerson was not belief in a divine principle, for that he had never lost, but a sense that he could once again claim to belong to a community of believers. The very outrages to the moral sentiment that the law created would some day prove its undoing. At the close of his second address on the Fugitive Slave Law, delivered in 1854 in New York, he looked forward to a future in which individuals and states were enlisting at last in the cause of justice, and hence of belief:

> The Antislavery Society will add many members this year. The Whig party will join it. The Democrats will join it. The population of the Free States will join it. I doubt not, at last, the slave states will join it. But be that sooner or later, — and whoever comes or stays away, — I hope we have come to an end of our unbelief, have come to a belief that there is a Divine Providence in the world which will not save us but through our own cooperation.[62]

60. Emerson, *Journals and Miscellaneous Notebooks,* 11:362.

61. Emerson, *Journals and Miscellaneous Notebooks,* 11:358. Because they are important here, I have included the words Emerson wrote and then cancelled in this passage (cancelled words are contained between broken brackets).

62. Emerson, "Seventh of March Speech on the Fugitive Slave Law, 7 March 1854," in *The Later Lectures of Ralph Waldo Emerson 1843-1871,* ed. Ronald A. Bosco and Joel Myerson (Athens: University of Georgia Press, 2001), 1:347.

# "Rare and Delectable Places":
# Thoreau's Imagination of
# Sacred Space at Walden

*John Gatta*

## Spirits of Concord

Few classic works of American literature are so intensely identified with
a particular geographic site as Thoreau's *Walden*. Today the setting of
this experiment in solitary living near the village of Concord, Massachusetts, remains a tourist mecca — and qualifies, for many, as a literary
shrine. In fact, an energetic woman who resided in my corner of Connecticut helped for some years to lead a group called Walden Forever
Wild, Inc., in its efforts to designate the pond area a Massachusetts State
Sanctuary on the grounds that "its spiritual sanctity should be preserved
beyond demands for local use."[1] Textual evidence suggests that Thoreau
too regarded the pond precincts as sacred space but in a more complicated — and, I think, more deeply Transcendental — way. His most celebrated book underscores the belief that this place he had known from

---

1. Brochure from Walden Forever Wild, Inc. issued from P.O. Box 275 in Concord.
The group's quarterly newsletter, "Voice of Walden," has had an editorial office in Storrs,
Connecticut. Mary Sherwood, a forester who championed preservation of the Walden
plot and had formerly lived in Concord, was 95 when she died in July 2001. In *The Environmental Imagination: Thoreau, Nature Writing, and the Formation of American Culture* (Cambridge: Belknap Press of Harvard University Press, 1995), Lawrence Buell comments extensively on the process of Thoreau's extraliterary canonization (pp. 311-69) and observes
that he is now widely recognized as "The patron saint of American environmental writing" (p. 115).

23

childhood, this remnant of a wilder New England so close to civilization, was not just an attractive place to live cheaply and freely. As the focal point of Thoreau's romantic naturalism, it was also the locus of his worship and spiritual discovery. In other published writings Thoreau offers descriptive commentary on diverse sites he had visited, including Cape Cod, the Maine Woods, the Concord and Merrimack Rivers, and Wachusett Mountain. But in the singular case of that book originally subtitled "life in the woods," Thoreau reflects at length on a place he had not only visited, but inhabited.

Much has been written, of course, about the crucial matter of Thoreau's response to the nonhuman world. That Thoreau sustained a lifelong belief in the spiritual significations of nature, despite the heightened attention he showed after 1850 toward scientific details of his material environment, has generally been acknowledged.[2] But what did it actually mean for Thoreau to regard Walden Pond and the surrounding woodlands as sacred space? For that matter, just how might one define Thoreau's sense of the sacred, as conjoined with his fundamentally religious apprehension of nature? And how, finally, did Thoreau's syncretistic, largely non-Christian theology of nature nonetheless incorporate selected themes of biblical Christianity?

Consistent with the richly allusive character of *Walden,* Thoreau sounds several dimensions of the sacred in his portrayal of the pond and its environs. While the Transcendental belief at issue here is largely "pagan" in orientation, a faith commonly described as pantheistic and as substantially influenced by Asian philosophy and religion, Thoreau also drew heavily on scriptural and other elements of Christian tradition to map the distinctive spiritual geography represented in Walden. There is, for exam-

2. See, for example, Buell, *Environmental Imagination,* especially p. 117; and Walter Harding, *The Days of Henry Thoreau: A Biography* (1965; repr. New York: Dover, 1982), pp. 290-93. Some of Thoreau's later natural history writings, including "The Dispersion of Seeds" and "Wild Fruits" — published in *Faith in a Seed: The Dispersion of Seeds and Other Late Natural History Writings,* ed. Bradley P. Dean (Washington, D.C.: Island Press/Shearwater Books, 1993) — are indeed highly scientific and largely but not entirely secular in orientation, as discussed by Ronald Wesley Hoag, "Thoreau's Later Natural History Writings," in *The Cambridge Companion to Henry David Thoreau,* ed. Joel Myerson (New York: Cambridge University Press, 1995), pp. 152-70.

ple, clear biblical precedent — especially throughout the Exodus narratives — for the paradoxical tension Thoreau sustains between devotion to his own "Holy Land" of Concord and his self-description as a "saunterer" journeying perpetually through the world without attachment to home or property.[3] He is at once well rooted to place, or (as he puts it in "The Bean-Field" chapter) "attached . . . to the earth," and the unencumbered sojourner. He has, in short, "travelled a good deal in Concord."[4] Despite Thoreau's rejection of organized religion and his unceasing jibes against Christian churches and clerics, his allusions to biblical texts actually became more pervasive in *Walden* than they had been previously in the *Week*.[5]

3. Henry David Thoreau, "Walking," in *Excursions* (1863; repr. Gloucester, Mass.: Peter Smith, 1975), pp. 161, 214.

4. Henry David Thoreau, *Walden*, in *The Writings of Henry D. Thoreau*, ed. J. Lyndon Shanley (Princeton: Princeton University Press, 1971), pp. 4, 155; hereafter cited in the text as *W.*

5. William J. Wolf, *Thoreau: Mystic, Prophet, Ecologist* (Philadelphia: United Church Press, 1974), p. 93. In addition to Wolf's book, other general assessments of Thoreau's religious beliefs can be found in Walter Harding and Michael Meyer, *The New Thoreau Handbook* (New York: New York University Press, 1980), pp. 130-32; Catherine L. Albanese, *Nature Religion in America: From the Algonkian Indians to the New Age* (Chicago: University of Chicago Press, 1990), pp. 87-93; Alexander C. Kern, "Church, Scripture, Nature, and Ethics in Henry Thoreau's Religious Thought," in *Literature and Ideas in America: Essays in Memory of Harry Hayden Clark*, ed. Robert Falk (Athens: Ohio University Press, 1975), pp. 79-95; and Edward Wagenknecht, *Henry David Thoreau: What Manner of Man?* (Amherst: University of Massachusetts Press, 1981), pp. 155-72. Relevant but more specialized commentaries linked to specific Thoreauvian texts include John B. Pickard, "The Religion of 'Higher Laws,'" *Emerson Society Quarterly* 39 (1965): 68-72; Reginald L. Cook, "Ancient Rites at Walden," *Emerson Society Quarterly* 39 (1965): 52-56; and Jonathan Bishop, "The Experience of the Sacred in Thoreau's *Week*," *English Literary History* 33 (1966): 66-91. See also Philip F. Gura, *The Crossroads of American History and Literature* (University Park: Pennsylvania State University Press, 1996), pp. 228-33 and 246-49, for illuminating remarks about Thoreau's religious responses to foxfire and other signs of "'certain *transcendentia*'" in the creaturely world during his travels in Maine. Thoreau's eclectic and largely self-fashioned interest in Asian religions, which I do not attempt to analyze here, has been ably discussed elsewhere — by Arthur Christy, *The Orient in American Transcendentalism: A Study of Emerson, Thoreau, and Alcott* (New York: Farrar, 1972), pp. 185-233; and by Arthur Versluis, *American Transcendentalism and Asian Religions* (New York: Oxford University Press, 1993), pp. 79-99. Another noteworthy account of Thoreau's religious imagination, Alan D. Hodder's book on *Thoreau's Ecstatic Witness* (New Haven: Yale University Press, 2001), appeared while my own study was assuming its final shape. I regard Hodder's ap-

And despite disdainful remarks about God's "personality,"[6] Thoreau's version of nature mysticism incorporates elements of traditional Christian belief in a personal Creator and in the world as divine creation.

Did Thoreau, then, believe in a personal God? Because of his fondness for Transcendental inconsistency and distaste for articulated doctrine, the question admits of no simple answer. On the one hand, his writing commonly personalizes the deity through its pronoun references and its figurative portrayals of God as Creator, as the "original proprietor" of Walden Pond — and as congenial artisan, speaker, or musician. The journal confirms that in his maturity, Thoreau was more often willing than Emerson was at a comparable phase to address God as a presence beyond himself, as a someone he could imagine being both the object and the source of love. Not surprisingly, this affective dimension of Thoreau's tentative theism appears more prominently in journal entries recorded soon after the gruesome death of his brother John in 1842, when the pain of Henry's loneliness was most acute. On the other hand, it is hard to know just how seriously or literally to take Thoreau's playful images of divinity — or for that matter, his related personifications of the Pond and other features of nature. Moreover, other references in the journal and elsewhere seem to support the more typically Emersonian conception of a thoroughly internalized or impersonal deity. Though the coloration of Thoreau's beliefs changed over time, he remained emphatic in his rejec-

---

proach as different from yet fundamentally compatible with mine. Hodder emphasizes Thoreau's responses to Orientalism (pp. 142, 174-217), his religious appreciation of "ecstasy" (that is, "experiences of inspiration and euphoria in the natural world," p. 21), and his lifelong "spiritual biography" (p. xiv) as reflected in the journal and *A Week* as well as in *Walden*. My treatment is more concerned with close reading of certain sections of *Walden* (particularly the sand foliage passage), with the influence of biblical Christianity and hermeneutics on Thoreau's religious outlook, and with the author's sense of place and internalization of developmental science. It should be apparent, however, that I share Hodder's insistence on "the intensely religious character" of Thoreau's "personal transactions with nature" and "the emphatically religious character of so much of his life and writing" even though he was "no friend of organized religion" (pp. 300, 20, 3).

6. In the "Sunday" chapter of *A Week on the Concord and Merrimack Rivers,* Thoreau inveighs with some passion against anthropomorphic images sponsored by Jewish and Christian theism. But this earlier polemic against divine "personality," which corresponds to Emerson's Transcendental principle that the "soul knows no persons," gives way to a less consistent, more complex theological language in *Walden*.

tion of Jesus' unique divinity and of the Hebraic image of a stern and jealous "Jehovah." In a journal entry recorded in April or May of 1850, he expressed his preference for the "purer more independent and impersonal knowledge of God" he saw represented in the contemplative writings of Vedic Hinduism;[7] yet Hindu tradition is itself elusive and elastic with regard to concepts of divine personality or polytheism.

Above all, Thoreau insisted that "God," if authentically divine and transcendent, must transcend all human images and description. This apophatic awareness of God as truly ineffable Being appears in many sacred texts of Hinduism and Buddhism (including the Upanishads and Zen works not known to Thoreau by the time he wrote *Walden*) as well as in Christian writings such as the *Mystical Theology* by Pseudo-Dionysius the Areopagite, a sixth-century Syrian monk, and the fourteenth-century *Cloud of Unknowing*. For Thoreau, however, the personal God that Christian churches of his day purported to worship was nothing more than a frightfully enlarged human person, a grossly anthropomorphic projection. "All the gods that are worshipped have been men," he declared in his journal for 1849, "but of the true God of whom none have conceived — all men combined would hardly furnish the germ" (*PJ* 3:7). If he could not describe such a Being, he nonetheless regarded naturalistic experience as his chief means of pursuing "the true God." *Walden* marks a critical stage in his lifelong quest to embrace a sacred reality whose essence he could not hope to explain.

Perhaps the first thing to notice, rhetorically, in approaching *Walden* is the regularity with which Thoreau uses the word "sacred" — to evoke not a distinct supernatural order, but a transcendent dimension of this physical world antithetical to the "profane."[8] For Thoreau, the "profane"

7. Henry David Thoreau, *The Writings of Henry D. Thoreau: Journal*, ed. John C. Broderick et al. (Princeton: Princeton University Press, 1981), 3:61; hereafter cited in the text as *PJ*.

8. Mircea Eliade's classic study, *The Sacred and the Profane: The Nature of Religion*, trans. Willard R. Trask (New York: Harcourt, 1959), likewise defines the sacred as "the opposite of the profane" (p. 10). At least one previous commentator has confirmed Eliade's pertinence to *Walden*, particularly with reference to the "book's persistent dialectic between the sacred and the profane" (p. 268). See David E. Whisnant's "The Sacred and the Profane in *Walden*," *The Centennial Review* 14 (1970): 267-83.

is associated not just with overt degradation but also with commonplace dullness or inertia, with failure to realize the divine fullness of Transcendental imagination. Often, too, he links the profane quite physically to human alterations or deformations of the landscape. He remarks, for example, on how "the woodcutters, and the railroad, and I myself have profaned Walden" (*W* 197).

In Mircea Eliade's classic formulation, sacred space is a place set apart as "exceptional," a spot regarded as auspicious for experiencing some opening toward the transcendent. For Eliade, the sacred place "constitutes a break in the homogeneity of space, so that archaic peoples readily perceive it to stand symbolically as the Center of the World and nearest abode to heaven."[9] And insofar as the sacred corresponds most broadly to an experience of the numinous — that is, to encounter with something "wholly other," beyond the usual bounds of human culture, the nonhuman world of nature is evidently allied to the numinous. Confronting nature's "wildness" has at least a potential religious value, then, insofar as it helps us, in Thoreau's words, "to witness our own limits transgressed, and some life pasturing freely where we never wander." Despite his occasional labor as a surveyor setting boundaries, Thoreau is most intrigued by the human hunger for boundlessness, our desire "that all things be mysterious and unexplorable, that land and sea be infinitely wild, unsurveyed and unfathomed by us because unfathomable" (*W* 317-18).

Eliade's description of how "primitive peoples" ritualize space is, I think, strikingly applicable to Thoreau's project of reaching beyond the desacralizing tendencies of post-Enlightenment civilization to recover a spiritually archaic or "original relation to the universe."[10] It is particularly relevant to the second chapter of *Walden,* which is replete with place references, both geographic and figurative. When Thoreau presents his central statement on "Where I Lived and What I Lived For," even the chapter title ties his broader search for existential purpose to a particular locale. Just as Thoreau's reasons for living at Walden go well beyond his initial plan to finish writing *A Week on the Concord and Merrimack Rivers*

9. Eliade, *Sacred and Profane,* pp. 37, 39.

10. Ralph Waldo Emerson, *Nature,* in *The Collected Works of Ralph Waldo Emerson,* ed. Robert E. Spiller and Alfred R. Ferguson (Cambridge: Harvard University Press, 1971-), I:7.

there, so also his cognizance of the place itself — or, as we might say colloquially, of "where he's at" — expands beyond the mapspace to further planes of perception. In this key second chapter we are urged to believe that meditating on *where* the author lived will also clarify just *what* makes life worth living. After first describing the physical coordinates of his address — by a small pond, low in the woods, about "a mile and a half south of the village of Concord" (*W* 86), Thoreau looks toward loftier horizons of space and time to see himself seated indeed at the divine center of things. What he calls "one of the best things which I did," his morning practice of bathing daily in the pond, becomes a "religious exercise" (*W* 88) not only of interior self-renewal but also of ritualized connection to his outdoor environment. Like the communal purification rites of traditional peoples, yet in terms consistent with Christian understanding, such activity becomes for Thoreau a true "sacrament" — that is, an "'outward and visible sign of an inward and spiritual grace'" (*W* 69).[11] If *where Henry lives,* legally speaking, is only a parcel of Waldo's real estate,[12] he has nonetheless claimed it by power of imagination — and by squatter's rights of occupation — as the property of his own spirit.

11. Despite Thoreau's somewhat facetious reference to the Bible as "an old book" (*W* 5), sacramental language linked to Christian imagery is surprisingly abundant in his writing. In 1845, for example, he reported feeling that through his fruit and nut diet, "eating became a sacrament — a method of communion" and of "sitting at the communion table of the world" (*PJ* 2:165). As discussed by R. W. B. Lewis in *The American Adam: Innocence, Tragedy, and Tradition in the Nineteenth Century* (Chicago: University of Chicago Press, 1955), pp. 20-27, Thoreau significantly revised St. Paul's understanding of sacred mystery in formulating "his own sacramental system" (p. 22). But Lewis interprets Thoreau's nature-centered ritualism as a total inversion of Paul's emphasis on overcoming "nature" and the "natural man." I consider the relation to be more complicated and problematic — not only because of major linguistic shifts in meaning from Paul's first-century "natural man" (1 Corinthians 2:14 in KJV) to Thoreau's nineteenth-century "nature," but also because of the highly ambivalent anthropology Thoreau manifests in "Higher Laws." The tendency to confuse pre-modern references to "nature," as a philosophic term unrelated to outdoor landscapes, with biota in the modern sense persists in many current discussions of environmental issues. In Paul's typical usage, for example, the "natural" or "unspiritual" is best understood as antithetical not to culture or civilization but to "spiritual" persons and things.

12. On Emerson's circumstance as proprietor, see Walter Harding's edition of *The Variorum Walden and the Variorum Civil Disobedience* (New York: Simon, 1968), p. 268, n. 132, together with Harding's remarks in *The Days of Henry Thoreau,* pp. 179-80, 191, 216.

One way Thoreau imaginatively establishes Walden's status as a sacred place is through his application of temple imagery to the pond, to the pine groves and forest topography, and especially to the author's self-constructed house. "Verily," he writes in his journal for 1845, "a good house is a temple — A clean house — pure and undefiled, as the saying is. I have seen such made of white pine" (*PJ* 2:156). For Thoreau, of course, the temple's aura of localized sanctity derived from Greco-Roman and Asian religious systems as well as from Hebrew scriptures and Christian tradition. Yet Walden, envisioned with vital particularity in all seasons, is clearly Thoreau's place of worship — his church, in the physical sense of a finite space. Punning on the place-name of this "Walled-in" refuge from competitive society (*W* 183), the author envisions the shores of his pond — elsewhere litanized as "God's drop" (*W* 194) — to be set apart from the profane world. Walden is "a gem of the first water" (*W* 179), a reservoir of original cosmogonal purity said to be bottomless.[13] Here indeed "the morning wind forever blows, the poem of creation is uninterrupted" (*W* 85). Though we are "wont to imagine rare and delectable places" of divine presence in the far reaches of outer space, Thoreau discovers that his "house actually had its site in such a withdrawn, but forever new and unprofaned, part of the universe." If "in eternity there is indeed something true and sublime," Thoreau confirms that "all these times and places and occasions" of transcendence "are now and here" since "God himself culminates in the present moment and will never be more divine in the lapse of all the ages" (*W* 88, 97).

Thus, Thoreau's contemplative engagement with Walden, supported by the physical involvement of his daily immersion ritual, amounts to a centering exercise. For Thoreau, the pond defines "where I lived" not only geographically but also on that spiritual, existential plane at a right angle to the *axis mundi*. Walden qualifies all the more as a sacred center because the author can imagine the unpeopled space around him to be "as much Asia or Africa as New England" (*W* 130).

But just how welcome, in the face of our current environmental predicament, should we find Thoreau's emphasis on the sacred potential of

13. For elaborative commentary on the pond's connection to sacred cosmology, see David E. Whisnant, "Sacred and Profane," pp. 277-80.

wildness? Should we really believe that in "Wildness is the preservation [or, in Aldo Leopold's telling misquotation, the "salvation"] of the World"?[14] How helpful to our circumstance is Thoreau's insistence on preserving "rare and delectable places" at some remove from urban society? Not very, according to some recent commentators. In fact, the impulse to valorize wilderness terrain as uniquely godly by contrast with the presumably fallen, corrupted state of all settled landscapes has been called unfortunate and even pernicious. Some, including the distinguished environmental historian William Cronon, have blamed Thoreau for contributing to this enduring myth of the romantic sublime. According to such critics, present-day wilderness advocates inspired by Thoreau typically fail to recognize that wilderness is always a cultural construct and that the ideal of recovering a pristine, sanctified face of nature is always illusory. Nature is, by its very nature, ever-changing. So to make a fetish of protecting roadless territories from human influence will only distract us, say some, from the real environmental challenge, which is learning how to make our home wisely in this physical world. Thus Cronon includes in his published edition of symposium pieces on the theme of "reinventing nature" an essay of his own significantly titled "The Trouble with Wilderness; or Getting Back to the Wrong Nature."[15]

Now it is certainly true, as we've already noted, that Thoreau sacralizes features of his physical landscape, often drawing on temple imagery in the process. For him the leaves of the wild andromeda were, according to one journal entry, "stained windows in the cathedral of my world" (PJ 4:471). It is likewise evident that some of the author's descriptions of untamed nature, including his well-known account of ascending Mount Katahdin in *The Maine Woods*, reflect an awestruck fascination with wilderness — responses linked to notions of the sublime that had become commonplace by the eighteenth century.[16]

14. Thoreau, "Walking," p. 185; Aldo Leopold, *A Sand County Almanac* (New York: Oxford University Press, 1966), p. 141.

15. William Cronon, "The Trouble with Wilderness; or, Getting Back to the Wrong Nature," in *Uncommon Ground: Toward Reinventing Nature*, ed. William Cronon (New York: Norton, 1995), esp. pp. 69, 71, 74-75.

16. On the intellectual history of sublime landscapes, see, for example, Cronon's *Uncommon Ground*, p. 73, and Barbara Novak, *Nature and Culture: American Landscape Painting*,

Yet in several key respects, Thoreau's spirituality of place transcends those naive versions of romantic wilderness worship with which it is often equated. Instead of fetishizing the Concord woods as exotic or monumentally sublime, Thoreau cherishes them as his home ground. The authorial consciousness of *Walden* shows an elaborate self-awareness of how imagination, in the spirit of Wordsworth, half-creates what it perceives about a place's hierophantic power. Particularly in his concluding chapters, Thoreau presents Walden's landscape — despite his fondly detailed delineation of it — as more exemplary than unique. This place, in other words, becomes for him at once exceptional and commonplace — and as Transcendental commonplace, opens toward anyone's spiritual epiphany much as the village common does in the first chapter of Emerson's *Nature.* By centering attention now on two epiphanic moments in *Walden,* we might begin to grasp how this work imaginatively re-creates the author's spiritual relation to his environment.

## Active and Contemplative Religion

The first telling episode is Thoreau's account of morning meditation toward the beginning of the chapter "Sounds." Having first declared his love for a "broad margin" to his life, the author relates how he had sometimes confined himself quite narrowly within the frame of his doorway for an entire summer morning. There he simply sat in the sun, "rapt in a revery, amidst the pines and hickories and sumachs, in undisturbed solitude and stillness, while the birds sang around or flitted noiseless through the house." Thus oblivious to the passage of time, he says he "realized what the Orientals mean by contemplation and the forsaking of works" (*W* III-12).[17] The sacred character of such repose is confirmed by journal

---

*1825-1875* (New York: Oxford University Press, 1980). The more depressing and intimidating aspect of Thoreau's response to Katahdin does not, however, entirely fit conventional notions of the sublime.

17. Thoreau's personal claims to attaining yogic status remained tentative and qualified. Yet two elements of Hindu religious tradition strike me as particularly relevant to the Thoreauvian faith highlighted in my subsequent discussion: (1) a sense of physical creation as continuous process, emanating directly from God; (2) a perception of the

entries in which he aspires to be "as still as God is," or praises that animal contentment that he supposes "comes of resting quietly in God's palm" (*PJ* 1:349, 371).

Particularly noteworthy for our purposes is the way Thoreau sets his account of meditative engagement with nature squarely inside a domestic portal. The open doorway, like the window at which the observer-listener sits later on in "Sounds," corresponds to Eliade's image of the mythical threshold. It marks a boundary not only between two physical spaces, but also between "two modes of being, the profane and the religious."[18] For Thoreau, though, the doorway becomes a fluid, not fixed, frontier between indoor and outdoor environments, just as the chapter as a whole recollects a mélange of sounds produced by civilized commerce and nonhuman creatures. While birds pass freely *into* his house, the author's soul passes outside its wood frame to encounter the uncut pines, hickories, and sumacs. As Sherman Paul and others have stressed over the years,[19] Thoreau's primary interaction with nature's wildness at Walden occurs not amid geophysical wilderness but in more settled territory. For Thoreau, as for Aldo Leopold, "wildness" is not synonymous with "wilderness." *Walden* conspicuously lacks the emphasis on exoticism, on images of scenic grandeur, associated with most

---

yogi's vocation as co-creator with God. As Robert Kuhn McGregor observes in *A Wider View of the Universe: Henry Thoreau's Study of Nature* (Urbana: University of Illinois Press, 1997), Thoreau would have encountered the dynamic principle associated with the first point from his early reading of "The Laws of Manu" (p. 98). And in a journal entry for 1851, Thoreau asserts that "the Yogin, absorbed in contemplation, contributes for his part to creation . . . Divine forms traverse him without tearing him, and united to the nature which is proper to him, he goes he acts, as animating original matter" (*PJ* 3:216).

18. Eliade, *The Sacred and the Profane,* pp. 24-26.

19. Sherman Paul, *The Shores of America: Thoreau's Inward Exploration* (Urbana: University of Illinois Press, 1958), esp. pp. 306-7. More recently, several commentators have emphasized the non-pristine character of Thoreau's physical environment at Walden and have analyzed more closely the marginal social circumstances (as regards race and class) of his human neighbors. See, for example, Robert Sattelmeyer, "Depopulation, Deforestation, and the Actual Walden Pond," in *Thoreau's Sense of Place: Essays in American Environmental Writing,* ed. Richard J. Schneider (Iowa City: University of Iowa Press, 2000), pp. 235-43; McGregor, *A Wider View of the Universe,* esp. pp. 7-31; and David R. Foster, *Thoreau's Country: Journey through a Transformed Landscape* (Cambridge: Harvard University Press, 1999).

wilderness travel literature. And it is certainly concerned with how to make a home in nature, starting at the most graphically literal plane of construction.

Thoreau, unlike some present-day deep ecologists, does not condemn every human alteration of the landscape as a deformation. This point is evident from his willingness to cultivate the earth in chapter seven, "The Bean-Field." Beyond the practical value of raising crops such as beans and corn, his spade labor in a "half-cultivated field" (*W* 158) near his house connects him more solidly to the soil — and to the original dust of his own nature. It also reinforces his spiritual kinship with Native Americans who once worked the same plot, likewise raising beans and corn. While censuring typical farming practices of his day, Thoreau insists that agriculture qualified in ancient tradition as "a sacred art," and that something of the sacred calling of "husbandry" might still be recovered through morally reflective engagement with the soil.

Granted, Thoreau's own garden version of farming never became a full-time occupation or sole means of support. His hoeing and weeding in the dirt nonetheless offer a much earthier picture of encounter with sacred nature than does the tourist's awestruck gaze at some titanic cataract. Thus, the author's much-discussed pastoralism bears religious as well as socio-cultural significance. Though American pastoral often supports an unreflective and regressive ideology of nostalgia,[20] the version of agrarianism cultivated most assiduously in "The Bean-Field" is self-consciously religious insofar as it offers a ritual discipline, a practical means of working out one's salvation. Growing beans not only helped Thoreau heal his culturally inherited alienation from the earth; it also mediated his limited connection with human society through the market economy. Unlike the subsistence farmer, this planter bartered his beans for rice.

That Thoreau typically calls his habitation a house, not a cabin or shack,[21] underscores his willingness to enrich his life in the woods with what he takes to be the best things of civilization — including books and writing instruments. Toward more intrusive activities of the industrial

20. See Buell, *The Environmental Imagination,* pp. 31-52.

21. See Philip Van Doren Stern's remarks in *The Annotated Walden* (New York: Clarkson Potter, 1970), p. 45.

world, such as the noisy rush of the Fitchburg Railroad or the winter work of ice cutters on the pond, he betrays attitudes ranging from scornful satire to cheerful acceptance. Even commerce, though, can sometimes find a place in Thoreau's sacral vision of nature. After telegraph wires reach Concord in 1851, Thoreau testifies in his journal to the delight and "revelation" he experiences in hearing celestial music of the "telegraphy harp" (*PJ* 4:89-91, 5:436). In *Walden*, he muses with satisfaction that when New England merchants sell pond ice to India, the "pure Walden water," which he likes to consider "as sacred as the Ganges," might mingle in fact "with the sacred water of the Ganges" (*W* 192, 298).

## Sandbank Visions of Numinous Evolution

Nowhere is this comprehensive quality of Thoreau's vision more apparent than in the justly renowned railroad-cut passage found in the book's penultimate chapter, "Spring." This stunning etymological rhapsody starts from the simple act of observing the flow of sand and clay on the bankside of the rail cut, at the pond's western edge, during spring thaw. Warmed by sunlight, the icy sand flows down "like lava." The cosmogonic story continues as sandstreams form themselves into leaves and vines. Then, swept by a copious stream of linguistic correspondences emanating from the word "lobe," these vegetative leaves turn into fatty leaves suggestive of animal parts and, finally, of the human body. For, after all, "what is man but a mass of thawing clay?" (*W* 307).

What Thoreau envisions in this common earthbank, which is clearly an artifact of rail commerce rather than a fact of wilderness nature, is nothing less than Lucretius's nature of all things. With benefit of imagination, one gazes here into the mystery of life itself. Before Thoreau's eyes, the world evolves almost instantly from chaos to cosmos, from primordial energy to the leaves of his own book in progress. The full course of Creation appears, in a progression from lava sand through vegetable leaf to human consciousness as imaged in the great tree of language.[22]

22. In *The Roots of Walden and the Tree of Life* (Nashville: Vanderbilt University Press, 1990), Gordon V. Boudreau surveys the enormous quantity and range of commentary that

Exposed through the centering omphalos of the deep cut are both Culture and Nature, art and animality.

Within this dynamically evolutionary tableau of creation, Thoreau nonetheless finds room for a divine maker with personal attributes. Rather than pantheism, such a theology has been aptly termed panentheism, because it regards the whole universe as a divine milieu while recognizing the presence of a transcendent God who in some manner exceeds the bounds of this created universe.[23] Earlier, Thoreau had playfully described his pleasure at receiving winter visits from that "old settler and original proprietor, who is reported to have dug Walden Pond, and stoned it, and fringed it with pine woods; who tells me stories of old time and of new eternity" (*W* 137). This congenial deity had, the author teases, used a "divining rod" (*W* 182) to site the excavation for Walden's well. Through another pun, Thoreau had likened a legal bequest to the determinations of a personal creator who "rounded this water with his hand, deepened and clarified it in his thought, and in his will bequeathed it to Concord" (*W* 93). Now he is moved to describe a God who combines the scientist's *sapientia,* in this case involving zeal for experimental knowledge, with the artist's love of cosmos, or beauty:

> What makes this sand foliage remarkable is its springing into existence thus suddenly. When I see on the one side the inert bank, — for the sun acts on one side first, — and on the other this luxuriant foliage, the creation of an hour, I am affected as if in a peculiar sense I stood in

---

this section of *Walden* has elicited. As Boudreau observes, "in the latter half of the twentieth century the sand foliage passages have become a critical proving ground for Freudian and Eriksonian critics" (p. 2). For historically based analysis focused on philological implications of the passage, see Philip F. Gura, *The Wisdom of Words: Language, Theology, and Literature in the New England Renaissance* (Middletown, Conn.: Wesleyan University Press, 1981), pp. 132-37. Though the section's religious import has rarely been emphasized, Boudreau's book offers useful suggestions toward constructing such a reading.

23. See Edward Wagenknecht, *What Manner of Man?* pp. 170-72; and William Wolf, *Thoreau,* pp. 151-62, 172-75. Although Horace Greeley's influential (and disparaging) description of *Walden's* philosophy as pantheistic might seem to be confirmed by the explicit homage to Pan that Thoreau had recorded in *A Week,* Wolf (p. 157) points out the etymological fallacy involved in this linkage. Hodder presents another view of the matter in *Thoreau's Ecstatic Witness,* pp. 143-44.

the laboratory of the Artist who made the world and me, — had come to where he was still at work, sporting on this bank, and with excess of energy strewing his fresh designs about. I feel as if I were nearer to the vitals of the globe, for this sandy overflow is something such a foliaceous mass as the vitals of the animal body. You find thus in the very sands an anticipation of the vegetable leaf. No wonder that the earth expresses itself outwardly in leaves, it so labors with the idea inwardly. The atoms have already learned this law, and are pregnant by it. The overhanging leaf sees here its prototype. *Internally*, whether in the globe or animal body, it is a moist thick *lobe*, a word especially applicable to the liver and lungs and the leaves of fat.

Thus it seemed that this one hillside illustrated the principle of all the operations of Nature. The Maker of this earth but patented a leaf. What Champollion will decipher this hieroglyphic for us, that we may turn over a new leaf at last? This phenomenon is more exhilarating to me than the luxuriance and fertility of vineyards. True, it is somewhat excrementitious in its character, and there is no end to the heaps of liver lights and bowels, as if the globe were turned wrong side outward; but this suggests at least that Nature has some bowels, and there again is mother of humanity. (W 306-8)

In the cutaway moment, Thoreau comes to a place where the Creator is "still at work." While he ends up recapitulating the entire course of temporal cosmology, he testifies above all to the essential dynamism of *bios*, the encapsulated drama of a continuous creation. And within this drama he, too, plays a discernible role. Thoreau's representation of numinous nature advances, therefore, from more conventionally static images of sacred space to this dynamic icon of sacred mystery. To perceive the wonder of inhabiting a continuously regenerative and divine creation is, above all, to appreciate the wildness of life as *bios*. For "it is in vain," Thoreau tells his journal in 1856, "to dream of a wildness distant from ourselves. There is none such. It is the bog in our brain and bowels, the primitive vigor of Nature in us, that inspires that dream."[24] The elemental *bios* revealed in the railroad cut, which runs from the excremental depth of bowels to the mental heights of humankind's cranial "lobe," en-

24. Thoreau, quoted in Foster, *Thoreau's Country*, p. 5.

compasses more than botany and zoology to embrace those interlayered zones of reality that philosopher Ken Wilber discusses under the headings of physiosphere, biosphere, and noosphere.[25] Geography, then, is consequential but never sacred unto itself. The railroad deep cut, though discovered near Walden, could run as well through the Bronx or anywhere else.

The sand foliage passage seems to me remarkable not for its exposé of the author's personal psychology — or pathology, as some analysts would suggest — but for its bold intellectual synthesis, its bid to re-envision nature's numinousness in the new light of evolutionary theory. Some years before encountering Darwin, Thoreau had already begun to reflect seriously on competing views of evolutionary change (or, in the contemporary idiom, of "development") debated in scientific works such as Robert Chambers's *Vestiges of the Natural History of Creation* (1844), Asa Gray's *Manual of the Botany of the Northern United States* (1848), and Louis Agassiz's *Principles of Zoology* (1851, co-authored with Augustus Gould).[26] Like most of the new biology, and likewise consonant with the new geography of Alexander Humboldt and new geology of Charles Lyell, Thoreau's naturalism had by midcentury recognized the vast expanse of time required for changes in landforms and species. In an earlier but revised journal version of the sand foliage passage, while pondering that grand "interval" between earth's preorganic state and the appearance of "luxuriant vegetation," Thoreau refers incredulously to Bishop Ussher's quaint chronology in which God "is reputed to have built this world 6000 years ago" (*PJ* 2:577). Yet Lyell could observe by 1830 that even geologists needed to revise drastically their estimation of time after discovering they had misread physical signs of change once believed to take "thousands of years where the language of nature signified millions."[27] In the same era, higher criticism was highlighting the

25. Ken Wilber, *A Brief History of Everything* (Boston: Shambhala, 1996).

26. See William Rossi, "Thoreau's Transcendental Ecocentrism," in *Thoreau's Sense of Place*, pp. 29-40; and Robert Sattelmeyer, *Thoreau's Reading: A Study in Intellectual History* (Princeton: Princeton University Press, 1988), pp. 82-87.

27. Charles Lyell, *Principles of Geology*, vol. 1 (1830-1833; Chicago: University of Chicago Press, 1990), p. 79. See also Laura Dassow Walls, *Seeing New Worlds: Henry David Thoreau and Nineteenth-Century Science* (Madison: University of Wisconsin Press, 1995), pp.

historical, time-conditioned circumstances of biblical revelation. Just as scientists were discovering the vast temporal scale of natural history and the prevalence of process rather than permanence in environmental analysis, theologians were advancing an evolutionary hermeneutic that found the Bible's eternal truths incarnated in ever-changing circumstances and fallible personages.[28]

Though gathered into a single moment, then, the evolutionary vision Thoreau perceives in the sandbank is expansive across immense intervals of time. It is also teleological and spiritual rather than purely materialistic. Like Robert Chambers, Thoreau had largely disavowed traditional versions of natural theology that featured an argument from design, the special creation of diverse species, and belief that God frequently intervened in physical processes. In fact, the anonymous author of *Vestiges of the Natural History of Creation* was widely suspected of teaching pernicious atheism. Privately, Chambers apparently did wrestle with religious skepticism,[29] but his book nonetheless affirmed that God was "ever present in all things." Although the First Cause did not create by "some sort of immediate or special exertion," the organic universe reflected an unfolding of divine will in accord with primal law, including "advances of the principle of development" through "the whole train of animated beings." For Chambers, the observable facts of life "clearly shew how all the various organic forms of our world are bound up in one — how a fundamental unity pervades and embraces them all" in a system conceived from one "law or decree of the Almighty" though "it did

---

42-44. In addition to Walls (pp. 76-130), Ning Yu offers useful analysis of how Thoreau responded to Humboldt's holistic understanding of science in "The Hydrological Cycle on Katahdin: Thoreau and the New Geography," *ESQ: A Journal of the American Renaissance* 40 (1994): 1-25.

28. In this regard, Coleridge's prose writings offered Thoreau the rare example of evolutionary perception on both planes. In *Confessions of an Inquiring Spirit* and *Aids to Reflection*, Coleridge unfolded his hermeneutics of biblical interpretation, while less prominently in these works but directly in *Hints Towards a More Comprehensive Theory of Life*, he reflected on the language of God presented scientifically by an ascending scale of natural process that reaches from inanimate matter to human consciousness.

29. For Thoreau's exposure to this work, see Robert Sattelmeyer, *Thoreau's Reading*, pp. 86-87; and for a recent assessment of Chambers, see Janet Browne, "Anonymous Author Who Left *Vestiges*," *Times Literary Supplement*, July 13, 2001, pp. 6-7.

not all come forth at one time." So the creative flux of development is on-going, just as the processes by which bodies come to be formed in space are "still and at present in progress."[30] Chambers's account of a continu-ous creation, of an evolution inspired from within matter rather than manipulated successively and supernaturally from without, anticipates Thoreau's own portrayal of sacred cosmology toward the close of *Walden*.

A century later, the scientist-theologian Pierre Teilhard de Chardin would find ways of reconnecting such an evolutionary theology of radi-cal immanence to overtly Christian spirituality. But Thoreau, and subse-quently Whitman, were the first Americans to turn a theology of natural "development" into poetry. As Gordon Boudreau suggests, "perhaps the emergent Darwinian view of nature demanded a muse that had its ex-pression in Thoreau, for *Walden* attains its climactic vision over a thawing bankside in a way to anticipate the tangled bank in the concluding teleo-logical and — dare it be said? — transcendent vision in *The Origin of Spe-cies,* published five years after *Walden*."[31]

Yet the microcosmic revelation of the deep cut only reveals itself by virtue of a human interpreter. If "this one hillside illustrated the princi-ple of all the operations of Nature" so that "The Maker of this earth but patented a leaf," such disclosure requires a discerning reader of the hill-side — and, by extension, of Thoreau's text. Thus, the sand foliage pas-sage must in some sense be read through the book's chapters on "Read-ing" and "Sounds." There Thoreau insists that serious reading involves a reflective discipline capable of leading us to gaze upon divinity and, as he subsequently affirms, to look "always at what is to be seen." Since "much is published, but little printed," one must learn to read nature by decod-ing its visible and aural signs — just as one must know the "particular written languages" of books to discern their meaning (*W* 99, 111). To read birds, for example, requires familiarity with the articulated sounds of each species. Learning to look with understanding at what is already "be-fore you" in the text, field, or sandbank is essentially, then, a problem of

30. Robert Chambers, *Vestiges of the Natural History of Creation and Other Evolutionary Writings,* ed. James A. Secord (Chicago: University of Chicago Press, 1994), pp. 185, 153, 196, 203, 197, 21.

31. Boudreau, *Roots of Walden,* p. 128.

hermeneutics. For Thoreau, the material facts of nature are usually signifiers, but their transcendental import is never self-evident. Sustained reflection is needed to discern those "essential facts of life" lurking in Walden's woods. So while Thoreau's linguistic, psychological, and other concerns have been usefully discussed in connection with the sand foliage passage, I think its most innovative contribution to the environmental imagination is hermeneutical.

In this light, the episode dramatizes a highly developed recognition that humans always and inevitably interpret the facts of nature. Thoreau's ideal is to read — and thereby to live — deliberately, so that the interpretive act becomes fully self-conscious. In so interpreting nature, the integrative imagination reunites the divided realms of human and nonhuman life. When the poet "takes a fact out of nature into spirit," he becomes conscious of that grander, cosmic consciousness in which nature speaks "along with him" (*PJ* 69).

Of course, the idea of "reading" the book of nature in a manner comparable to that of scriptural revelation had already been entertained by many in America. In a previous century, Edwards had found "the Book of Scripture" to be "the interpreter of the book of Nature." In Thoreau's own day, Emerson had not only responded to new biblical approaches associated with the "higher criticism" of Herder and Eichhorn, but had gone so far as to envision Nature and the "aboriginal self" replacing Scripture as the primary locus of "revelation."[32] Yet Emerson's theory of correspondences implied a smoothly incremental progression from nature to language to spirit. And as originally formulated, Emerson's Transcendentalism discounted the world's physicality in favor of an Idealism that regarded Nature as a function of human perception, an "apocalypse of the mind."[33]

While accepting much of Emerson's formulation, Thoreau ordinarily displayed more acute awareness of the split between material na-

32. See Barbara Packer, "Origin and Authority: Emerson and the Higher Criticism," in *Reconstructing American Literary History,* ed. Sacvan Bercovitch (Cambridge: Harvard University Press, 1986), pp. 67-92; and Richard A. Grusin, *Transcendentalist Hermeneutics: Institutional Authority and the Higher Criticism of the Bible* (Durham: Duke University Press, 1991), pp. 1-7, 81-114.

33. Emerson, *Nature,* 1:29.

ture and the dynamics of human interpretation. Insofar as the physical world presents "inhuman" and "unfathomable" sites in which to "witness our own limits transgressed" (*PJ* 339; *W* 318), Nature retains a transcendent otherness, a resistance to assimilation by the self.[34] "I love nature," he insisted in 1853, "partly *because* she is not man, but a retreat from him" (*PJ* 5:422). Accordingly, Thoreau was more insistent than Emerson about humanity's need to decipher nature's hieroglyphics. In the "Spring" chapter of *Walden,* he himself becomes the Champollion graced to transliterate the meanings inscribed in leaf and hillside.[35] And in etymological terms, to approach the nonhuman world as *hiero-glyph* (from Greek *hieros,* or sacred, and *glyph,* carving or script) was already to affirm its religious signification as sacred script. But deciphering this script required an imaginative fusion of subjective and objective sources of revelation. While thus developing his own views concerning a hermeneutics of nature, particularly around 1848 when he was shaping early drafts of the sand bank passage, Thoreau found notable inspiration in his reading of Coleridge.[36]

Since Emerson was more involved than Thoreau in ecclesiastical

34. In *Thoreau as Romantic Naturalist: His Shifting Stance toward Nature* (Ithaca: Cornell University Press, 1974), James McIntosh emphasizes Thoreau's disinclination to follow "the logic of Emerson's subordination of nature, even while he remains aware of this logic with a part of his mind" (p. 9).

35. In recasting Champollion as an interpreter of nature's rather than of ancient Egypt's hieroglyphics, Thoreau may have been influenced by Lyell. In his *Principles of Geology,* vol. 1, Lyell mentions Champollion by way of reminding his readers that prior contextual knowledge (in this case, knowledge of geological history and anthropology) is needed rightly to interpret signs presented by the physical world (p. 76). Further examples of Thoreau's disposition to correlate written texts with biotic signs can be found in several journal entries preceding the publication of *Walden: PJ* 1:47-48, 1:131, 2:163, 2:178, 3:62, 4:28, and 4:392.

36. See Robert Sattelmeyer and Richard A. Hocks, "Thoreau and Coleridge's *Theory of Life,*" in *Studies in the American Renaissance,* ed. Joel Myerson (Charlottesville: University Press of Virginia, 1985), pp. 269-84; and Boudreau, *Roots of Walden,* p. 33. As Sattelmeyer and Hocks point out, Thoreau copied out substantial extracts from this work soon after its posthumous publication in 1848. In *Thoreau's Reading,* Sattelmeyer discusses Thoreau's "marked interest" (p. 30) in other Coleridge prose works — *Aids to Reflection, The Statesman's Manual,* and *Confessions of an Inquiring Spirit* — that he encountered between January and April 1841.

controversies of the day, one should not expect Thoreau to react directly to questions about the authority of biblical interpretation raised by higher criticism. Yet clearly he did respond to Coleridge, and not only by way of accepting the famous Reason vs. Understanding distinction from *Aids to Reflection.* Coleridge's views on biblical hermeneutics are relevant, therefore, to appreciating Thoreau's project of developing a hermeneutics of nature even though Thoreau modified the Christian suppositions apparent in works such as *Confessions of an Inquiring Spirit* and *Hints Towards a More Comprehensive Theory of Life.*

A Coleridgian principle of scriptural exegesis directly applicable to nature is the need to interpret each particular element of the text "by the Spirit of the whole." The letters or words written in the "plain sense" of Scripture cannot, therefore, be simply equated with God's revelatory Word. To avoid naïve "bibliolatry," one must look beyond historical literalism to discern the animating "Spirit of the Whole." Thus, a kind of ecological vision of the Bible's variegated life forms is needed to read the text rightly. And for Coleridge, it is through the subjective exercise of determining what "finds me" in the text that one verifies the Bible's objective authority as vehicle of the Holy Spirit: "Revealed Religion (and I know of no *religion* not revealed) is in its highest contemplation the Unity (the identity or coinherence) of *Subjective* and *Objective.*"[37]

For Thoreau, naturalistic science would replace the church and biblical historicism as the objective component in this equation. Hence "the religion I love is very laic" (*PJ* 1:289). Rather than the company of visible saints, the visible facts of creation became his chief source of revelation and spiritual authority beyond the human soul. His individualistic temper led him to reject Christianity's social frame of worship, its tradition of collective textual exegesis and communal spirituality.[38] Yet his exegesis of biospheric signs maintained a teleological and decidedly religious cast. The sandbank passage fulfills extravagant claims made earlier in *Walden*

37. *Confessions of an Inquiring Spirit,* in *The Collected Works of Samuel Taylor Coleridge: Shorter Works and Fragments,* part 2, ed. H. J. Jackson and J. R. de J. Jackson (Princeton: Princeton University Press, 1995), 11:1156, 1121, 1168.

38. The solitary bias of Thoreau's religious perspective, particularly as evidenced in *A Week,* is persuasively defined by Jonathan Bishop in "The Experience of the Sacred," pp. 83-85.

that "God himself," at play within the full breadth of natural history, "culminates in the present moment" and that "it is the chief end of man here to 'glorify God and enjoy him forever'" (*W* 97, 91).[39] But only a contemplative disciple of true science can see beyond prosaic materialism to find the earth revealed as "living poetry" (309). Elsewhere, Thoreau expresses the simple ambition of devoting "his life to the discovery of the divinity in Nature." His vocation as Transcendental scribe is to report "the glory of the universe" (*PJ* 4:390). The Hebrew prophet Habakkuk testifies that he stood waiting on the tower of Jerusalem for a final vision of the Lord's glory. Thoreau likewise commits himself to watching metaphorically "a whole year on the city's walls," but actually amid earth's "rich & fertile mystery," for "some trace of the ineffable." Such revelation, he insists, is more joyous than that reported by the Hebrew prophets. Yet his "profession" is comparable to theirs insofar as he commits himself "to be always on the alert to find God in nature — to know his lurking places" (*PJ* 4:53-55, 315).

As we have seen, Thoreau pursued this spirit quest with an acute awareness of the subjective, imaginative grounds of his response to nature. At the same time, he was determined to respect the objective materiality of the nonhuman world, tirelessly presenting concrete facts to demonstrate how the *bios* of Walden sustained what Coleridge would call "a life of its own."[40] Thus, the lofty account of personal contemplation that

39. The irony of Thoreau's citation here from the Calvinist inflected Shorter Catechism is multi-layered. Although plainly satirizing what he takes to be the oversimplified assurances of this version of Christian orthodoxy, he is even more disdainful of unreflective believers — that is, those who have *"somewhat hastily"* reached their doctrinal conclusions on the basis of authority, without benefit of existential inquiry or experience. Curiously, though, Thoreau's book *does* end up affirming, in its own unorthodox but serious religious terms, that "it is the chief end of man to 'glorify God and enjoy him forever.'" Doubtless Thoreau would insist that *Walden* demonstrates more authentic *enjoyment* of God than does the Westminster Catechism. For fuller contextual elucidation of the citation and its relation to *The New England Primer,* see Sargent Bush, Jr., "The End and Means in *Walden:* Thoreau's Use of the Catechism," *ESQ: A Journal of the American Renaissance* 31 (1985): 1-10.

40. Writing to William Sotheby in 1802, Coleridge declares that "Nature has her proper interest; & he will know what it is, who believes & feels, that every Thing has a Life of it's own, & that we are all one Life." Quoted in *English Romantic Writers,* ed. David Perkins (New York: Harcourt, 1967), p. 526.

opens "Sounds" is followed presently by an earthy catalogue of seasonally differentiated plants — including groundnut, goldenrod, pitch pine, and sand-cherry *(cerasus pumila)* — growing beside his house. The book's bestiary features not only conventionally inspiring cases such as the wild-sounding loon and the hawk sporting freely in "fields of air," but also insects such as the ant and mosquito. In "Where I Lived, and What I Lived for," Thoreau even claims that he relished hearing "the faint hum of a mosquito" passing through his living quarters at dawn. That a mosquito buzz could stir recollection of "the heroic ages" and suggest "something cosmical" about "the everlasting vigor and fertility of the world" sounds at first preposterous. More incredibly still, an earlier journal draft of the passage equates this trumpeting of a solitary mosquito directly with Θειου — that is, with divinity (*PJ* 2:235). My students want to know: what's with this guy, anyway, that he brushes aside the obvious annoyance of insect bites so as to find God in a mosquito? Can this be for real?

Part of Thoreau's idea here, surely, is to extend the romantic definition of nature beyond picturesque landscapes and appealing fauna to embrace that wealth of commonplace facts and organisms contained within the earthly "cosmos." So the mosquito becomes a homely synecdoche for Emerson's array of "natural facts" as well as a token of that biotic vigor Annie Dillard would later describe more darkly as "fecundity."[41] In addition, Thoreau wants to press the logic of Transcendental correspondences, though not so antagonistically as Melville or Dillard, to see whether meditative scrutiny of "particular natural facts" might confirm the supposition that "Nature is the symbol of spirit." If God is immanent throughout the *cosmos* of this planet's ecological systems, then why not indeed within the *bios* of every species, including small and reviled insects? What better test case for a non-anthropocentric view of ecology than to try imagining the mosquito from something like God's point of view?

Or, by way of returning to the sandbank episode, how better to demolish overidealized human constructions of nature than to imagine "excrements of all kinds"? Animal waste is, of course, a universal fact of material life on earth. It not only plays an essential role in ecological processes of

41. Annie Dillard, *Pilgrim at Tinker Creek* (1974; repr. New York: Harper, 1998), pp. 161-83.

growth and decay, but also supplies a graphic reminder of creation's objective ontology. It is implacably *there,* whether or not humans wish to think about it. But according to Julian of Norwich, the fourteenth-century English mystic, we can experience even the act of elimination as a sign of God's homely love and care for creation. Excremental imagery likewise pervades writings influenced by the biblical and Reformed religious tradition of Puritan New England. Though commonly related there to the fallen condition of the world and humankind, it can also bear more positive allegorical association with God's bowels as the seat of divine mercy. Edward Taylor, for example, portrays in one memorable poem a saving kinesis in which "Gods Tender Bowells run / Out streams of Grace."[42] Similarly, the "excrementitious" character of Thoreau's sandbank vision reflects the divinely deep origin of regenerative processes in the bowels of a living earth, for "Nature has some bowels, and there again is mother of humanity." Just as Whitman cheers himself by remembering that his corpse will eventually make "good manure," so also Thoreau exults in imagining that insofar as we are dungishly linked to earth, its great bowel movements "will heave our exuviae from their graves" (*W* 309). Most impressively from the standpoint of religion, such images of physical elimination help define a view of natural evolution that is at once material *and* spiritual. Surely, then, there is nothing ethereal — and "nothing inorganic" (*W* 308) — about the spirituality of creation Thoreau witnesses in the sandbank. To regard the world as sacramental is to believe that spirit reveals itself through rather than despite materiality.

Thoreau's sense of place in *Walden* embraces a comparable paradox. "Where he lived" is a real location as well as a state of mind and soul. His book depicts a physical site, objectively situated a mile and a half from Concord, as well as an idyllic refuge, which he constructs subjectively and imaginatively. Part of the work's genius lies in its self-conscious preservation of this polarity, the interplay between nature's resistant auton-

---

42. "Meditation 8 (First Series)," in *The Poems of Edward Taylor,* ed. Donald E. Stanford (New Haven: Yale University Press, 1960), p. 18. Karl Keller discusses Taylor's varied use of excremental and erotic imagery in *The Example of Edward Taylor* (Amherst: University of Massachusetts Press, 1975), pp. 91-220. Biblical examples of language (as rendered by the King James Version) in which divine mercy is associated with bowels include Isaiah 63:15, Philippians 1:8 and 2:1, Colossians 3:12, and 1 John 3:17.

omy (allied to what Coleridge called life's "tendency to individuation") and humanity's rage for unifying order.[43] The hermeneutical breakthrough Thoreau achieved in *Walden* was to demonstrate how nature could be read and reinterpreted imaginatively as a sacred text in the new light of developmental science combined with recent forms of critical exegesis applied to biblical texts. But to rediscover divine revelation in and through the Creation, one had to study nature correctly — not merely by accumulating scientific data but by learning to perceive "her true meaning" so that "the fact will one day flower out into a truth."[44]

Particularly in the book's final chapter, Thoreau likewise reminds his audience that the experience of discovering God's presence in Nature cannot be geographically restricted to Walden — or, for that matter, to any other single location. Despite his thorough involvement with local landscapes, Thoreau ends by urging readers to look beyond New England boundaries because "Thank Heaven, here is not all the world." Finding our place in the scheme of things first requires, apparently, recognizing our own ignorance of the globe, discovering that "We know not where we are" (*W* 320, 322). A wild nature preserve might disclose the numinous not by any potency of the place itself but, once again, by enabling us to "witness our own limits transgressed."

So if part of Thoreau's sensibility coincides with more ritualized traditions of Christianity, according to which the sacred can be physically connected to sanctified space, Thoreau's ancestral link to more iconoclastic traditions of Protestantism suggests a countervailing tendency. This Protestant impulse would resist any attempt to confine movements of the spirit within a given location. It insists that the power of the sacred does not reside materially in the place or thing itself but rather, as Emerson observed, in the interactive harmony between nature and the human imagination. Thus, it promotes an attitude more phenomenological than the archaic essentialism presumed by Eliade's theory. It might even regard the fixation of present-day tourists on Walden Pond, to the exclu-

43. "Formation of a More Comprehensive Theory of Life," in *Selected Poetry and Prose of Coleridge,* ed. Donald A. Stauffer (New York: Random House, 1951), p. 578.

44. See Robert D. Richardson, Jr., "Thoreau and Science," in *American Literature and Science,* ed. Robert J. Scholnick (Lexington: University Press of Kentucky, 1992), pp. 110-27. Richardson (p. 110) quotes here from Thoreau's *Journal.*

sion of less crowded and degraded landscapes, as a species of idolatry. Accordingly, Thoreau in his "Higher Laws" chapter follows something of a Pauline argument by displacing his temple imagery away from structures or places in the outer landscape to the human body. "Every man," he asserts, "is the builder of a temple, called his body, to the god he worships, after a style purely his own, nor can he get off by hammering marble instead" (*W* 221).

Few writers have recorded so richly sensual an immersion in the particularities of place as Thoreau does in *Walden*. Nonetheless, the book consistently urges readers to apprehend the geography of the sacred in terms that transcend the literalism of physically defined mapspace. If Thoreau saw his Walden house planted figuratively at the world's center, he also understood himself to be living on the margins of society. If the deep cut lays bare the very center of Nature's splendor as *bios*, it lies also at the physical periphery of Walden's estate. That Thoreau should see the world not so much in Blake's grain of sand but on the sideslope of Fitchburg Railroad's sandbank, a byproduct of mechanized industry, may reflect a suitable adaptation to the largely de-centered mythological perspective of Western culture by 1854. One suspects the author would, in any case, heartily endorse the reluctance of another New England writer and nature-lover, the contemporary poet Mary Oliver, to follow his footsteps to the actual scene of Walden Pond. As Oliver writes in her poem titled "Going to Walden," some regard her as "half a fool" for refusing the chance to make her own daytrip to Concord. "But," she concludes,

> . . . in a book I read and cherish,
> Going to Walden is not so easy a thing
> As a green visit. It is the slow and difficult
> Trick of living, and finding it where you are.[45]

Thoreau himself, by the time he published *Walden*, no longer located his life in the house by the pond. But by then he had made another dwelling place, a text that would offer readers, too, a site from which they could learn to read nature as *hiero-glyph*, or holy writ, and to witness their own limits transgressed.

45. Mary Oliver, *New and Selected Poems* (Boston: Beacon, 1992), p. 239.

# Charity and Its Discontents:
## Pity and Politics in Melville's Fiction

*Michael Colacurcio*

IN OUR PRESENT moment of intense — quite often conscientious — correctness, it seems difficult to imagine how any work of literature could possibly be "apolitical." Literary language is, after all, language, so that, however complex the structure, however multiform the rhetoric, however steadfastly ironic the speaking persona, the poem or the story always says something; and if it appears to say just nothing at all about the life-arrangements of its particular time and place, the reader may suitably infer that the author is satisfied well enough with those arrangements. And judge this conservatism accordingly. So natural does this all seem, so inevitable, that our historical sense may find it worthwhile to remember the moment when just the opposite was so — when Hawthorne's "My Kinsman, Major Molineux," for example, was declared to be not much concerned with the Revolution; or, to take an example closer home, when Melville's "Benito Cereno" *could* not be about race or slavery because writers of Melville's imaginative power simply *did* not address themselves to the local and the practical. Thus a well-published and rather influential critic of American fiction felt altogether safe in concluding that "Benito Cereno" was about the problem of "perception" or, more substantively, the ambiguous fact that nothing in life is really either black or white.[1]

---

1. See Richard Harter Fogle, *Melville's Shorter Tales* (Norman: University of Oklahoma Press, 1960), pp. 116-47.

Nor was this New Criticism the only alternative to politics. Hawthorne's stories, like "Molineux," were rich in image and symbol, and seemed to advertise the ambiguity of their own meaning on every page; yet the adept interpreter of dreams could read their "traumatic" reference without let or hindrance. Probing "deeper" than politics, Hawthorne's meanings were psychological, even psychoanalytic.[2] Melville's were, too — with the difference that Melville's dreams went even deeper, unveiling not only the unhappy fact that the "ego is not master in its own house" but, gloomier still, the urgent but usually repressed suspicion that man's psychic dis-ease is only one more evidence that creation and chaos are not altogether opposing conditions. For Hawthorne this was clear in "the haunted mind"; for his friend and one-time disciple, it was the encompassing condition of a universe that haunts us with the thought of what may lie behind a universe that feeds on its own flesh and takes no notice whatsoever of the virtue of its "Gentoos and corn-eaters."[3] Perhaps it was the politics of the *universe* that most needed investigating.

Accordingly, of the works that come down to us from the classic period of Melville criticism, one of the more exemplary is a book-length study called *Melville's Quarrel with God.* Its author, Lawrance Thompson, may seem a little too impressed by William Empson's (or Blake's) "Satanist" reading of Milton, and a little too proud of his own theory of Melville's multi-layered rhetoric, which means to dupe the pious but unwary and compliment the literary intelligence of the ungodly. But surely he was right to emphasize the fact that Melville's is a mind that never could be convinced that all's right with the world, or that human beings, with even the best will they can manage, can ever make it right enough to satisfy any very strict standard of justice. Not only do really terrible things happen to decent enough people — regularly enough to support Hume's

2. For representative moments in the too-confident psychologizing of Hawthorne's tales, see Richard P. Adams, "Hawthorne's 'Provincial Tales,'" *New England Quarterly* 30 (1957): 39-57; Seymour Gross, "Hawthorne's My Kinsman, Major Molineux," *Nineteenth-Century Fiction* 12 (1957): 97-109; and Frederick Crews, *Sins of the Fathers* (New York: Oxford University Press, 1966), esp. pp. 3-79.

3. The memorable formula occurs in Emerson's "Experience." The Library of America edition — *Essays and Lectures,* ed. Joel Porte (New York: Library of America, 1983) — has "Gentoos and Grahamites" (p. 481).

claim that the God of this world cannot be both all-good and all-powerful — but the system of the world itself, orderly enough in its physical workings, is yet insufficient to ratify an ethic of universal benevolence.[4] Thompson's tone often suggests that Melville may have been a little sophomoric in his discovery that "the world was put together wrong" and that "God was the scoundrel."[5] And no doubt he allows for too little distance between Melville and Ahab, the prime prosecutor of his quarrel. Still, that quarrel did not write itself. Nor is *Moby-Dick* the only Melville work that sounds as if it were written by a man exasperated, finally, by the logic of the deliberate "affliction" of God's formally chosen, or by the encompassing assurance that, within the plan of sin freely permitted and salvation offered to the same liberty, God always manages to bring good out of evil.[6]

As that sense is not present in complete form from the beginning of Melville's career, one worthy task might be to try to discover, with more care and precision than Thompson cared to exercise, just where the exasperation began and under what influence it found the nerve to express its impious resistance with full fury. Thompson's Melville seems never not to have known the brilliant perversity with which Pierre Bayle treats the problem of evil, but Bayle's suggestion that an old-time Manicheanism might have handled the question more satisfactorily than did the orthodoxy to which it lost out suggests the possibility of a project called "Melville and Monotheism." Or even "Melville and Theism," as the "problem of evil" may simply fail to appear where there is no *a priori* assumption of a universal control that is both competent and benevolent.[7] There are, to be sure, certain hints in Melville's earliest works of that cosmic paranoia

4. For modern discussion of the problem of evil as it derives from Leibniz and Hume, see William L. Rowe, ed., *God and the Problem of Evil* (Malden, Mass.: Blackwell, 2001).

5. Lawrance Thompson, *Melville's Quarrel with God* (Princeton: Princeton University Press, 1952), p. 356. At one point Thompson permits himself to refer to Melville's theological resistance as "spiritual gastritis" (p. 18).

6. Just so, somewhat oddly, does Aquinas offer to answer the objection that the actual existence of evil precludes the possibility of a being by definition infinitely good; see *Summa Theologica*, V. I, Q. 2, a.3.

7. For the model of Melville's similarity to Pierre Bayle, see Thompson, *Melville's Quarrel*, pp. 26-31.

that pushes the theory of original sin beyond the limit of orthodox apology. But a careful study of its development would require much more than the brief summary attempted here — where the point is to examine that self-constructed fault line in Melville's short fiction, where the problem of universal defect comes face to face with the question of human obligation.

## Imperfect Trial, Infallible Error

*Typee,* to begin with the earliest example, is mostly content to conclude that "the penalty of the Fall presses very lightly" (*T* 229)[8] on the people of Polynesia and to ascribe whatever depravity may appear among them to the process of de-nationalization begun by the misguided intrusion of missionaries. Only once, as I read that curious mixture of captivity narrative and comparative sociology, does the idea of cosmic injustice without cosmic retribution threaten to disturb the surface of recognizable Enlightenment protest. After recounting some of the almost unbelievable "enormities perpetrated" by the French "upon some of the inoffensive islanders," the more political of the book's two narrators proposes that the track of "many a pretty trader" can be traced

> from island to island . . . by a series of cold-blooded robberies, kidnappings, and murders, the iniquity of which might be considered almost sufficient to sink her guilty timbers to the bottom of the sea. (*T* 37-38)

The strategic insertion of an "almost" is meant to save the sentiment for ordinary rationality, one supposes, but the disturbing figure of the "guilty timbers" manages to suggest the idea of an evil reaching deeper than any-

---

8. Citations of Melville's text refer to the various volumes of The Library of America: *Typee, Omoo, Mardi,* ed. G. Thomas Tanselle (New York: Library of America, 1982); *Redburn, White-Jacket, Moby-Dick,* ed. G. Thomas Tanselle (New York: Library of America, 1983); and *Pierre, Israel Potter, The Confidence-Man, Tales,* and *Billy Budd,* ed. Harrison Hayford (New York: Library of America, 1984). Each novel and story will be cited parenthetically by page number within the text: *Typee* as *T, Mardi* as *M, Redburn* as *R, White-Jacket* as *WJ, Moby Dick* as *MD,* and selected short stories as *Tales.*

one's individual will. Men are to blame, of course, but the barely repressed plea for the Universe itself to intervene in an affair not well enough noticed by the regular and mostly incompetent agencies of human justice amounts to an almost perfect anticipation of the moral inquisition Ahab will make of the severed but sphinx-like head of a sperm whale — as if to confirm a madness provoked by the inability of other agencies to explain why Nature's laws reveal no hint of moral discrimination.

In *Typee,* however, the moment passes, almost unnoticed, and nothing in *Omoo* provides a convincing sequel. The attack on intruders is renewed — on missionaries and those altogether less sacred wanderers who follow in their footsteps — but it seems part of the book's strategy that its narrator shall not recognize that he and his companion are part of the problem he turns aside, at times, most violently to protest. Their sexual ecology altogether disturbed by some ugly combination of Presbyterian morality and sailor boy sexuality, the Tahitians are indeed dying off at an alarming rate, but no one is there to blame the nature of things for the evident genocide. The closest anyone can come to capturing the irony of their painful death within a world of surpassing softness and beauty is the little poem "chanted, in a low, sad tone, by aged Tahitians":

> The palm-tree shall grow,
> The coral shall spread,
> But man shall cease. (*T* 519)

And in context the pathos of the sentiment is easily overwhelmed by the priapic adventures the narrator regularly ascribes to "my Long Ghost" — proving, I suppose, that when Melville cannot quite justify the ways of God he can always make fun of the phallus. In any event, the universe continues not to notice.

*Mardi,* of course, is quite another kind of book — one that works its way into a place where all sorts of questions just like "the problem of evil" can be inquired about, explicitly and at length, by a narrator who, having lost a young heart's desire but not given up on some maidenly image of it, is occupying himself with a discussion group formed of the handiest South-Sea versions of a king, a philosopher, a historian, and a poet. Unpredictably, perhaps, the talk can be quite wonderful: where else

— unless in some postmodern play — can we expect to find a debater under duress instruct his adversary that "My tropes are not tropes, but yours are"? But as the book is being written under the watchful eye of a genteel wife, a pious father-in-law, and the orthodox friend who has been lending Melville the very books he wishes to incorporate, we are not to expect it to blurt out or even insinuate, Shakespeare-like, any of those "deep, far-away things . . . which we feel to be so terrifically true, that it were all but madness for any good man, in his own proper character, to utter, or even hint of them."[9] Cautiously, therefore, the book talks its way to the discovery that evil is a problem we may have to live with, provokingly, and never even begin to solve.

The theism of *Mardi* seems secure. So does the truth of Christianity, despite the doubts of one Pani, whom fate has placed in the unhappy situation of guiding the faithful through scenes of religion whose significance he himself also doubts. For when the assembled Questers reach the land of Serenia they are instructed, in terms that echo the liberal Christian arguments of William Ellery Channing, that the principles of Serenia's redeemer were known "long previous to the Master's coming," and that this exemplary "Alma" merely "opens unto us our own hearts." Indeed,

> were his precepts strange we would recoil — not one feeling would respond; whereas, once hearkened to, our souls embrace them as with the instinctive tendrils of a vine. (M 1288)[10]

9. Thus Melville expresses his own wish to avoid censored expression in "Hawthorne and His Mosses": quoted in Hershel Parker and Harrison Hayford, eds., *Moby-Dick* (New York: Norton, 2002), p. 522. For the presence of Evert Duyckinck in the near background of *Mardi*, see Merrill R. Davis, *Melville's Mardi: Chartless Voyage* (New Haven: Yale University Press, 1952), pp. 35-42, 62-64; also the "Historical Note" to the Northwestern-Newberry Edition of *Mardi* (Evanston: Northwestern University Press, 1970), pp. 661-66; and Hershel Parker, *Herman Melville: A Biography*, vol. 1, *1819-1851* (Baltimore: Johns Hopkins University Press, 1996), pp. 534-36, 559-60, 577, 585-87, 626-27.

10. For Channing's most concise formulation of the "recognition" argument, see "The Evidences of Revealed Religion," in David Robinson, ed., *William Ellery Channing: Selected Writings* (New York: Paulist Press, 1985), p. 143. For elaboration of that argument by "Transcendentalist" Christians such as Orestes Brownson, George Ripley, and Theodore Parker, see Perry Miller, ed., *The Transcendentalists: An Anthology* (Cambridge: Harvard University Press, 1950), pp. 205-46. For commentary, see my own "Better Mode of

A specifically Calvinist version of the problem of evil remains: what are we to make of those who — like Melville's father, perhaps — "die unregenerate"? "Why create the germs that sin and suffer, but to perish?" Ah, but this is "The last mystery which underlieth all the rest" (M 1296), the strict and philosophic Babalanja is forced to concede. Yet this most resistant of Taji's companions appears satisfied when he learns from a dream that "Great Love is sad; and heaven is Love" (M 1299). No one *quite* says that God must be thought to suffer the travail of his own creation, but probably we are as close to the idea of a limited God as the nineteenth century was able to come.[11]

But if this surrender of power in the name of goodness satisfied the faith of those whose library and credo had a part in the theodicy of *Mardi,* no such pious compromise is invoked in *Redburn* — or anywhere else in a career rapidly losing control over its own moral momentum. A naïve Redburn may pray, in a timely fashion, that he himself may never turn into a terminally alienated "Ishmael," but his story is already prepared to let us see exactly what a figure of incorrigible hatred and resentment might look like. A dying sailor named Jackson coughs up and spits out the bitterness of a life come to nothing but meaningless pain, and not much effort is made to explain where all this malignity might have come from. His quarrel is simply a fact:

> He seemed to be full of hatred and gall against every thing and every body in the world; as if all the world was one person, and had done him some dreadful harm, that was rankling and festering in his heart. (R 71)

Redburn is tempted to call him "crazy," but he seems to recognize that, in any case so advanced, the moral fact is more significant than the rational explanation.

And perhaps there is *no* explanation for this mystery of iniquity. Re-

---

Evidence," *Emerson Society Quarterly* (1969): 12-22; and more recently, "Pleasing God," in *Doctrine and Difference: Essays in the Literature of New England* (New York: Routledge, 1997), esp. pp. 140-54.

11. As Ishmael expresses the thought in Chapter 106 of *Moby-Dick,* "the gods themselves are not for ever glad. The ineffaceable, sad birthmark in the brow of man, is but the stamp of sorrow in the signers" (355).

coiling from his nihilist belief that "everything [is] to be hated, in the wide world," Redburn describes him as "spontaneously an atheist and an infidel" (R 117); but the reader who presses on to the famous scene of starvation and familiar death in the squalor of old-world Liverpool is hardly left without imaginative resource. Presided over, as it were, by a policeman whose motto might be some local variation of a more cosmic laissez faire,[12] and far more aggressively graphic than the slow withering and death at a distance of the natives in *Omoo*, the untimely yet somehow systematic death of mother and children seem a representative fact of the world — not yet in Redburn's America, perhaps, but not so far away as to escape moral notice. If indeed there were any justice.

Except perhaps for the moment of self-maddened hatred which tempts its Narrator to annihilate both himself and his Captain, should that petty tyrant dare lay the lash to his immaculate manliness,[13] *White Jacket* appears content to expose the peculiar usages of the U.S. Navy; but the moral inquisition of first Ishmael and then Ahab is in no way restricted to evils that beset men who, like Redburn's friend Harry Bolton, have fallen into the business of whaling when other resources have failed. From the moment of his fictional self-naming — Call me bastard-outcast of the universe, the man who fell outside the Covenant despite the pleas of a most faithful father — Ishmael tries to be ironic about his personal desperation: a whaling voyage in the place of a ritual suicide and a jaunty acceptance of nothing more significant in "the grand programme of Providence" (MD 799). But his urgent wish "to sail forbidden seas" and odd desire to "be social with . . . a horror" (MD 800) suggest a more confrontational view of the relation between lonely man and hostile forces. So, most plainly, does his approval of the invincibly restless Bulkington. Indeed, when the time comes to dismiss that character in favor of one whose oppositional energy has run all the way to a madness, in a chapter that begins with the *Pequod* thrusting "her vindictive bows into the cold

12. For the subtle presence of Adam Smith in *Redburn*, see John Samson, *White Lies* (Ithaca: Cornell University Press, 1989), pp. 98-103, 109-11, 115-20, 126-27.

13. This terrific exception to the *realpolitik* of *White Jacket* may support Melville's claim that, in writing a book "for money," as other men are forced to "sawing wood," he had nevertheless "not repressed [him]self much": see *Correspondence* — vol. 14 of *The Writings of Herman Melville* (Evanston: Northwestern University Press, 1993), pp. 138-39.

malicious waves" (*MD* 906), Melville cannot resist the opportunity to have Ishmael preach a eulogy whose distinct but perverse echoes of Calvin suggest that, in his final phase, humanity's representative man will challenge Decree itself.[14] No wonder then if, after Ahab's ridicule of Starbuck's intimation of blasphemy, Ishmael's own vindictive shouts "had gone up with the rest" (*MD* 983).

The perfection of the monomaniac's conscientious blasphemy comes in Chapter 119, no doubt, where Ahab, speaking from Melville's rare knowledge of Manichean lore and missing his "sweet mother" Sophia, challenges his "fiery father" to appear in any form other that of "speechless, placeless power" (*MD* 1334). Thompson fails to emphasize the point, but the close student of the moral history of New England can see the long shadow of Puritan resentment finding expressive fulfillment here. Speaking back to several American centuries of Calvinist insistence that man stands in no position to pronounce upon the ways of a sovereign God, a most mild-mannered liberal had steeled his nerves to announce that a God of sheer power can be no God to us — that our moral sense "forbids us to prostrate ourselves before mere power, or to offer praise where we do not discover worth." God deserves "veneration" only as he "discovers himself to us in characters of benevolence, equity, and righteousness."[15] Amen to that, saith a more maddened and less repressed Ahab:

> Come in thy lowest form of love, and I will kneel and kiss thee; but at thy highest, come as mere supernal power; and though thou launchest navies of full-freighted worlds, there's that in here that still remains indifferent. (*MD* 1333-34)

If Ahab blasphemes, exactly where Channing worships, the reason is that he has failed to find even an approximate "coincidence of his will and government with those great and fundamental principles of morality

14. For Ishmael's defiance of the "howling infinite" as a specific insult to Calvinist theology, see Thomas Werge, "Moby-Dick and the Calvinist Tradition," *Studies in the Novel* 1 (1969): 484-506, and T. Walter Herbert, *Moby Dick and Calvinism: A World Dismantled* (New Brunswick, N.J.: Rutgers University Press, 1977), esp. pp. 117-58.

15. Channing, "The Moral Argument Against Calvinism," in *Selected Writings*, p. 114.

written on our souls."[16] Man begins to be moral, Ahab's doctrine would imply, only when he decides to be more kindly than the universe. In which case he might well have aided the *Rachel* in searching for her lost children.

If we look for the basis of Ahab's distracted defiance anywhere but in the unmanning loss of a leg and in the objectification of its dead-bone replacement, we find it revealed, at a flash, in his final dialogue conversation with Starbuck: "Look! see yon Albicore! Who put it into him to chase and fang that flying-fish?" But this is only the final moment of his determination to have the murdering judge of the universe "himself . . . dragged to the bar" (*MD* 1375). And his abrupt, elliptical questions of Starbuck have already been asked, in a fuller, more feeling, even sentimental form, of the suspended head of a sperm whale "in the midst of so intense a calm, it seemed the Sphynx's in the desert." Fundamental to the wicked/spotless logic of the book, it deserves quotation in full. Especially as Melville — hell-bent here on the unsupportable poignancy of a vision in which the famously impartial sun and rain seem positively to prosper the wicked — will live to parody his own unabashed rhetorical effect.

> "Speak, thou vast and venerable head," muttered Ahab, "which, though ungarnished with a beard, yet here and there lookest hoary with mosses; speak, mighty head, and tell us the secret thing that is in thee. Of all divers, thou hast dived the deepest. That head upon which the upper sun now gleams, has moved amid this world's foundations. Where unrecorded names and navies rust, and untold hopes and anchors rot; where in her murderous hold this frigate earth is ballasted with bones of millions of the drowned; there, in that awful waterland, there was thy most familiar home. Thou hast been where bell or diver never went; hast slept by many a sailor's side, where sleepless mothers would give their lives to lay them down. Thou saw'st the locked lovers when leaping from their flaming ship; heart to heart they sank beneath the exulting wave; true to each other, when heaven seemed false to them. Thou saw'st the murdered mate when tossed by pirates from the midnight deck; for hours he fell into the deeper mid-

16. Channing, "The Moral Argument Against Calvinism," p. 114.

night of the insatiate maw; and his murderers still sailed on unharmed — while swift lightnings shivered the neighboring ship that would have borne a righteous husband to outstretched, longing arms. O head! Thou hast seen enough to split the planets and make an infidel of Abraham, and not one syllable is thine!" (*MD* 1126-27)

The logic here, more a web of passionate associations than a set of strict inferences, is as tendentious as it is sentimental: surely the elements do not always prosper the pirates, and now and then a righteous husband does make it home safe; but Melville's maddened protagonist is in no mood for statistics. Knowing that each of us has our own anthology of injustice, however, Melville himself feels no need to repent the overstatement. Few men may imagine performing an act in which "the judge himself is dragged to the bar," but most can confess to believing that God has a little explaining to do. Nor would the literature of religion be complete without the record, somewhere, of that New Prometheus who has felt "all the general rage and hate felt by his whole race from Adam down" (*MD* 989). An Anti-Christ that hero seems determined to be, but a Representative Man nonetheless.

More so than the foolish-noble Pierre, no doubt, who thinks he can reestablish the universe's moral quotient — compensate for God's silence and the world's indifference — by taking the burden of perfect self-sacrifice upon himself. A plausible cynic named Plotinus Plinlimmon knows it's not going to work: the world will support a modest enlightening of self-interest, but life lasts too long for a virtue that is its own reward. The reader also knows better, all along, from teachers as various as St. Paul and Nietzsche: righteousness is entirely a gift, and true virtue is just too hard for carbon-based life. Yet somehow Melville cannot resist telling the whole tale of imperfect trial and infallible error — extravagantly, in prose that will not take yes for an answer. Humans may rue the absence of a Model of Christian Charity written into the nature of things — or despair when the universe fails to answer a desperate prayer for moral guidance[17] — but they must know as well that their own moral

17. In Book VII, section v, Pierre lies under a perilously balanced stone, praying that it will fall on him if the decision he is about to make is not virtue but moral outrage. His only answer is a cheerfully chirping bird.

power is insufficient to right the uneven balance. Perhaps they ought indeed to adjust their expectations, learning to thank the system of natural being for the gift of natural life itself — and to regard universal protest both as naïve and as a form of ingratitude rather than of piety.

## The Limits of Pity

All this should be clear enough. Nor should it require a special revelation to observe that in the best pointed and most controlled short stories written in the years 1853-1856, the rampant energies of *Moby-Dick* and *Pierre* may be felt to subside — almost as if the prose required to maintain the conventions of Heroism and Romance had left Melville a little out of breath. After so much sound and fury, what? By default, it almost seems, Melville appears to have discovered, all at once, the essentially modern Mode of Irony,[18] in which all issues are painfully reduced and nothing is really expected to work out very well; and where, with the idea of a superintending God all but out of the picture, the appropriate question is no longer who is to blame for, but can anything in fact be done about, the sad human cases over which one keeps stumbling, even in the suburbs of human significance. To be sure, Ahab might have helped the *Rachel* "in her retracing search after her missing children" (*MD* 1408); and one is left to wonder what domestic urgency prevents Redburn from aiding in the Americanization of Harry Bolton. But the issue of personal obligation is not placed at the center of our interpretative intention in either of these cases — as it most certainly is in stories like "Bartleby the Scrivener," "Cock-a-Doodle-Doo," and "The Piazza."

The cases are similar enough to constitute a sort of thematic group: each of these stories presents us with one of those non-standard yet not really so rare instances of suffering that look like they might be pretty hard to alleviate and might discourage us in the process. The question, at its most primitive, involves the duty of an observer to intervene in a situ-

---

18. For the classic derivation and theoretic description of irony as an entire literary mode, see Northrop Frye, *Anatomy of Criticism: Four Essays* (Princeton: Princeton University Press, 1957), pp. 33-67.

ation where somebody is already *in extremis* — through no fault of the observer, it may be, and possibly through no fault of the sufferer as well. Must the Samaritan try to help *every* observant Jew he finds beaten up and lying in a ditch? The question has, of course, its melodramatic side: what if the guy you are saving from the swollen river is not the Christ Child but the thug who has just killed the only son of a well-bred black comedian? But even where nothing like heroic risk seems remotely thinkable, a subtle question remains: what are we supposed to do when there is nothing useful to be done? And how are we to compose our affect when the case proves itself beyond our competence? Writing a whole book on neighborly duty, Cotton Mather once suggested that, "if you have nothing else to bestow upon the miserable, bestow a *tear* or two upon their miseries."[19] One might look here for a distant motive behind a Narrator's quietist decision to stick to his "piazza deck, haunted" by the face of incurable suffering, yet neither he nor any of Melville's other narrative agents appears to be "sentimental" in just this way.

One can contend, of course, that in "Bartleby the Scrivener" the Narrator's attempts to intervene in the case of the hapless scrivener involve a charity both too chilly and too late to be of any use; but it can also be observed that he gives a more respectable performance of the "corporal works of mercy" than most of us would be able to manage — especially with our reputation for worldly good sense at issue.[20] To be sure, he eventually abandons Bartleby to the tender mercies of what Melville understands as "the world"; he may even back himself, like another frightened disciple, into the situation of a threefold denial. Before this, however, he has found a way to put up with behaviors scarcely tolerable in any well-run business. And our students, ignorant at first, then suspicious

19. Cotton Mather, *Bonifacius,* ed. David Levin (Cambridge: Belknap Press of Harvard University Press, 1966), pp. 57-59. The other tales that invoke Cotton Mather are "The Lightning-Rod Man" and "The Apple-Tree Table."

20. For a sharp attack on the Narrator of "Bartleby" as "representative of a world of prudent privilege," see Kingsley Widmer, *The Ways of Nihilism: A Study of Herman Melville's Short Novels* (Los Angeles: California State Colleges, 1970), pp. 104-20. For an account of other critics who blame the Narrator, see Lea Bertani Vozar Newman, *A Reader's Guide to the Short Stories of Herman Melville* (Boston: Hall, 1986), pp. 65-66; and for a critical estimate of these and other approaches, see Dan McCall, *The Silence of Bartleby* (Ithaca: Cornell University Press, 1989), esp. pp. 99-154.

of any talk about the "Christ-figure," regularly imagine the Narrator may be as cracked as Bartleby himself. Look at the conduct of his office, after all: tolerant of workers who can manage to perform useful work for only half-a-day each, and swayed now and then by the sort of fellow-feeling that has relieved itself in the gift of an old coat to one of these sub-standard performers, the Narrator is a soft touch indeed. He professes to be a disciple of John Jacob Astor, but that self-made personage would surely be horrified by one look at this unlikely assemblage of damaged persons. It's like something out of Dickens![21] Indeed we begin to suspect that the Narrator has, from the outset, made so much of his quiet safety precisely because he knows that, in the story he is about to tell, the worldly reader may well accuse him of a certain recklessness.

His first account of his religious motives is just plain silly: no one *consciously* practices virtue in order to secure "delicious self-approval" (*Tales* 647).[22] But his Sunday-morning recognition of Bartleby's "miserable friendlessness and loneliness" (*Tales* 651) rings more solid, and it seems right somehow that he is unable to attend his fashionable Anglican church that day. And finally, when he refers his sense of responsibility for Bartleby to his timely recollection of the New Testament's "new commandment . . . that ye love one another," we can be pretty sure that his ethic is a degree or two less worldly than that of the average millionaire fur-trader. He blurs the purity of his motive by remarking that "charity" is a very "prudent principle," as it has prevented the "old Adam" (*Tales* 661) of his mounting frustration from expressing itself as deadly anger, but the exceptions he has already made for Bartleby's outrageous behavior have well exceeded the bounds of all good business sense. Evidently what the Narrator describes as a "superstitious knocking at my heart" (*Tales* 654) may well be taken in a specifically Christian sense; and no doubt H. Bruce Franklin is right to read the entire story as a sort of oblique gloss on Matthew 25: "whatever you do to the [forlornist] of

21. For the pressure of Dickens on "Bartleby the Scrivener," see Robert Weisbuch, *Atlantic Double-Cross: American Literature and British Influence in the Age of Emerson* (Chicago: University of Chicago Press, 1986), pp. 36-54.

22. For a revealing study of the epistemology of self-deception, see Kenneth Marc Harris, *Hypocrisy and Self-Deception in Hawthorne's Fiction* (Charlottesville: University of Virginia Press, 1988), esp. pp. 1-14.

mine, you do unto me."[23] Bartleby, that is to say, is "Christ figure" in the only sense the New Testament will safely sponsor: not a look-alike or a fractured type with the bad luck to appear long after the fulfillment, but simply a person in need of aid and comfort. With an historical identity past discovery — and acting more like an anorectic whose negative preferences anticipate a Nirvana that is the suspension of all personal will than a reformer seeking to transform the notion of "kingdom" — Bartleby nevertheless figures Christ to the Narrator. And, like a man trying to imitate Christ with only the gifts of the Old Adam to go on,[24] the Narrator tries his underpowered best to relieve the exemplary suffering of the uncommunicative person he has dared introduce as an "avatar."

To no avail, as we sadly recall. Bartleby ends up starving himself to death in "The Tombs," and his last words to the Narrator offer guilt rather than understanding or forgiveness: "I know you, . . . and I want nothing to say to you" (*Tales* 669). But the Narrator really has tried. Informed that Bartleby has remained behind in the quarters he has lately quitted, he has even offered — as we ourselves never do, to the panhandler we suspect will misspend the change out of our pocket — to take his forlorn scrivener into his own home. Balked in that offer, he suffers the devices of the world to arrange the end of this cosmic misfit. More significant than this sadly familiar outcome, however, is the fact that the Narrator has attempted his ill-fated Christian enactment in spite of a powerful intuition of his almost uncertain failure. From the moment he makes the melancholy Sunday morning discovery that Bartleby is in fact living in his law-offices, storing his few pitiful possessions in an old bandana handkerchief, he is all but overcome with a sense of his exemplary hopelessness. In a speech rather well thought out for a man of no speculative tendency, he observes that, as a rule, there is a point beyond which "the sight of misery" no longer "enlists our best affections." And this owes, he insists, not to the "inherent selfishness of the human heart" but to a "certain hopelessness of remedying excessive and organic ill."

23. See H. Bruce Franklin, *The Wake of the Gods: Melville's Mythology* (Stanford: Stanford University Press, 1963), pp. 126-36.

24. The inspired formulation was suggested to me by Professor Roger Lundin of Wheaton College — whose sponsorship of a series of lectures at the University of Notre Dame called this essay into existence.

We help when we can, he theorizes, but when we see at last that our "pity cannot lead to effectual succour, common sense bids the soul be rid of it." Case in point: the "innate and incurable disorder" (*Tales* 653) of Bartleby.

"Innate" is no longer a word we like to use, but "disorder" is precisely the term by which modern psychotherapy tries to conceal its own etiological uncertainty. Of course we need not take the momentary reflection of a thoroughly fictionalized Narrator as the gospel teaching of modern literature's arch-theorist of "woe," particularly when that Narrator goes right on to try to *help* the unhelpable. But some version of the Narrator's sentiment may survive its own ironic transumption, particularly in a writer well known to be on the lookout for problems no one can solve and for sufferings no natural calculus can regularize. Painful to behold, Bartleby's disorder seems nevertheless "organic" — not in the bodily sense, perhaps, as if to prejudice the enduring question of organism and psyche — but in the sense of the endemic or inevitable, given the limits of a certain system, as if evil of a certain sort were the penalty of creation in that same sort.

But while we are estimating the cogency of this theology, or meditating the paradox of a Narrator painfully trying to fix the recognizably unfixable, the determined political reader of the story — which is to say the Marxist — will now and then step in to declare that all the ink we spill over the quality and efficacy of the Narrator's goodwill is so much misplaced sentiment, just like the philosophical commentaries on Edwards's rejection of Locke's preference for the word "prefer,"[25] or the more widespread if less systematic attention given to the symbol of "the wall." The story is, after all, "A Story of Wall Street," the capital of American capitalism: what matters about Bartleby is less "his solitude" than "his poverty" (*Tales* 651). Obviously alienated from the repetitive labor of mere copying, his salary is furthermore insufficient to afford him a meaningful life. The quiet charity of the Narrator's private heart might offer him a superfluous overcoat, as it did with Turkey, but the problem is a system that

25. See Allan Moore Emery, "The Alternatives of Melville's 'Bartleby,'" *Nineteenth-Century Fiction* 31 (1976): 170-87; also instructive on the philosophical question of "will" is Daniel Stemple and Bruce R. Stillians, "'Bartleby the Scrivener': A Parable of Pessimism," *Nineteenth-Century Fiction* 27 (1972): 268-82.

generates capital wealth on the condition of the strategic abuse of labor. And only those hopelessly in love with metaphysical explanations will fail to see what Bartleby means when he replies to the Narrator's repeated demands for explanation with the following unusually wordy response: "Do you not see the reason for yourself" (*Tales* 656).[26]

Such strong political interventions have been made fairly regularly over the lengthening history of "Bartleby," and their failure to stem the tide of abstruse interpretation proves at least that ideology we have always with us. But their failure may also suggest that systems of political economy are not the only ones Melville has in mind. Nor has the rise and fall of Marxist societies generally weakened our sense that the universe has more dark corners than the besom of economic reform can possibly sweep clean. And perhaps some such suspicion may be increased in the reader who comes to the story of "Bartleby" from the one that prefaces it in the strategic organization of Melville's *Piazza Tales*.[27]

The structure is pretty much the same: repeatedly observing a gleam of light in the mountainous distance, a convalescent narrator, ordinary enough to represent our own ironic selves, comes, at the end of a quest he hoped would lead to his "Fairyland," face to face with a wan and wasted embodiment of extraordinary sadness whom Shakespeare, Tennyson, and now Melville himself have all named Marianna.[28] Far from Wall Street, and living in a cottage notable for its ramshackle disrepair,

26. For a timely lodging of the Marxist protest, see David Kuebrich, "Melville's Doctrine of Assumptions," *New England Quarterly* 69 (1996): 381-405. And for a sober recognition that Christian theology and the church may indeed have "felt more committed to a socially irrelevant love of neighbor than to political enlightenment and activity," see Hans Küng, *Does God Exist? An Answer for Today*, trans. Edward Quinn (1980; repr. New York: Crossroad, 1995), p. 253; and *passim*, pp. 215-61.

27. Written late in the period of Melville's tales, "The Piazza" was nevertheless composed to serve as the introduction to a collection called *The Piazza Tales* (1856), including all the tales Melville had published in *Putnam's Magazine*, beginning with "Bartleby the Scrivener"; see Merton R. Sealts, "The Chronology of Melville's Short Fiction," in *Pursuing Melville, 1940-1980: Chapters and Essays* (Madison: University of Wisconsin Press, 1982), pp. 221-31. And for the argument that, after writing and failing to publish a book called *The Isle of the Cross*, Melville wrote "Bartleby the Scrivener" and "Cock-a-Doodle Doo" as an "Idealist Turned Would-Be Stoic," see Hershel Parker, *Herman Melville: A Biography*, vol. 2, *1851-1891* (Baltimore: Johns Hopkins University Press, 2002), pp. 162-89.

28. For a review of the scholarship on "Marianna," see Newman, *Guide*, pp. 310-11.

she is easily recognizable (by those who have been there) as an aggravated instance of Appalachian poverty. Deprived of his fiction of fairyland, the Narrator might yet be criticized for his failure to offer this solitary maiden much beside banal advice already too familiar. But what? Proposing marriage seems a sexist solution and, as one of my students soberly suggested, offering her a stage-ticket to the mills of Lowell would only substitute one sort of suffering for another. In short, the reader is not easily convinced that Marianna's sadness is not also "excessive and organic," designed to arouse our sympathy but balk our wish for persons to redeem or politics to prevent.

Unlike Bartleby, however, Marianna is voluble and expressive, if only in an oblique and symbolic way, so that we get some glimpse of the problem we are asked to consider if not to solve. Orphaned long since, living only with a brother, absent every day at his task of wood-cutting and dead tired at night, and in a place visited by "Birds . . . seldom" and "boys, never" (*Tales* 633), Marianna is left entirely to herself — and to the remarkable fantasies she keeps for company. She too has seen a gleam in the distance, the Narrator's own glistening roof, as it turns out; and though we feel at once the force of his declining to identify himself and thus disillusion her, we quickly get beyond the clichéd sense that the other grass is always greener. For the cases are not quite parallel: long aware of the risk, the Narrator has nevertheless gone off to explore the real-life basis of his sustaining illusion, but Marianna's life appears to permit no such mobility. Indeed, as her situation passes, without allegorical marker, from the sadly social to the soberly philosophical, she comes to seem an almost perfect shut-in, seldom getting up from her sewing, deprived of everything one would wish to dignify with the name of reality, and identifying herself only as the scene of fancies — altogether private but familiar enough to have their own names.

At night she calls her relentless disturbance "Thinking, thinking — a wheel I cannot stop" (*Tales* 633). Insufficiently aware that he is getting out of his depth, the Narrator recommends prayer and a fresh hop pillow to cure this noetic insomnia. Well beyond that advice, Marianna points instead at two hop-vines that would have "joined over in an upward clasp, but the baffled shoots, groping awhile in empty air, trailed back whence they sprung" (*Tales* 633). Not quite "Ah Bartleby! Ah humanity," perhaps, but sign enough that "souls never touch their objects,"[29] particularly when Marianna's daytime mentality has revealed itself as an exquisite exercise in the discrimination of shadows: "You watch the cloud," says Marianna, interrupting the Narrator's Poe-like identification of the shape of "some gigantic condor." "No, a shadow," he replies —

> "A cloud's, no doubt — though that I cannot see. How did you know it? Your eyes are on your work."
>
> "It dusked my work. There, now the cloud is gone, Tray comes back."
>
> "How?"
>
> "The dog, the shaggy dog. At noon he steals off, of himself, to change his shape — returns, and lies down awhile, nigh the door. Don't you see him? His head is turned round at you; though, when you came, he looked before him."
>
> "Your eyes rest but on your work; what do you speak of?"
>
> "By the window, crossing."
>
> "You mean this shaggy shadow — the nigh one? And, yes, now that I mark it, it is not unlike a large, black Newfoundland dog. The invading shadow gone, the invaded one returns. But I do not see what casts it."
>
> "For that, you must go without." (*Tales* 631-32)[30]

Out of the *cave*, even our primitive knowledge of Plato readily suspects. But as the Narrator goes home to moralize about the dark and the light of life, we are left to make the epistemological application for ourselves.

The most well-read Narrator, who surely knows that Tray is a dog out of Shakespeare, does not seem to know that his minor-romantic faculty has met its major-philosophic match.[31] If imagination has been to

---

29. Thus Emerson nods to the problem of solipsism in the first (Illusion) section of "Experience"; see *Essays and Lectures*, p. 473.

30. Given the repeated reference to shadows, the reference to the inside and outside of Plato's cave seems evident — even though "go without" also suggests Marianna's familiarity with deprivation.

31. For the Narrator's astonishing range of allusion, particularly to the genre of romantic quest, see Helmbrecht Breinig, "The Destruction of Fairyland," *ELH* 35 (1968): 254-83. And for readings that approach the tale as a study of art and epistemology, see

him a way to color with vermilion his gray-granite world, or to sustain an occasional inland voyage to fairly-land, away from the world where "millions of strange, cankerous worms" (*Tales* 626) infect the beauty of the Chinese creeper growing near his piazza, to Marianna it has been no less than a life-saving device. Plato's mythic optimism to the contrary, neither of these two poetic reflectors gets out of the cave that dooms all men to muse on the meaning of shadows cast by we know not what. But Marianna's neck is more tightly chained than that of the Narrator: free to roam about and inspect all the compartments in the cave, and to read the reflections of other more privileged cave-dwellers, he has had the odd luck one day to stumble across the chamber of one whose inventive faculty has had to preserve the integrity of consciousness itself. Beneath the fertile academic topic of fancy vs. imagination lies the root fact of fantasy, the power to construct a life worth living. Subject to "Romantic" abuse, we soberly learn from Dr. Johnson, but impossible to forbid, particularly to the poor.[32] And who but Melville could identify — in a region somewhere between upstate New York and the "Tartarus of Maids" — a disease we can identify only as Platonic schizophrenia? Psychotropic drugs might help Marianna with her sleeplessness, but where in modern epistemology is remedy for knowledge that cannot exceed its own tropes?

And so we find ourselves, prematurely no doubt, on the verge of a critical dogma: Melville is identically that writer who deeply knows that, as mortal being is inherently imperfect, its disease is bound to appear from time to time in forms we may curse but never cure. Pity is for a time the only humane response, but what visitor of the sick or re-distributor of wealth will hold that a new coat will cover the naked soul of Bartleby or Marianna? And for a further, perhaps paradigmatic, example, who will

---

Nancy Louise Roundy, "Fancies, Reflections, and Things," *College Language Association Journal* 20 (1977): 539-46.

32. For naming the theme we know as "the dangerous hungers of the imagination," we have to thank Samuel Johnson's neo-classic poem, "The Vanity of Human Wishes." For a political second thought, see Nathaniel Hawthorne, "The Hall of Fantasy," where it is observed that "with all its dangerous influences, we have reason to thank God, that there is such a place of refuge from the gloom and chilliness of actual life." *Tales and Sketches*, ed. Roy Harvey Pearce (New York: Library of America, 1982), p. 739.

not wince when, in the inspired rewrite of a modern poet, the ever-jovial Amasa Delano is heard to tell a demoralized and nearly demented Benito Cereno that with the freshening of the wind "Everything is going to go better and better"?[33] But if we wish to stop here, restricting charity and its extension as politics to the less theological side of Melville's genius, we had better not go on to read "Cock-a-Doodle-Doo," the strangely indecorous story about sex and death Melville wrote immediately after "Bartleby." It also asks us to estimate the behavior of an ordinary narrator in the face of familiar poverty and extreme suffering. And it convicts both him and us in the security of our mounting quietism.

## Marx and Melville

Unlike the two narrators we have encountered so far, the rural landholder who relates to us the strange case of his sometime woodcutter is himself full of express resentment against the world. Bartleby's businesslike historian is irritated by the thought of "incurable disorder," and the strolling esthete who promises to remember Marianna resents it when his shrubs are attacked by worms; but the man who celebrates the austere life and triumphant death of one Merrymusk is from the beginning an accomplished hater of what he takes to be cosmic imperfection and indeed injustice: his spring brings only a "damp, disagreeable air" (*Tales* 1203), while surrounding hills prevent the dispersion of small-town smoke, itself serving only to hide "many a man with the mumps, and many a queasy child" (*Tales* 1204). Meanwhile, in the human world, revolutions fail and despotisms thrive; friends die by accidents of "locomotive and steamer," vaunted "improvements of the age" (*Tales* 1205); insatiable creditors mercilessly dun this much-beset and long-suffering observer of the slings and arrows of man's worldly life. Multifarious they are, yet economic ills bother him especially: "A miserable world! Who would take the trouble to make a fortune in it, when he knows not how long he can keep it?" The enemy, it appears, is not the moth and rust well known to corrupt so much capital wealth but the "villains and asses who have the manage-

33. See Robert Lowell, *The Old Glory* (New York: Farrar, 1965), p. 180.

ment" of those murderous railroads and steamboats. So that — in an amateurish version of the plot called "If Man Were God" — if he were made "Dictator in North America" (*Tales* 1204) he'd string them all up.

A faithful source criticism has suggested that this gouty reader of Burton's *Anatomy of Melancholy* would do well to take that author's advice: get some exercise and try a more healthy diet.[34] But what appears to cheer him up, almost at once, is the lusty crowing of some neighboring but unseen cock: "Cock-a-Doodle-Doo!" What a remarkably uplifting sound! Would that he might own that inspiriting prophet of dawn and day. Untutored searching in the "neighboring country" (*Tales* 1211) finally reveals that the cock's owner is none other than his own part-time yardman. Once himself lusty enough to father four children — and still able to give a sly wink over the question of who may and may not be said to possess a magnificent cock — Merrymusk is now poor to the point of starvation. Yet he refuses to sell the treasured bird, from the undaunted optimism of whose cry both he and his failing family take some sort of religious hope or assurance. "Glory to God in the Highest," they all hear this barnyard prophet declare, even to the point of their own death. The Narrator hears other messages, from time to time, such as "Let the world and all aboard it go to pot. Do you be jolly, and never say die" (*Tales* 1216); and, less explicitly, slap another mortgage on the old homestead, order more Philadelphia Porter and Herkimer cheese, and never let the bill-collector see you sweat. But in learning to bear the assaults of first the dun and then the civil-process server, he imagines he is learning the lesson of faith and hope the Merrymusk family hear in the crowing of the cock to whom they have given the apocalyptic name of "Trumpet."

Unable to purchase the prophetic bird, he is nevertheless restored by some odd mistranslation of its remarkable cry. It helps him bear the "hard world" in which he, "as good a fellow as ever lived," by his own estimate, finds himself "forlorn — unjustly used — abused — unappreciated" (*Tales* 1215). One thing it does *not* do, however, is make him more sensitive to the "neighborly" need of the Merrymusk family. To be sure, he has now and then offered his woodcutter "a dish of hot pork and

34. See Allan Moore Emery, "The Cocks of Melville's 'Cock-a-Doodle-Doo,'" *Emerson Society Quarterly* 28 (1982): 89-111.

beans, and a mug of cider" in place of the "stale bread" and "salt beef" (1217) he has brought along for his lunch; and no doubt this underlies his sense of being "hospitable — open-hearted — generous to a fault" (*Tales* 1215). But we also notice, despite the Narrator's casual reporting of the fact, that he does not always pay Merrymusk on time or in the full amount owed. Indeed the Narrator first mentions the question of the "extraordinary cock" to Merrymusk when the woodcutter, "having long previously sawed [the] wood," finally comes back for his pay, of which the Narrator, not having "the full change," pays him only a part. So that — "one fine morning" (*Tales* 1218) an indeterminate time later — his first visit to the Merrymusk shanty is for the purpose of giving him the remainder of what was long overdue. And no doubt we are to remember these small economic facts when we come to the end (and to the Narrator's moral) of the Merrymusk story.

At first meeting, the Narrator assures us that, thanks to Merrymusk's steady labor, his "family never suffered for lack of food"; but he also lets on that the cow they bought so as to have "plenty of wholesome milk for the children" had died "during an accouchement," that they "could not afford to buy another," and that in fact the children appear "rickety" (*Tales* 1218). Evidently the economic condition of the Merrymusk family has been worsening over time, and with it the quality of their diet. Certain it is that, when the Narrator makes his penultimate (and crucial) visit to the Merrymusk home, the whole family seems desperately ill of that malnutrition the nineteenth century knew as rickets. More than resigned to the prospect of their imminent demise, indeed glorying in the prospect of death and resurrection to which their crowing prophet continues triumphantly to testify, they may be deliberately refusing to prolong their impoverished lives — if we are to believe the Narrator's report of seeing a supply of jerked beef, potatoes, and Indian meal in their rafter-less and earth-floored home (*Tales* 1221). Their case is grim, at very best. Perhaps they are indeed too far along in some mad regimen of holy anorexia — past the point of charitable intervention, perhaps, in a world where individual good will can never keep pace with the Malthusian spread of rural poverty.[35]

35. For Melville's response to the poverty-economics of Thomas Robert Malthus, see Beryl Rowland, "Sitting Up With a Corpse," *Journal of Australian Studies* 6 (1972): 69-83.

Near the end, however, a curious opportunity appears to present itself: "Is there any hope of your wife's recovery?" the Narrator asks Merrymusk, suitably enough. "Not the least," comes back the fateful answer. "The children?" the Narrator presses on. "Very little" (*Tales* 1223), Merrymusk replies, leaving very little room for timely intervention. Very little, but not none. Just here, some concerned person — some "neighbor," enacting that Samaritan charity of which a conscientious politics would be only the natural extension — might have said, "For God's sake, man, what is that hope, and how may one help? Shall we not run at once to fetch the village doctor?" But the Narrator, short on memory of the parables and too impressed, perhaps, by Merrymusk's declaration that the luridly cheerful crowing of "Trumpet" is "Better than a 'pothecary," responds only with the weakly philosophical comfort that "It must be a doleful life, then, for all concerned" (*Tales* 1223).[36] And so the moment passes, too slight for most critical notice, assuring the pathetic/triumphant death of the entire family.

Crowing wildly at the end of his strange story, the Narrator wishes to recall and apply their example as the proper spiritual antidote for his besetting melancholy, but the careful reader may wish to remember instead that the Narrator has missed an earlier opportunity to intervene in the course of the unmerited suffering that marks for him this hard and indeed unjust world. The revelation of this chance that was wasted comes almost inadvertently, at the end of the Narrator's longest and most detailed rehearsal of his quarrel with this world for its lack of proper governance. Beginning with a protest over his own financial difficulty, but moving on to an ironic imitation — indeed a parody — of Ahab's mighty protest, the passage is worth quoting in its entirety:

> I can't pay this horrid man; and yet they say money was never so plentiful — a drug in the market; but blame me if I can get any of the drug, though there never was a sick man more in need of that particular sort of medicine. It's a lie; money ain't plenty — feel of my pocket. Ha! here's a powder I was going to send to the sick baby in yonder hovel,

36. If "Bartleby the Scrivener" emplots Matthew 25, then "Cock-a-Doodle-Doo" surely suggests a gloss on Luke 10, containing the parable of the Good Samaritan: the inter-textual irony might be thought to center on the Narrator's shallow claim to be "hospitable."

where the Irish ditcher lives. That baby has the scarlet fever. They say the measles are rife in the country too, and the varioloid, and the chicken-pox, and it's bad for teething children. And after all, I suppose many of the poor little ones, after going through all this trouble, snap off short; and so they had the measles, mumps, croup, scarlet-fever, chicken-pox, cholera-morbus, summer-complaint, and all else, in vain! Ah! there's that twinge of the rheumatics in my right shoulder. I got that one night on the North River, when, in a crowded boat, I gave up my berth to a sick lady, and staid on the deck till morning in drizzling weather. There's the thanks one gets for charity! Twinge! Shoot away, ye rheumatics! Ye couldn't lay on worse if I were some villain who had murdered the lady instead of befriending her. Dyspepsia too — I am troubled with that. (*Tales* 1205-06)

What we notice, first of all, is the way the various versions of the Narrator's complaint trail away — first into the trivial and then the merely personal: babies suffer from the deadly scarlet fever all the way down to the discomfort of teething and "summer-complaint"; and the vain suffering of children who make it through childhood diseases only to die before they become adults gives way to the injustice of the Narrator's latest flare of rheumatism, the thanks he gets for an act of chivalry and the latest proof that no good deed goes unpunished. And don't forget his upset stomach. Compared to the savage protest of Ahab, however, the tone here is comic: the smallest phonograph player in the world is playing "Oh how you must suffer." What survives from this baby-quarrel, therefore, is less a cogent re-formulation of the problem of evil and more a reminder that our self-pitying Narrator does not always walk the walk. Why not deliver that powder to some sick baby, in one hovel or another, after all?

And, while we are at it, we may find ourselves wondering what that powder might have been? Not an antibiotic, since the discovery of that life-saving killer will have to wait for another cleaner, better-lit century. Not even aspirin, which came into common use some decades after the fictional life and death of the Merrymusk family.[37] A "drug," the Narra-

---

37. Though natural substances such as willow bark, later found to contain salicylic acid, were used, more or less ineffectively, since antiquity, its synthesis and use in powder

tor's pun keeps insisting: a pain-killer, no doubt, in a world where bodies in pain knew more about how to deaden sensation than to preserve and restore health. Quite likely it is the powder used to make up the tincture of laudanum, famous enough as the nineteenth century's nearly universal cure for pain of all sorts; an opium-derivative that eased the suffering of quite a few well-known authors — Coleridge, De Quincey, Poe, to name only the self-confessed users.[38] So that when Marx taught, with enduring authority, that "religion is . . . the opium of the people," he clearly presumed our understanding that the opium of the literary class is, identically, opium. Intellectuals, suffering the loss of fresh sensation or the death of God, can well afford the means to blunt the pang of their own belatedness. The poor have no such luck, only the hope of resurrection and an afterlife to assuage the bodily and spiritual pain of their earthly existence. Fair enough, the faithless literati appear to believe. Yet why not deliver the powder to some poor family or other? Would a little ease disturb the balance of their settled resignation? Surely it would not end all suffering, but it might be well received for all that.

Or if, as with the Merrymusk family, the case is too far advanced, if systematic poverty and endemic suffering have made the long-trumpeted afterlife of otherworldly religion seem the only resource, then the Narrator might at least notice the irony of the system in which he finds himself caught up. Consciously, though without much spiritual discernment, he is trying to feed his faith and hope on the vigor of Merrymusk's own, much as Wordsworth was able to cheer himself at the sight of an aged but still lucid and competent leech-gatherer — a poetic incident to which the story by grotesque misquotation openly refers.[39] But where Words-

form began only in the 1860s, its effective production and distribution only in the 1870s. The acetylsalicylic acid tablet we know as "aspirin" dates from 1897. See David B. Jack, "One Hundred Years of Aspirin," *Lancet* (1997): 350, 437-39.

38. Coleridge's account of how "Kubla Khan" came to be written in "an opium dream" is almost as explicit a part of literary history as is Thomas DeQuincy's *Confessions of an English Opium Eater* (1822). For the (limited) scope of Poe's non-fictional use of opium, see Kenneth Silverman, *Edgar A. Poe: Mournful and Never-ending Remembrance* (New York: Harper, 1991), p. 481.

39. Editor Warner Berthoff calls Melville's allusion to Wordsworth's "Resolution and Independence" an "alarming parody-reference"; see *Great Short Works of Herman Melville* (New York: Harper, 1966), p. 75.

worth's leech-gatherer exhibits only a sort of indestructible animal faith, Merrymusk appears to have passed from that lusty natural state to one of utter and desperate otherworldliness. Himself a willing-enough part of an economic process that has pushed a poor man and his family to a positively manic wish to leave the material world behind, the Narrator then turns to the victim as a sustaining spiritual resource, the meaning of which he totally misunderstands. An ironic outcome, wherever Melville got the plot.

There is no proof that Melville knew, from the Preface to *A Contribution to the Critique of Hegel's Philosophy of Right* (1844), Marx's often misquoted (and regularly misinterpreted) formulation: "Religion is the sigh of the oppressed creature, the heart of a heartless world, and the soul of soulless conditions. It is the opium of the people." Or that such sentiments were clearly recalled in sayings of a certain, socially concerned "Parson Lot": "We have used the Bible as if it was . . . an opium . . . for keeping beasts of burden patient while they are being overloaded."[40] The matter of Malthusian poverty and Socialist proposal was pretty well covered in various intellectual magazines Melville was known to read from time to time; and though Merrymusk cannot be got to describe himself as an "oppressed creature," the Narrator — complaining a little too much about what genuine poverty would recognize as capitalist self-deception — certainly protests a world that is both "heartless" and "soulless."[41] Yet

40. Now justly famous, Marx's observation about the people's "otherworldly" religion as opium is quoted in Lewis Feurer, ed., *Marx and Engels* (Garden City, N.Y.: Anchor, 1959), p. 263. The "echo" is from Parson Lot's "Letter to the Chartists, No. ii," in *Politics for the People* 4 (May 27, 1848): 58; Parson Lot is the familiar penname of the Rev. Charles Kingsley, also known as the author of the children's novel *Waterbabies* (1863) and, earlier, the economic-reformist novel *Alton Locke* (1850).

41. Readers of *Mardi* will recall that by 1848 Melville had already begun to express his responses to the program of the Chartists in England and to the various revolutions of 1848. Closer to home, the story of Marianna takes place "not long after 1848," when various kings had "voted for themselves" (*Tales* 623); and "Cock-a-Doodle-Doo" itself begins by recalling that, worldwide, "many high-spirited revolts from rascally despotisms had of late been knocked on the head" (*Tales* 1203). For the state of not-quite-Marxist commentary in England, one might see (for example) the omnibus review of Kingsley (as Parson Lot and as himself), Proudhon, and several others in the *Edinburgh Review* 93 (Jan. 1851): 1-33. Oddly enough, Marx might have been known better in America than in England in the 1850s, though not quite as such: the many articles he published in the *New York Tribune* be-

the case is even more curiously interesting if Melville was not aware of Marx; for in that case he would have written, in "Cock-a-Doodle-Doo," a tale that intuits all on its own the Marxist relation between oppression and apocalypse. For clearly the sort of religion Marx has in mind is precisely that which offers salvation in another world as the only fit recompense for so much suffering in this one.

Conservatives might continue to insist, in paragraphs now painful to read, that only profound and widespread religious conversion could lead the world out of its present dilemma of progress and poverty. American liberals, such as those who had been for a time Transcendentalists, might reply, bravely but with experience on their side, that "priests and pedagogues" have had their turn long since, that the social evils of the nineteenth century are not in the last analysis "individual in character" but are "inherent in all our social arrangements"; so that "could we convert all men to Christianity in both theory and practice, . . . the evils of the social state would remain untouched."[42] It remained to Marx, however, to argue that religion — at least in its familiar, otherworldly form — was not only no solution but was in fact a large part of the problem. And perhaps to Melville as well. For all Marx could add to "Cock-a-Doodle-Doo" would be the observation that the assurance of a better life beyond death is all that prevents the poorest classes from rising up against an injustice not altogether the result of divine incompetence or inattention — surely an amendment Melville could easily adopt.[43]

---

ginning in 1851 all appeared anonymously; some were translated from the German by Engels; and, under the watchful eye of Charles A. Dana, they stuck to the reporting of foreign political affairs and avoided religious insult.

42. Separating themselves from the liberal wing of the Unitarian Church, George Ripley and Theodore Parker both abandon the talking cure for some more direct political involvement — communitarianism in the one case, abolitionism in the other. It remained for Orestes Brownson, however, to use language that would remind social historians, even distantly, of Marx; see "The Laboring Classes," in Miller, ed., *Transcendentalists*, pp. 436-46.

43. For an account of Melville's *Moby-Dick* as a response to the Revolutions of 1848, see Larry Reynolds, *European Revolutions and the American Literary Renaissance* (New Haven: Yale University Press, 1988), pp. 97-124.

## The Indefinite Interim

To say that Melville wrote a story that perfectly enacts the logic of "early Marx" is not to claim that Melville ever looked to revolution as the way to right the imbalance of suffering in the world, or even that he finally abandoned theodicy in favor of politics. It is only to say that, in the period of his magazine tales at least, when the extravagances of his heroic and romantic rhetoric had given way to the keener pleasure of irony, his relentless inquiry marked out a space in which the political might justly appear. Following in the footsteps of an empathy which might betray a natural rather than a "true" virtue, it was not to be neglected for that abstruse "Edwardsian" reason.[44] And neither could the failure of material creation to solve all the problems it appeared to generate ever justify the lapse of that always endangered instinct. If the universe taught indifference, the natural imagination nevertheless continued to put itself in the place of the injured and excluded.

Yet as this accession of the political is gradual and in the end partial, so the exact formula is proving very hard to write. For all the correctness of our present sensitivity, a tale like "Benito Cereno" — where a Narrator encounters not one but two exemplary cases of suffering off scale — manages to understand but refuses altogether to endorse the violence let loose in an exemplary slave revolt; and *Battle Pieces,* the most explicitly political of all Melville's works, emphatically declines an after-the-fact sponsorship of patriotic gore in the name of righteous abolitionism.[45] Cautionary as well, "The Tartarus of Maids" throws the veil of St. Veron-

44. The polar opposite to Melville's Plotinus Plinlimmon is, of course, Jonathan Edwards, whose *Nature of True Virtue* (1755) sets itself the problem of defining true virtue as nothing short of "benevolence to Being-In-General" — without discounting at the same time a "mere" natural virtue.

45. The dominant modern reading of "Benito Cereno," that of Eric Sundquist, makes it clear that the tale goes out of its way to imply the entire history of "New World Slavery." *To Wake the Nations: Race in the Making of American Literature* (Cambridge: Belknap Press of Harvard University Press, 1993), pp. 135-82. What is not so clear, however, is Melville's underlying political intention. For a dissent pointing in the direction of an encompassing theology, see Allan Moore Emery, "The Topicality of Depravity in 'Benito Cereno,'" *American Literature* 55 (1983): 316-31. See also Maurice Lee, "Melville's Subversive Political Philosophy," *American Literature* 72 (2000): 495-519.

ica over the gender-specific sufferings of the sex that bleeds the human race into being, but it stops well short of imagining that brave new time when babies come from test tubes. From a world of rural poverty very like that of "Cock-a-Doodle-Doo," "The Poor Man's Pudding" observes a scene of forced labor and bereft motherhood not far different from that of slavery. But, while not forgiving the rich men who moralize its necessity and even its curious pleasures, it also forces the reader to notice the poor family's copy of the *Submission to Divine Providence in the Death of Children,* one of the many works in which Dr. Philip Doddridge offered the orthodox explanation, from the seventeenth century to the nineteenth, of why catastrophic things so regularly happen to such well-meaning people. And down the road a few years, a puzzled divinity student named Clarel will have more than political injustice to thank when, returning from a search for the authentic footsteps of the Redeemer, he finds his intended wife dead of one more meaningless skirmish over a desert landscape remaining holy but in ironic name.[46] Guilty men continue to play their part in Melville's mature drama of depravity, but some structure beyond that of caste and class remains keenly at issue — even as the question of "The Personality of the Deity" recedes into the background and almost into silence.

What this suggests is that, though the problem of Evil may well appear logically as the result of an explicit theism, it does not always disappear with the gradual eclipse of that particular hypothesis. Or so we seem to learn from the example of Melville, in which the feeling of sympathy with those who fall afoul of a universe not designed to repent or even to take notice never loses its original sense of disproportion and even of resentment. As if one were to blame God for failing to exist.[47] Or,

---

46. On Melville's reference to Doddridge, see Rowland, "Sitting Up," pp. 78-79, and Maurice Lee, "Melville's 'Mistakes,'" *ESQ: A Journal of the American Renaissance* 41 (1995): 153-75. And for a reading of *Clarel* as frank and determined theodicy, see Stan Goldman, *Melville's Protest Theism: The Hidden and Silent God in "Clarel"* (DeKalb: Northern Illinois University Press, 1993), esp. pp. 147-72.

47. Jack Miles refers us to a scene in *Mistler's Exit* by Louis Begley, where the protagonist, dying of cancer and aware that the universe is not going to notice, "craves the vindication of repudiating the God in whom he does not believe." *Christ: A Crisis in the Life of God* (New York: Knopf, 2001), p. 10.

if that should prove an empty paradox, then we may say at least that Melville never becomes quite the "naturalist" he appears in Milton Stern's *Fine-Hammered Steel of Herman Melville,* the other very strong reading from the classic period of Melville criticism. Somewhere in Melville there lives indeed the suspicion that those "idealists" who try to impress a single, usually godly, meaning in the universe are quite likely to become a danger to themselves and those who happen to be standing around.[48] But something else remains as well. Not quite Job's "I will love him though he slay me." More like: I trust he will not destroy me for pursuing without cynicism the moral evidences that call into question our best metaphysical proofs. Not quite the "definite belief" a morally companionable Hawthorne would prescribe, in 1856, as the only cure for Melville's spiritual dis-ease; yet a position that left ample room for faith, should it ever be given.[49] And one that, in the indefinite interim, never forgave those who would sit in judgment on the organization of the world and not live up to the standard of their own moral word.

48. For the intellectual and moral dangers of idealism in Melville, see Milton Stern, *The Fine Hammered Steel of Herman Melville* (Urbana: University of Illinois Press, 1957), esp. Ch. 1, "The Absolute and the Natural."

49. For Hawthorne's estimate of the troubled seriousness that made Melville "better worth immortality than most of us," see *The English Notebooks 1856-1860,* ed. Thomas Woodson (Columbus: Ohio State University Press, 1997), p. 163.

# Nimble Believing: Dickinson and the Conflict of Interpretations

*Roger Lundin*

"**O**N SUBJECTS of which we know nothing, or should I say *Beings* —" Emily Dickinson wrote in the spring of 1882, four years before her death, "we both believe, and disbelieve a hundred times an Hour, which keeps Believing nimble."[1]

This assertion about a subject of incessant concern to Dickinson appears as an aside in an intimate letter she wrote to the one man, 69-year-old Otis Phillips Lord, whom we know for certain she considered marrying. We might not expect to come upon a meditation on belief and unbelief in such a spot, wedged in as it is between passionate avowals of love and visions of sexual delight, yet such was the custom for Dickinson in her poetry and her letters. Gnomic assertions repeatedly break from her compressed verses or irrupt into discussions of unrelated matters in her correspondence. Encountered singly, these images and asides seem like riddling signs of Dickinson's baffling brilliance; considered in their complex entirety, her explorations of religious experience offer one of the most incisive accounts we have of the transformation of belief in the modern age.

It would be hard to glean this fact about Dickinson through the reading of many accounts of her life. Consider, for instance, the three most

---

1. Emily Dickinson, *The Letters of Emily Dickinson*, ed. Thomas H. Johnson and Theodora Ward (Cambridge: Belknap Press of Harvard University Press, 1958), 3:728; hereafter cited in the text as *Letters*.

comprehensive Dickinson biographies of the past quarter century — Richard Sewall's *Life of Emily Dickinson,* Cynthia Griffin Wolff's critical biography, and Alfred Habegger's *My Wars Are Laid Away in Books.* Of the three, only Sewall treats Dickinson's religious beliefs with considerable historical nuance. Yet even he flattens the peaks of her religious experience and floods the dark nights of her soul with talk of the "sunshiny God" of love whom Dickinson supposedly admired.[2]

In a similar manner, excellent as it is in so many respects, Habegger's biography of Dickinson calls to mind Alan Wolfe's recent observation that "no aspect of life is considered so important to Americans outside higher education, yet deemed so unimportant by the majority of those inside, as religion."[3] Habegger packs 764 pages with the results of exhaustive documentary research and provides frequently illuminating readings of Dickinson's poems. Yet intellectual history and the life of the mind play minor roles at best in the drama of her life as he represents it. His biography of the poet, for instance, contains no references to the dramatic changes in science that rocked the world in her lifetime and shaped her vision in innumerable ways. In addition, religious belief and practice appear almost exclusively as importuning forces that threaten to crimp her personal life and poetic style. Habegger judges Dickinson's religious vision to have been "consciously 'pagan.'" He concludes that she "was contesting the kind of belief that claims sure knowledge of ultimate things. If heaven and all the rest were down pat ahead of time, our faith would be 'foreclosed' and our minds shackled. It is our ignorance that enlivens us and makes possible our greatness." As Habegger portrays her, Emily Dickinson is drawn to the subject of belief, but only if it forsakes its claim to any object of belief; she is captivated by faith, but only if that faith seeks nothing more than the restless activities of its own probing ignorance.[4]

Habegger's interpretation of Dickinson on religion has a long his-

---

2. Richard Sewall, *The Life of Emily Dickinson* (1974; repr. New York: Farrar, 1980), p. 601.

3. Alan Wolfe, "Faith and Diversity in American Religion," *The Chronicle Review,* 8 Feb. 2002, http://chronicle.com/free/v48/i22/22b00701.htm.

4. Alfred Habegger, *My Wars Are Laid Away in Books: The Life of Emily Dickinson* (New York: Random, 2001), pp. 617, 620.

tory dating back to the earliest responses to her work. From the beginning many readers resisted taking the religious range of her verse at face value and chose instead to consider her as a psychological type or as a forerunner of one secularizing movement or another. This proved to be the case, for example, when a man named Samuel Ward read the first edition of Dickinson's poetry, which was published four years after her death. Ward was a wealthy banker who in early adulthood had been an associate of Emerson and his Concord circle, and when he came across this slender volume of poems, he was so taken with them that he wrote at once to the book's co-editor, Thomas Wentworth Higginson.

In this letter, which Higginson called "the most remarkable criticism yet made on E. D.," Ward reported that he was, "with all the world, intensely interested in Emily Dickinson." Yet as Sewall, Wolff, and Habegger were to do a century later, Ward pursued his interest by transposing Dickinson's complex religious concerns into a simpler story of psychological inwardness. He told Higginson she was the "quintessence" of Puritanism, and with this term he was designating a set of cultural patterns and personal habits rather than a body of religious beliefs or liturgical practices: "We came to this country to think our own thoughts with nobody to hinder. . . . We conversed with our souls till we lost the art of communicating with other people. The typical family grew up strangers to each, as in this case. It was *awfully* high, but awfully lonesome." When the "gift of articulateness" was "not denied, you had Channing, Emerson, Hawthorne, a stupendous example, & so many others. Mostly it was denied, & became a family fate. This is where Emily Dickinson comes in. She was the articulate inarticulate."[5]

Although they correctly note Dickinson's healthy skepticism about doctrinal systems as well as her profound aversion to church membership, Ward, Habegger, and others fail to engage her serious, sustained passion for the subject — and objects — of belief. Jane Donahue Eberwein rightly observes that "the driving question of Emily Dickinson's life was the one she apparently directed to the Reverend Washington Gladden: 'Is Immortality true?' Everlasting life was the one

---

5. Samuel Ward, quoted in Millicent Todd Bingham, *Ancestors' Brocades: The Literary Debut of Emily Dickinson* (New York: Harper, 1945), pp. 169-70.

great promise of Christianity that she kept testing in her poems, letters, and conversations."[6] Or as James McIntosh has framed the issue in a recent study, "believing for intense moments in a spiritual life without permanently subscribing to any received system of belief, is a key experience, an obsessive subject, and a stimulus to expression for Dickinson."[7] She could not and would not let go of the subject of belief.

The argument of this essay is twofold and involves both a retrospective view and a prospective vision. First the retrospect: throughout her adult life, in both her poetry and her letters, Dickinson most often approached the question of belief by way of a key nineteenth-century distinction between verifiable knowledge and religious belief. She took seriously the advances in scientific theory and practice that had been made over the previous two centuries and that continued to unfold in her own lifetime. Like others in her cultural cohort, Dickinson considered scientific judgments about reality to be axiomatic, and she accepted it as a fact that modern science had made knowledge a matter of the tangible and had turned belief into an affair of the ineffable. Under the considerable influence of this tacit assumption, she would come to hold that we can *know* that which we can track with our senses or trace through the labyrinth of memory and consciousness, while we can *believe* that which our appetite desires and our spirit requires.

Ever a keen student of family discord, Dickinson was fascinated by the history behind the modern divorce of knowledge and belief. She grasped the historicity of religious thought and experience, just as she understood how the contours of belief could change within the development of an individual life. Further, she sensed intuitively something that we now understand historically, which was that in her own lifetime open unbelief had become an intellectually viable and socially acceptable option. The emergence of such unbelief represented a radical development in the cultural history of the West. It introduced the issue of choice into

6. Jane Donahue Eberwein, "Emily Dickinson and the Calvinist Sacramental Tradition," *ESQ: A Journal of the American Renaissance* 33 (1986): 67-81; reprinted in *Emily Dickinson: A Collection of Critical Essays*, ed. Judith Farr (Upper Saddle River, N.J.: Prentice-Hall, 1996), p. 104.

7. James McIntosh, *Nimble Believing: Dickinson and the Unknown* (Ann Arbor: University of Michigan Press, 2000), p. 1.

the most intimate questions of belief, and it made *not believing* for the first time a readily available alternative. Although Dickinson struggled with the consequences of this new freedom, she nevertheless embraced it as a good and searched for a way of encompassing the experience of unbelief within that of belief.[8]

The prospective portion of my argument will draw upon Dickinson's poetry and letters as well as Paul Ricoeur's analysis of historicity and hermeneutics (in *Freud and Philosophy* and *The Conflict of Interpretations*) to situate her thought in a broader intellectual and cultural context. I will argue that Dickinson incorporated the experience of unbelief within her understanding of belief by shifting the question of truth from history to eschatology, thereby turning truth into a matter of hope rather than one of fact. In doing so, she cut against the grain of most late nineteenth-century Protestant theology, which saw truth as emerging in the processes of history and had abandoned any hope of a final revelation at history's apocalyptic end. In the early years of the twentieth century, the German theologian Ernst Troeltsch reported approvingly that "the eschatological office is for the most part closed," its services no longer being required as a result of the triumph of nineteenth-century liberalism on every front. Several decades later, in the aftermath of two world wars, Hans Urs von Balthasar wittily replied to Troeltsch with the observation that the office now appears to be "working overtime."[9] Balthasar was referring, among other things, to the powerful renewed emphasis

---

8. In discussing the dynamics of belief and unbelief, I am indebted to James Turner's superb study of the subject. "Historically the dominant sense of 'believe' has been confidence in a person, not credence in a statement," Turner observes. But after the Reformation, "church leaders . . . did greatly expand the role of creed and doctrine in belief." They "realigned belief more toward the realm of specifiable logical judgments and thus brought it closer to the new cast of mind displayed so well in natural philosophy." The unbelief that emerges in the second half of the nineteenth century is related to the phenomenon of doubt but distinct from it. "Doubt" has to do with temporary uncertainty, while "unbelief" points more to a recurrent or persistent denial. *Without God, Without Creed: The Origins of Unbelief in America* (Baltimore: Johns Hopkins University Press, 1985), pp. 24, 25.

9. Ernst Troeltsch and Hans Urs von Balthasar, quoted in Helmut Thielicke, *The Evangelical Faith*, vol. 3: *Theology of the Spirit*, trans. and ed. Geoffrey W. Bromiley (Grand Rapids: Eerdmans, 1982), p. 379.

upon eschatology that Karl Barth had ushered in with his commentary on Romans in 1918. "If Christianity be not altogether thoroughgoing eschatology," Barth thundered, "there remains in it no relationship whatever with Christ."[10]

Emily Dickinson was already at her desk in the eschatological office in the late nineteenth century, puzzling over the riddles of belief and eagerly waiting for any news that might arrive. In a real sense, she anticipated the eschatological turn that Barth and others were to make in the twentieth century, and she did so by conceiving of truth as a mystery to be unveiled at the end of the age, which for the solitary woman from Amherst meant in death. Figures of sorcery, mystery, secrecy, and the uncanny abound in her poetry, and through the use of such images Dickinson fashioned her own distinct view of truth and developed a creative solution to what Ricoeur was to call "the conflict of interpretations."

In her response to the intellectual challenges posed to Christian belief, Dickinson showed prophetic insight of a kind that was rare in the nineteenth century. Like Herman Melville, Fyodor Dostoevsky, and Friedrich Nietzsche — contemporaries with whom she merits comparison — she was among the first to take the full measure of the loss of God. As Dostoevsky in particular did, she took that loss to involve the possibility of a temporary though terrifying reversal, and she did not see it as a matter of irreversible historical necessity. Instead of acceding to the inevitability of unbelief, for the whole of her adult life Dickinson sought to articulate a vision that could incorporate that loss within a more expansive understanding of faith.

## The Fine Inventions of Belief

Dickinson's breathless aside about believing and disbelieving a hundred times an hour has at its core a crucial assertion about belief. It is the claim that "we *know* nothing" about the subjects, the "Beings," that are the objects of that belief. Almost a century before Dickinson, Immanuel Kant

---

10. Karl Barth, *The Epistle to the Romans*, 6th ed., trans. Edwyn C. Hoskins (1918; London: Oxford University Press, 1933), p. 314.

had argued, in the preface to the second edition of *The Critique of Pure Reason,* that "all possible speculative knowledge of reason is limited to mere objects of *experience,*" and "we cannot *know* these objects as things in themselves."[11] To be sure, Dickinson never read Kant, but like many other educated Americans of her day, she knew her Kantianism well, having absorbed its lessons from the pages of Emerson and the Transcendentalists.[12] What she derived from that reading dovetailed with the conclusions she was reaching on her own, primarily by means of her understanding of science.

Kant had built a path to the transcendent on the rugged trail of the categorical imperative, and Emerson had touted the broad highway of intuition as a road to the divine, but by the time that Dickinson came to her intellectual maturity, those passages to the truth were blocked. She would not have carried the argument as far as Ludwig Feuerbach did when he traced "all religious ideas . . . back into their foothold in the senses, from which they originally proceeded: the symbolic bread into palpable bread, the symbolic wine into real wine."[13] Nevertheless, Dickinson did conclude that whatever the ultimate status of divine beings may be, we can know nothing for certain about them. The noumenal realm is closed to our senses, no matter how phenomenal those senses may seem to be, just as it is closed to our general intuitive capacities. "'Faith' is a fine invention/For Gentlemen who *see!*" Dickinson wrote in an early, playful verse, "But Microscopes are prudent/In an Emergency!"[14]

---

11. Immanuel Kant, *Critique of Pure Reason,* trans. Norman Kemp Smith (New York: St. Martin's, 1965), p. 27.

12. For the connections between Kant and the Transcendentalists, in particular, and the larger currents of nineteenth-century American thought, see Bruce Kuklick, *Churchmen and Philosophers: From Jonathan Edwards to John Dewey* (New Haven: Yale University Press, 1985), pp. 133-39, 146-60, and John J. Duffy, introduction to *Coleridge's American Disciples: The Selected Correspondence of James Marsh,* ed. John J. Duffy (Amherst: University of Massachusetts Press, 1973), pp. 23-27.

13. Karl Löwith, *From Hegel to Nietzsche: The Revolution in Nineteenth-century Thought,* trans. David E. Green (1964; repr. New York: Columbia University Press, 1991), p. 338.

14. Emily Dickinson, *The Poems of Emily Dickinson: Reading Edition,* ed. R. W. Franklin (Cambridge: Belknap Press of Harvard University Press, 1999), p. 95. This poem is #202 in the Franklin numbering scheme; all further references to Dickinson's poetry will give the Franklin number and will be cited within the text.

That is not to say that Dickinson was content with this situation. She would have paid dearly to be able to steal a peak at whatever those "Gentlemen" had perused with their eyes of faith. For example, at the age of nineteen she analyzed her failure to catch sight of God, when she wrote to a friend about a revival then underway in Amherst. "Christ is calling everyone here," she explained, and apparently everyone, including her own sister Vinnie, was answering the call. They "have been seeking, and they all believe they have found; I cant tell you *what* they have found, but *they* think it is something precious. I wonder if it *is?*" Young Emily found this sanctification "strange." It "works such a marvelous change" by "bring[ing] Christ down," and under its influence, "the faces of good men shine, and bright halos come around them; . . . It *certainly* comes from God — and I think to receive it is blessed — not that I know it from *me,* but from those on whom *change* has passed" (*Letters* 1:94).[15]

That specific change, which involved an explicit experience of conversion, never was to pass over Dickinson, and in her poems seekers most often fail to find the signs of the divine for which they have been searching. "My period had come for Prayer —", for example, opens with its speaker recognizing that she "missed a rudiment" of prayer — "Creator — Was it you?" Having been told that "God grows above," she "stepped opon the North/To see this Curious Friend —." Yet she finds nothing but blankness to gaze upon, for God has neither a "House" nor a "sign" by which one might "infer his Residence." All that her eye can take in are "Vast Prairies of Air/Unbroken by a Settler —." The fruitless search prompts a frustrated question: "Infinitude — Had'st Thou no Face/That I might look on Thee?" Stranded in the "Silence" without a sign, the speaker reports that she was "awed beyond my errand —/I worshipped — did not 'pray' —" (#525). Here worship seems to entail a sober, even frightened acknowledgment of impersonal power, and it is not anything like a personal encounter with God.[16]

---

15. The serious tone in this letter from 1850 contrasts with the sardonic treatment that Dickinson would later give to the 1873 "awakening" in Amherst. In commenting on that latter revival, she was jocular and dismissive. In her forties, Dickinson still took religion seriously, but she no longer regarded the evangelical model of conversion and revival as something substantial with which she had to reckon.

16. In representing nature as a storehouse of signs, Dickinson drew upon the typo-

Like other Dickinson poems on the subject, "My period had come for prayer" appropriates a crucial Kantian distinction between knowledge and belief. In a well-known statement from the preface to the *Critique,* Kant had written, "I have therefore found it necessary to deny *knowledge* in order to make room for *faith.*"[17] The word that Norman Kemp Smith translates as "faith" is "Glaube," which captures in German something of what is meant by "belief" as well as a good deal of what English intends by "faith." Through the use of this term Kant was seeking what Dickinson was to seek a century later: a practical faith that could be grounded in human need, whether that need be moral or spiritual. According to Charles Taylor, the exercise of moral freedom for Kant entailed "being able to decide against all inclination for the sake of the morally right."[18]

---

logical tradition that had inspired her Calvinist ancestors for two centuries. "The Puritan millennialists," writes Sacvan Bercovitch, "saw their errand into the wilderness as part of the final stage of history. In so doing, they distorted traditional forms of exegesis, but they were careful to justify themselves by recourse to scriptures. They always rooted their interpretations (however strained) in biblical texts, and they appealed to (even as they departed from) a common tradition of Reformed hermeneutics. Their Yankee heirs felt relatively free of such constraints." *The Rites of Assent: Transformations in the Symbolic Construction of America* (New York: Routledge, 1993), p. 147.

As one of those heirs, Dickinson treasured her freedom but also lamented the loss of certainty that came with it. Bercovitch argues that in the eighteenth century, "the meaning of Protestant identity became increasingly vague," and the "focus of figural authority" shifted "from Bible history to the American experience" (p. 147). For Dickinson in the nineteenth century, "the American experience" was less important as a source of figural authority than was the argument from design. The discrediting of the design argument most adequately explains the appearance in her poems of a sign-less nature and a silent God.

17. Kant, *Critique of Pure Reason,* p. 29. Kant believed his critique of reason would lead to the "inestimable benefit that all objections to morality and religion will be for ever silenced" (p. 30).

18. Charles Taylor, *Hegel* (Cambridge: Cambridge University Press, 1975), p. 29. Taylor notes that when "Kant said that he wanted to demolish claims to speculative knowledge about God to make room for faith, he was not just offering a consolation prize. His principal interest here was in the moral freedom of the subject, and this in a radical sense, that man should draw his moral precepts out of his own will and not from any external source, be this God himself. Thus in the *Critique of Practical Reason* Kant makes the point that it is fortunate for us that our speculative reason cannot take us farther. If we could

Dickinson traded upon the Kantian distinction but recast it for her own purposes. Knowledge for her had to do with sensory experience and the apprehensions of consciousness. What the eyes could see and the ears could hear in the immediacy of the moment, and what memory could steal and preserve from the vanishing past — these formed the substance of knowledge. And because the present so quickly faded into obscurity, memory bore for Dickinson the heaviest burden of knowing. "Memory is a strange Bell —," she wrote a month after her mother's death, "Jubilee, and Knell" (*Letters* 3:755). It was "Jubilee" because it raised the dead and lodged them in the mansion of the mind. "My Hazel Eye/ Has periods of shutting —/But, No lid has Memory," she believed, "for "Memory like Melody,/Is pink eternally —" (#869, #1614). Yet memory also sounded the death "Knell," tolling the loss of ones she had loved. "Remorse — is Memory — awake —" and whatever comforting presence memory conjures up can be countered by the fact that "The Grave — was finished — but the Spade/Remained in Memory —" (#781, #886). Because of memory's functional power as the engine of knowledge, Dickinson could not imagine living without it. "I think Heaven will not be as good as earth," she wrote to a friend late in life, "unless it bring with it that sweet power to remember, which is the Staple of Heaven — here" (*Letters* 2:651).

While *knowledge* could cling to reality through the powers of memory, for any understanding of the "Beings" beyond the ken of knowledge, only belief sufficed for Dickinson. But this was belief not as assent to doctrinal propositions or confidence in the promises of God; instead, belief for her involved the ability to trust that what the heart desires will one day come to pass. As she viewed it, belief was nourished almost entirely by hope and anticipation instead of by knowledge or possession, and appetite provided the fuel for that hope to feed upon. Where Emerson and Whitman could affirm belief as self-evident — "I know I am deathless," *Song of Myself* declares — Dickinson had to command belief

---

convincingly see God and the prospect of immortality, we would have always acted out of fear and hope, and would never have developed the inner motivation of duty, which is the crown of moral life." *Hegel,* p. 31. Dickinson played a variation upon this theme by positing metaphysical and aesthetic desire as life-giving powers nourished by the absence of God.

into being, as though desire and demand could in themselves create a state of satisfaction that God was no longer likely to deliver.

A hunger for belief lies behind the imperative voice employed in many of her poems about the subject. "So much of Heaven has gone from Earth/That there must be a Heaven," begins one of them. The greatest evidence of this heaven is our need for it, for "Too much of Proof affronts Belief." That belief resembles, of all things, a turtle who "will not try/Unless you leave him — then return —/And he has hauled away" (#1240). Or as a darker poem explains, it is the fact that "it will never come again" that "makes life so sweet." Because of that bittersweet truth, there is no point in "Believing what we dont believe," and life is "at best/An ablative estate —/That instigates an appetite/Precisely opposite" (#1761). Belief must savor whatever the "instigating appetite" can conjure up to satisfy the hunger of the heart.[19]

Dickinson's awareness of the historicity of unbelief was almost as keen as her understanding of the inner struggle between knowledge and belief. When she was born, the argument from design was securely in place on a six-thousand-year-old earth; at about the time that she began to write poetry on a regular basis, Charles Darwin published *On the Origin of Species,* the earth grew suddenly older, and its divine designer seemed ever more obscure and inaccessible. As her poems from the 1860s and 1870s repeatedly demonstrate, she was vexed by the loss of the providential assurance the design argument had provided. When a neighbor in 1882 asked

---

19. Joan Burbick offers a sharply different view of Dickinson's rhetoric of desire in arguing that the poet's "writings can be seen as expressing four logical, not chronological, visions of desire that imply a specific theory of use or economy." These range from the "joyful consumption of pleasure without regulation" to a deadly, self-mutilating abstinence. Burbick's structural reading of Dickinson's poetry pits her lonely search for "expressions of delight" against the oppressive network of forces "emerging from the Protestant vision of industrial capitalism." With Dickinson their largely helpless victim, these relentless "specters of regulation stalk the poetry." "Dickinson and the Economics of Desire," *American Literature* 58 (1986): 361, 363-64.

Such an interpretation does not account for the seriousness with which Dickinson took questions about the existence of God, the nature of belief, and the possibility of immortality. We may take that seriousness to be a mask for primary economic and sexual realities, but Dickinson would not have done so. See my *Emily Dickinson and the Art of Belief,* 2nd ed. (Grand Rapids: Eerdmans, 2004), pp. 11-18.

"if we didn't think it very shocking" that a Massachusetts political figure had "'liken[ed] himself to his Redeemer,'" the poet replied that she "thought Darwin had thrown 'the Redeemer' away" (*Letters* 3:728).

The shaking of her confidence in the authority of the Bible also contributed to Dickinson's spiritual anxieties in adulthood. Through her own reading, her correspondence, and her conversations with her brother Austin, she became conversant with higher criticism and began to question the Scriptures' historical claims. According to Robert Grant, doubts of this kind were in the air in the second half of the nineteenth century, with the growth of skepticism being driven more by "philosophical presuppositions" than by any other force. For most "historical interpreters," as well as for the likes of Emily and her brother, "the rationalist attitude toward miracles was taken for granted." In addition, Hegel's "distinction between external ideas and temporary forms was employed," and over the course of the nineteenth "century the differences between the biblical writings and any other writings came to be ignored."[20] Having assimilated these assumptions, Dickinson came to believe the Bible provided a weak foundation for the enterprise of faith. In a poem written near the end of her life, she concluded: "The Bible is an antique Volume — Written by faded Men / At the suggestion of Holy Spectres —" (#1577).

To give a name to the dramatic influence that evolutionary thought and biblical criticism, among other forces, were having upon the nature and experience of belief, Thomas Huxley coined the word *agnosticism* in 1869. This term was meant to denote what James Turner refers to as the "permanent suspension of belief in God" that was emerging as a cultural possibility in the late nineteenth century. According to Turner, "this settled inability to accept the reality of God, rather than positive atheism,

---

20. Robert M. Grant, *A Short History of the Interpretation of the Bible*, rev. ed. (New York: Macmillan, 1963), p. 154. In 1880, Emily reported to a friend, "Austin had told me confidentially 'there was no such person as Elijah.'" *Letters*, 3:667. The following year she wrote to her cousins about the suffering of the mortally wounded President Garfield: "When we think of his lone effort to live, and its bleak reward, the mind turns to the myth 'for His mercy endureth forever,' with confiding revulsion." *Letters*, 3:711. There might be "romance" in believing in the historicity of the biblical narratives, but it is obvious "in soberer moments / No Moses there can be" (#521).

became the distinctively modern unbelief." Up through the medieval period, "unbelief in God required so extreme an estrangement from 'obvious reality' as to be, if not strictly impossible, practically so." Nevertheless, "by the late nineteenth century unbelief had become a fully available option." And in the two decades when Dickinson wrote most of her poetry, the 1860s and 1870s, "disbelief in God [became], for the first time, plausible enough to grow beyond a rare eccentricity and to stake out a sizable permanent niche in American culture."[21]

## The Perfected Life, the Amputated Hand

Not surprisingly, as a champion of "nimble believing" Dickinson was of a divided mind about the historical emergence of unbelief, which she represented in her poems with images of everything from processes of stately progress to incidents of brutal transformation. One poem from 1863, for example, draws upon classic romantic images of self-development and the secularization of the spirit to depict the perfection of the self as a desirable consequence of the decline of belief. "The Props assist the House/Until the House is built," this poem begins. Eventually those props drop away, leaving a House, which being "adequate, erect" can "support itself." Yet that house also ceases to "recollect/The Augur and

21. Turner, *Without God*, pp. 4, 171. Turner sees historical contingency as a key to modern unbelief. Matters could have run a very different course: "The crucial ingredient, then, in the mix that produced an enduring unbelief was the choices of believers. More precisely, unbelief resulted from the decisions that influential church leaders — lay writers, theologians, ministers — made about how to confront the modern pressures upon religious belief" (p. 266).

For a dramatically different interpretation of the rise of unbelief, see Marcel Gauchet's account of this history. For Gauchet, the ancient decision to stress the utter transcendence of God in Judaism (and then Christianity) made the modern "disenchantment of the world" inevitable. Gauchet argues, "the seeds of this development are to be found in the unusual dynamic potentialities of the spirit of Christianity. They provide a coherent focal point that allows us to grasp the fundamental interdependence of such seemingly unrelated phenomena as the rise of technology and the development of democracy. Christianity proves to have been *a religion for departing from religion*." *The Disenchantment of the World: A Political History of Religion*, trans. Oscar Burge (Princeton: Princeton University Press, 1997), pp. 3-4.

the Carpenter." Such, then, is the "retrospect" of a "perfected Life": "A Past of Plank and Nail / And slowness — then the scaffolds drop / Affirming it a Soul —" (#729).

Religious images reverberate in this poem whose theme is the forgetfulness of the sacred. An "augur" is a pagan soothsayer or diviner, but there is also here a play on "auger," one of the primary tools of a carpenter, and the craftsman Dickinson has in mind lived and died in first-century Palestine. The poem presents us with a diviner of sacred signs, a sacrificial savior, plus the tools he used all bundled together, stored away, and forgotten, and it also offers a curious "retrospect" of the "perfected Life." It is a retrospect without a recollection, and although it looks to the past it also seeks to forget all that has gone before it. Like the culture in which it is embedded, this "Life" may at one time have required "A Past of Plank and Nail," but now it stands alone as a self-sufficient "Soul."

When she found herself in this phase of the cycle of nimble believing, Dickinson seems to have read the development of modernity along the lines drawn by one of her great artistic "preceptors," George Eliot. The English novelist, who explored nineteenth-century Protestant thought in her work on Feuerbach, D. F. Strauss, and others, presented the American poet with a finely delineated model for transforming Christianity into a secular *Bildungsroman*. The need for such a secularized reinterpretation of the Christian religion was made clear in a work that Eliot herself translated, Feuerbach's *The Essence of Christianity*. Here the German philosopher defines religion as "the disuniting of man with himself; he sets God before him as the antithesis of himself." As a result of this disunity, "in religion man contemplates his own latent nature," and "God as God . . . is only an object of thought."[22]

With God weakening as a force and vanishing as a presence, Eliot labored to salvage what she could of Christian ethical ideals from the ruins of Christian thought. "She sought," H. Richard Niebuhr notes, "to retain the ethos of Christianity without its faith, its humanism without its theism, its hope for man without its hope for the sovereignty of God."[23]

---

22. Ludwig Feuerbach, *The Essence of Christianity*, trans. George Eliot (1854; repr. New York: Harper, 1957), pp. 33, 35.

23. H. Richard Niebuhr, foreword to Feuerbach, *Essence of Christianity*, p. ix.

Dickinson commended Eliot for having performed heroic work in the absence of "the gift of belief which her greatness denied her" (*Letters* 3:700). When the novelist died, the poet memorialized her valiant efforts to bear the burdens of secularity:

> Her Losses made our Gains ashamed.
> She bore Life's empty Pack
> As gallantly as if the East
> Were swinging at her Back —
> Life's empty Pack is heaviest,
> As every Porter knows —
> In vain to punish Honey —
> It only sweeter grows — (#1602b)

This heroic secularity, however, is only one part of the story of unbelief, because although the subject of "The Props Assist the House" cares not to recollect the past, the speaker of the following poem cannot forget it. In this poem, the loss of belief entails a gruesome maiming and prompts a general diminishment, a disenchantment of the world. With a bloody image similar to the one employed by Nietzsche in the famous "death of God" passage in *The Gay Science,* Dickinson depicts a mangled deity and a lonely humanity. "Those — dying then,/Knew where they went —" begins the poem, which was written, as was the "nimble believing" letter, in 1882:

> They went to God's Right Hand —
> That Hand is amputated now
> And God cannot be found —
>
> The abdication of Belief —
> Makes the Behavior small —
> Better an ignis fatuus
> Than no illume at all — (#1581)

Dickinson refuses here to place the blame for the vanishing of belief. She renders the amputation of God's hand in the passive voice, and with the word "abdication" leaves it unclear whether this is an act of divine self-mutilation or parricidal human aggression. What is clear, however, is that the abdication of belief has left a palpable void.

Still, for every Dickinson poem that sees modern belief as a saga of decline, another depicts it as a chronicle of gain. Where some of her contemporaries, such as Melville, increasingly discovered the new uncertainties about belief to be wearying, Dickinson frequently found them to be exhilarating. Having recognized that belief in God had become optional in her lifetime, in numerous poems she employed that optionality as a tool of self-definition and self-defense. In doing so, she drew upon a long-established Puritan view of the church and of the role volition played in forming it. Edmund Morgan notes that the original settlers of the Massachusetts Bay Colony had developed a radical and novel approach to church membership, as they adapted the Reformation's "powerful impulse toward free consent as the basis of both state and church." The Reformers had largely "stopped short of a full acceptance of this principle," but the Puritans of early New England pursued it to its logical end. Where Catholicism, Eastern Orthodoxy, and most Protestant denominations continued to count on biology, geography, and genealogy to determine church membership, the New England Calvinists made self-conscious assent a prerequisite. By their standards, the church had to "contain only men [and women] who freely professed to believe, and tried to live according to, God's word. . . . A church could not be formed by governmental compulsion or by constraint of the wicked, but only by free consent of the good."[24]

This Puritan practice was to have an influence far beyond the bound-

24. Edmund Morgan, *Visible Saints: The History of a Puritan Idea* (1963; repr. Ithaca: Cornell University Press, 1965), pp. 29, 25. Nathan Hatch writes of the "inversion of authority" that took place in the religion of the early republic, as the advocates of voluntarism realized the radical potential of key Puritan ideas about free consent. Hatch explains that "the republican vision of the 1790s, as portrayed by Joyce Appleby, defended [a] classless view of society, hostility to rank and privilege, rejection of the wisdom of the ages, and buoyant confidence in the 'newly discovered capacity of human beings to develop constructively under the conditions of freedom.'" *The Democratization of American Christianity* (New Haven: Yale University Press, 1989), p. 46.

Mark Noll provides a useful and succinct overview of the growth of voluntarist notions in the theology of the early republic. See *America's God: From Jonathan Edwards to Abraham Lincoln* (New York: Oxford University Press, 2002), pp. 227-38.

aries of the seventeenth-century village church. In the mid-twentieth century, W. H. Auden noted that the presupposition for which America "has come, symbolically, to stand, is that liberty is prior to virtue." The distinction between liberty and license — so vital and necessary for Dickinson's New England forebears — was becoming difficult to sustain by the second half of the nineteenth century, because "freedom of choice" has become in modern America "the human prerequisite without which virtue and vice have no meaning. Virtue is, of course, preferable to vice, but to choose vice is preferable to having virtue chosen for one."[25] Or as David Riesman argued at the same time as Auden, autonomous freedom had become for many in American culture the primary or exclusive source of meaning. This was particularly the case for those whom Riesman called his "autonomous contemporaries." They stood in contrast to the "adjusted person" who is "driven toward his goals by a gyroscope over whose speed and direction" he has little control. On the other hand, the "autonomous contemporary" — Dickinson is a perfect fit for the type here — is "capable of choosing his goals, and modulating his pace. The goals and the drive toward them, [are] rational, nonauthoritarian and noncompulsive for the autonomous; for the adjusted, they [are] merely given."[26]

A number of Dickinson's poems about belief vigorously develop an argument along the lines of Morgan's historical analysis and Auden and Riesman's cultural assessments. This is the case with her famous account of her "second baptism":

---

25. W. H. Auden, *The Dyer's Hand* (1962; repr. New York: Vintage, 1989), p. 318.

26. David Riesman, with Nathan Glazer and Reuel Denny, *The Lonely Crowd: A Study of the Changing American Character*, abr. and rev. ed. (1961; repr. New Haven: Yale University Press, 2001), p. 250. The observations by Auden and Riesman are paralleled in Robert Langbaum's definition of modern commitment: "For it is not this or that political, philosophical, religious or even aesthetic commitment that marks the romanticist. It is the subjective ground of his commitment, the fact that he never forgets his commitment has been chosen. The commitment is as a result absorbed into a certain atmosphere of mind and sensibility, the essential meaning of which is that the commitment, no matter how absolutist and dogmatic, remains subordinate to the chooser." *The Poetry of Experience: The Dramatic Monologue in Modern Literary Tradition* (1957; repr. Chicago: University of Chicago Press, 1985), p. 21.

> I'm ceded — I've stopped being Their's —
> The name They dropped opon my face
> With water, in the country church
> Is finished using, now[.]

By 1862, when she wrote this poem, Dickinson like all Americans had become keenly aware of the risk of "ceding" and "seceding," of renouncing an established identity and confederating a new one. "They" who had "dropped" the water on her may now stow her name away, along with her "Dolls," her "Childhood," and the "string of spools," all of which she has undeniably outgrown. Those childish things had been chosen for her, and she is now ready to make her own choices:

> Baptized, before, without the choice,
> But this time, consciously, Of Grace —
> Unto supremest name —

Having willfully established her own identity, the speaker of the poem is prepared to stand

>     — Adequate — Erect,
> With Will to choose,
> Or to reject,
> And I choose, just a Crown — (#353)

Dickinson's strategy in this and a number of other poems provides an example of a linguistic process that Kenneth Burke has called a "borrowing back" of religious language. "Whether or not there is a realm of the 'supernatural,' there are *words* for it," he argues. Of necessity, those words are borrowed from the experiences "out of which our familiarity with language arises." There is a paradox to "this state of linguistic affairs," writes Burke, for "once a terminology has been developed for special theological purposes the order can be reversed." When we need to do so, we can reappropriate the language of the religious tradition, "again secularizing to varying degrees the originally secular terms that had been given 'supernatural' connotations." In this manner, what had become a "*theological* term" can "in effect be *aestheti-*

*cized."*[27] This reappropriation is the act at the heart of what Carlyle called "natural supernaturalism" and what M. H. Abrams has described as Romanticism's effort "to save traditional concepts, schemes, and values which had been based on the relation of the Creator to his creature and creation, but to reformulate them within the prevailing two-term system of subject and object, . . . the human mind or consciousness and its transactions with nature."[28]

In a number of her poems about belief, Dickinson effectively "borrows back" the language of the Calvinist tradition and places it in the service of self-definition. Although the conventional judgment holds that Dickinson spurned her religious heritage, it might be more accurate to say that she translated it.[29] That is to say she slipped from the theological grip of Calvinism by appropriating its language and concepts on her own terms and by putting them to her own uses. If she could not believe in Calvin's God, she might at least become like him:

> The Soul selects her own Society —
> Then — shuts the Door —
> To her divine Majority —
> Present no more —
>
> Unmoved — she notes the Chariots — pausing —
> At her low Gate —

---

27. Kenneth Burke, *The Rhetoric of Religion: Studies in Logology* (1961; repr. Berkeley: University of California Press, 1970), pp. 7-8.

28. M. H. Abrams, *Natural Supernaturalism: Tradition and Revolution in Romantic Literature* (New York: Norton, 1971), p. 13.

29. In Emily Dickinson's childhood, the Connecticut River valley was ruled theologically by a modified brand of Calvinism that sought "to blend the activist, voluntaristic, ambitious, fluid attitudes of nineteenth-century America with the religious doctrines of the Reformation. Broadly stated, this meant formulating into a religious ideology the culture associated with Whiggery." Daniel Walker Howe, *The Political Culture of the American Whigs* (Chicago: University of Chicago Press, 1979), pp. 159-60. In her struggle against Whig social ideals, Dickinson "borrowed back" key elements of Calvinist belief; against the sober order of the Whigs, she brought to bear the resources of Calvinist thinking on the subjects of divine sovereignty, the contingency of election/selection, and the stunning arbitrariness of ordinary experience.

Unmoved — an Emperor be kneeling
Opon her Mat —

I've known her — from an ample nation —
Choose One —
Then — close the Valves of her attention —
Like Stone — (#409)

The speaker's actions here have their analogue in the Calvinist doctrine of election, which tells of a God who chooses "[His] own Society," closes the "Valves of [his] attention," and then sits silently "Unmoved" by the plight of the unchosen.

This last poem presents an image of the soul as a satisfied and self-contained entity. Now that she has made her selection and has closed "the Valves of her attention —/Like Stone —" the soul retreats behind her gates, secure and delighted. Yet such contentment proves to be short-lived for many figures in Dickinson's poems, as they find themselves frightened within enclosed spaces or disoriented by their own inwardness. Often choosing to play the gothic victim instead of the sentimental heroine in her dramas of internal division, Dickinson "could exploit her chosen isolation to delve into psychological depths. She could confront her fears and cry out in terror."[30] For example, consider a poem that reads like a haunting sequel to "The Soul selects her own Society." (Dickinson in fact bound them together within the same fascicle.) Here we learn what awaits the self-selecting soul behind her closed doors:

One need not be a Chamber — to be Haunted —
One need not be a House —
The Brain has Corridors — surpassing
Material Place —

Where some Dickinson poems laud the perfection of the soul and celebrate the triumphs of the aesthetic consciousness, this poem puts consciousness to a severe test by pitting it against a foe that lurks in the background and proves to be more ancient than itself:

30. Jane Donahue Eberwein, *Dickinson: Strategies of Limitation* (Amherst: University of Massachusetts Press, 1985), p. 120.

> Ourself behind ourself, concealed —
> Should startle most —
> Assassin hid in our Apartment
> Be Horror's least —
>
> The Body — borrows a Revolver —
> He bolts the Door —
> O'erlooking a superior spectre —
> Or More — (#407)

## Will the Secret Compensate?

"Ourself behind ourself, concealed —/Should startle most" — in this and other instances, Dickinson's uncanniness may have less to do with compelling descriptions of present states or past developments than with the prospects this poem so presciently anticipates. I have in mind specifically the late nineteenth-century and early twentieth-century revolution in cultural history that Paul Ricoeur has outlined in *Freud and Philosophy,* the work in which he first developed his theory of the hermeneutics of suspicion and the conflict of interpretations. In both her troubled explorations of the divided self's dependence on desire and her restless exploration of the new polarities of belief and unbelief, Dickinson traced the outlines of theoretical arguments that Ricoeur and others would still be elaborating more than a century after she died.

In referring to the "hermeneutics of suspicion," Ricoeur was giving a name to revolutionary changes in thought and consciousness that had unfolded largely in Emily Dickinson's lifetime. The "masters" of suspicion were Karl Marx, Friedrich Nietzsche, and Sigmund Freud, and the radical decision that each made was "to look upon the whole of consciousness primarily as 'false' consciousness." Writing in the present tense of figures who worked a half to a full century before him, Ricoeur writes, "they thereby take up again, each in a different manner, the problem of Cartesian doubt, to carry it to the very heart of the Cartesian stronghold." The Cartesian tradition assumes that things are doubtful but rests in the assurance that consciousness can be trusted, because "in consciousness, meaning and consciousness of meaning coincide." But with Marx, Nietzsche, and Freud, "this too has become doubtful. After the doubt about things, we have started to doubt consciousness."[31]

Ricoeur says the "masters of suspicion" were "great 'destroyers.'" They dismantled consciousness in an effort to "clear the horizon for a more authentic word, for a new reign of Truth" that was to be made possible through "the invention of an art of *interpreting.*"[32] With the coming of Freud, Marx, and Nietzsche, he claims, "understanding is hermeneutics: henceforward, to seek meaning is no longer to spell out the consciousness of meaning, but to *decipher its expressions.*" The discovery of "Ourself behind ourself" — the uncovering of the unconscious signifying force that prompts and guides the conscious self — makes matters such that "a new relation must be instituted between the patent and the latent; this new relation would correspond to the one that consciousness had instituted between appearances and the reality of things." For the hermeneutics of suspicion, "the fundamental category of consciousness is the relation hidden-shown or . . . simulated-manifested."[33]

In "Existence and Hermeneutics," the opening essay of *The Conflict*

31. Paul Ricoeur, *Freud and Philosophy: An Essay on Interpretation,* trans. Denis Savage (New Haven: Yale University Press, 1970), p. 33.

32. The hermeneutics of suspicion has roots in Jewish and Christian monotheism: "Radical monotheism dethrones all absolutes short of the principle of being itself. At the same time it reverences every relative existent. Its two great mottoes are: 'I am the Lord thy God; thou shalt have no other gods before me,' and 'Whatever is, is good.'" H. Richard Niebuhr, *Radical Monotheism and Western Culture, with Supplementary Essays* (New York: Harper, 1960), p. 37. George Steiner sees the hermeneutics of suspicion as part of an extensive "anguished rebellion against the word": "As no others, therefore, Jews have perceived themselves and have been seen by others as being 'the people of the Book.' . . . To rebel against the holiness of the revealed and originating word (Derrida's 'there are no beginnings'), to put in question the Adamic equations between name and substance, to reject the unambiguous finalities of bequeathed meaning in the law, in prophetic mandates, to query the coherence and intentionality of narrative — was to seek emancipation at the most uncompromising level. . . . From the doubts of Lord Chandos, the desolate mockeries of Kraus or Kafka's parables on silence all the way to derridean deconstruction, modern Judaism has mutinied against its patriarchal-paternalistic legacy of textual prepotence." *Grammars of Creation: Originating in the Gifford Lectures for 1990* (New Haven: Yale University Press, 2001), pp. 281-82.

33. Ricoeur, *Freud,* pp. 33-34.

*of Interpretations,* Ricoeur speaks of the hermeneutics of suspicion by employing terms strikingly similar to those that Dickinson used to explore self-understanding and the dynamics of belief. "Existence," he argues, "is desire and effort. We term it effort in order to stress its positive energy and dynamism; we term it desire in order to designate its lack and poverty." Only through "deciphering the tricks of desire" can "the desire at the root of meaning and reflection [be] discovered." Yet no matter how vigilant we are, we cannot in the end get more "than hints" of this desire "behind the enigmas of consciousness. . . . It is behind itself that the *cogito* discovers, through the work of interpretation, something like an *archaeology of the subject.*"[34]

Ricoeur concludes "Existence and Hermeneutics" with a reflection on the deeper significance of the rise of this "archaeological subject." Is a hermeneutic of suspicion necessarily reductive and restrictive? Does it cancel out all other interpretive possibilities for texts or human experi-

---

34. Paul Ricoeur, *The Conflict of Interpretations: Essays in Hermeneutics,* ed. Don Ihde (Evanston: Northwestern University Press, 1974), p. 21. While Dickinson searched for signs of the divine in nature or experience, many of her poems also offered tropes depicting the inner life as a chaotic realm of unknowing. Consider, for example, the final lines of "I felt a Funeral, in my Brain," in which the images suggest obscurely the loss of knowledge and understanding:

> Then Space — began to toll,
>
> As all the Heavens were a Bell,
> And Being, but an Ear,
> And I, and Silence, some strange Race
> Wrecked, solitary, here —
>
> And then a Plank in Reason, broke,
> And I dropped down, and down —
> And hit a World, at every plunge,
> And Finished knowing — then — (#340)

The indecipherable world of this poem calls to mind Ricoeur's analysis of "the archaeology of the subject." Writing of that phenomenon, John Thompson argues that it "concedes the dispossession of immediate consciousness to the advantage of another agency of meaning, namely the emergence of desire. Yet desire is accessible only through the disguises in which it manifests itself; that is, it is only by interpreting the signs of desire that one can capture its emergence, and thus enable reflection to regain the archaic heritage which it has lost." *Critical Hermeneutics: A Study in the Thought of Paul Ricoeur and Jürgen Habermas* (Cambridge: Cambridge University Press, 1981), p. 47.

ence? Or, if it does not cancel them out, does it nevertheless relativize all interpretive frameworks? To each of these questions, Ricoeur would reply, "Not necessarily." For him, "rival hermeneutics are not mere 'language games,'" because "for a linguistic philosophy, all interpretations are equally valid within the limits of the theory which founds the given rules of reading." They remain language games "until it is shown that each interpretation is grounded in a particular existential function." To describe those functions we need "a hermeneutics" that can demonstrate that the "different modalities of existence belong to a single problematic." In Ricoeur's understanding of modernity, existence "always remains an interpreted existence. It is in the work of interpretation that this philosophy discovers the multiple modalities of the dependence of the self — its dependence on desire glimpsed in an archaeology of the subject, its dependence on the spirit glimpsed in its teleology, its dependence on the sacred glimpsed in its eschatology."[35]

To reconcile a religious understanding of the human person with material explanation, Ricoeur rejects what Mark Wallace calls "foundationalist, historicist, and physicalist" readings of human nature "in favor of a narrative hermeneutic of the human subject."[36] To use Wallace's terms, we might say that as the nineteenth century opened, foundationalist accounts of nature, experience, and knowledge held sway in the cultures of northwest Europe and North America. By the century's close, however, those accounts had been displaced by strong "historicist" and "physicalist" readings of nature, culture, and the self. Because nineteenth-century Christian apologetics relied so heavily upon the argument from design, it is not surprising that Darwinian naturalism was able to shake the foundations of belief as vigorously as it did.

The naturalistic premises of evolutionary theory seemed plausible enough to Dickinson, at least to a certain point. She thought the account offered by science should be accepted as an accurate detailing of the operations of nature. But when it claimed to be something more than that, Dickinson could be as skeptical of science as she was of sentimental pi-

---

35. Ricoeur, *Conflict*, pp. 23, 24.

36. Mark I. Wallace, introduction to Paul Ricoeur, *Figuring the Sacred: Religion, Narrative, and Imagination*, ed. Mark I. Wallace, trans. David Pellauer (Minneapolis: Fortress, 1995), p. 13.

ety. She would have understood, for example, Charles Taylor's cautionary words about the impact of material explanation upon moral reasoning and textual interpretation. "There is a great deal of motivated
suppression of moral ontology among our contemporaries," Taylor
writes, and this is due in part to the fact that "the pluralist nature of modern society makes it easier to live that way." The deeper reason for this
suppression, however, has to do with "the great weight of modern epistemology and behind this, [the weight] of the spiritual outlook associated with this epistemology."[37] There is at work in modern intellectual
life a powerful reductive force that seeks to expose the material and social
origins of all religious beliefs and experiences. Taylor challenges that
reductionism, and one can say confidently that Dickinson would have
been in sympathy with his efforts.

Indeed, what Ricoeur and Taylor elaborate philosophically, Dickinson largely articulated poetically more than a century ago through her
creative exploration of the new realities of belief. Although she never
heard of Marx and Nietzsche in her own day and knew nothing of the
Freud who was to come, Dickinson had a subtle understanding of the intellectual and cultural forces that shaped the masters of suspicion, and to
a considerable extent she shared their ambivalence about consciousness
and its representations. Yet she also would have resonated deeply with
the hope that Charles Taylor has, which is rooted in Christianity's "central promise of a divine affirmation of the human, more total than humans can ever attain unaided."[38]

With both her theory and her practice of "nimble believing,"
Dickinson was in effect seeking what Ricoeur refers to as a way of incor-
porating the experience of suspicion within that of faith. The polarity of
suspicion and belief, he claims, "is the truest expression of our 'modernity.'" We are torn between the desire to dismantle and the longing to re-
build, between the compulsion to doubt and the hunger to believe. As a
result of this division at the heart of our experience, language today faces
a "double solicitation and urgency: on the one hand, purify discourse, . . .

37. Charles Taylor, *Sources of the Self: The Making of the Modern Identity* (Cambridge: Harvard University Press, 1989), p. 10.

38. Taylor, *Sources*, p. 521.

liquidate the idols, go from drunkenness to sobriety, realize our state of poverty once and for all; on the other hand, use the most 'nihilistic,' destructive, iconoclastic movement so as to *let speak* what once, what each time, was *said,* when meaning appeared anew." According to Ricoeur, a double motivation animates genuine human understanding: "willingness to suspect, willingness to listen; vow of rigor, vow of obedience."[39]

Dickinson was ever so willing to suspect, and her work gives evidence of a stringent vow of rigor. Of her eagerness to listen there also can be no doubt, but she could not help but wonder whether there was anything to *hear.* She listened closely to nature and waited carefully to hear from God, but more often than not whatever sounds she detected seemed neither intended for human ears nor indicative of a higher harmony. In the words of one of her poems on the subject, it is frequently the way with human life that "The Morning after Wo" surpasses all others "For utter Jubilee." The sounds cascade upon the suffering person in such an indifferent fashion that it seems as if "Nature did not Care —." The suffering person aches to hear a melody instead of this cacophony:

> The Birds declaim their Tunes —
> Pronouncing every word
> Like Hammers — Did they know they fell
> Like Litanies of Lead —
>
> On here and there — a creature —
> They'd modify the Glee
> To fit some Crucifixal Clef —
> Some key of Calvary — (#398)

Skeptical of the idea of the word of God as something revealed in scripture or sacrament, loving Jesus as a fellow human sufferer but uncertain of his status in the Godhead, and bereft of her childhood faith in nature's power to speak an unambiguous spiritual language, Dickinson turned repeatedly to images of mystery and secrecy to speak of belief. Foremost in her treatment of that mystery was her fascination with death as the eschatological circumference of belief and truth. For her,

---

39. Ricoeur, *Freud,* p. 27.

death offered the greatest possibility for the revelation of what Ricoeur calls that "single problematic" that might forge a unifying truth from those "multiple modalities" that constitute for modern understanding the complexity of the self.

The letters and poems Dickinson wrote in the final decade of her life are filled with references to such mysteries and to the urgency of abiding within them to solve the riddle of belief. "After a while, dear," she wrote to a close friend whose husband had just died, "you will remember that there is a heaven — but you can't now. Jesus will excuse it. He will remember his shorn lamb" (*Letters* 3:713). Here as elsewhere in her late writings, Dickinson's confidence seemed poised between a substantial faith in God and a desperate recognition of desire. When another friend wrote of her "disillusion" in 1883, she called this "one of the few subjects on which I am an infidel. Life is so strong a vision, not one of it shall fail." The hope of the future, instead of the promise of the past, kept her spirits from flagging: "Not what the stars have done, but what they are to do, is what detains the sky" (*Letters* 3:794). In a poem written two years before her death, the poet reiterated her hope that the need to believe could prove the existence of the object of belief:

> Though the great Waters sleep,
> That they are still the Deep,
> We cannot doubt.
> No vacillating God
> Ignited this Abode
> To put it out. (#1641)

The death of Emily's nephew Gilbert in late 1883 proved more trying than any other in the poet's final years. When she had recovered sufficiently from her own shock and grief, she sent her sister-in-law Susan a remarkable letter full of heartbreak and hope. "Gilbert rejoiced in Secrets —" she told Susan, but "now my ascended Playmate must instruct *me*. Show us, prattling Preceptor, but the way to thee!" His death makes cruel sense, in a way, because for what reason "would he wait, wronged only of Night, which he left for us —." She closes her letter to Susan with a gentle plea to Gilbert:

Pass to thy Rendezvous of Light,
Pangless except for us —
Who slowly ford the Mystery
Which thou hast leaped across! (*Letters* 3:799)

These letters and poems show Dickinson's lyrics constituting a powerful series of discrete episodes set within a vast dramatic narrative, and within this story she saw her own part being played out.[40] The key to that narrative would be contained in its final chapter, which involved "fording the Mystery" that no one could understand fully this side of death. Weeks after her mother died in 1882, Dickinson wrote to her cousins, "We don't know where she is, though so many tell us. I believe," she went on, "we shall in some manner be cherished by our Maker — that the One who gave us this remarkable earth has the power still farther to surprise that which He has caused. Beyond that all is silence" (*Letters* 3:750). Or as she wondered in a poem written less than two years before her own death:

The going from a world we know
To one a wonder still
Is like the child's adversity
Whose vista is a hill,
Behind the hill is sorcery
And everything unknown,
But will the secret compensate
For climbing it alone? (#1662)

---

40. Margaret Dickie argues strongly that Dickinson's lyrics cannot be placed within a "master narrative," because her "lyric speakers have no narrative continuity, no social viability, no steadfast identity. In their squandering, melodrama, and excesses, they express an individuality that resists final representation and the control that signifies." Yet in making *evasion* rather than *indecision* a central category of Dickinson's poetry, Dickie must deny the palpable interest that Dickinson had in the subjects about which she wrote. Where Dickie discovers the essential quality of Dickinson's poetry in "its interest in the unaccountable surplus of individuality, in repetition as constituent of character, and in figurative excess as essential to self-presentation," one suspects Dickinson herself would have located that quality in things substantial rather than matters procedural. "Dickinson's Discontinuous Lyric Self," *American Literature* 60 (1988): 553.

According to Dickinson, this was the crucial question to be asked about belief and its objects. She believed that in death something, whatever it might be, would be disclosed to make sense of life and the mysteries of nimble believing. The only question was whether the truth to be revealed in death would compensate for the suffering that had been endured in life.

For some of Dickinson's otherwise astute interpreters, the answer to that question — in the form of a negative — is already in. As a case in point, Alfred Habegger concludes his story of the poet's life in a most un-Dickinsonian manner. With her death, he writes, "something with an unheard-of-brilliance and purity had come to an end, and something public, derivative, and dependent on a world of stumbling readers had begun." Habegger says that we can suppose that Dickinson would have found her fame "a contemptible substitute for the limitlessness and perfection she had spent life thinking about. But it doesn't look as if we are going to find out."[41]

Such an assertion seems to overlook several key facts about Dickinson's attitude toward fame. She banked on the possibility of posthumous fame and longed for the "stumbling readers" who would one day receive her work gladly. "Some — Work for Immortality —/The Chiefer part, for Time —" she wrote in 1863. It was clear for which one Dickinson wrote, for she was one of those "Beggars" who "Here and There" are "gifted to discern/Beyond the Broker's insight —/One's — Money — One's — the Mine —" (# 536). Or as she wrote to her sister-in-law in 1861, "Could I make you and Austin — proud — sometime — a great way off — 'twould give me taller feet —" (*Letters* 2:380). She craved the posthumous recognition of her genius as much as she coveted her earthly anonymity. Leo Braudy gets the matter exactly right: "We might call her the show-off of eternity for the innumerable ways she devised to humble herself in the world even as she asserted herself to posterity and to heaven."[42]

If Habegger believes that "it doesn't look as if we are going to find

---

41. Habegger, *My Wars*, p. 629.

42. Leo Braudy, *The Frenzy of Renown: Fame and Its History* (New York: Oxford University Press, 1986), p. 472.

out" the secret of Dickinson's posthumous response to her own posthumous fame, she hoped — indeed *believed* — to the end that she would learn the secret. Though it was desperate at times, Dickinson's hope remained a driving force in her life and prepared her for her death. That is another way of saying that in keeping her believing nimble, Dickinson found a way to live vitally with the conflict of interpretations and the uncertainties of modern belief. "Renunciation — is a piercing Virtue —" she once wrote, "The letting go/A presence — for an Expectation" (#782). Dickinson knew that the "letting go" of presence was a gamble, but she took the risk in hope. And in good measure, it was because she took that risk that she became one of America's most searing poets of suspicion as well as one of our most serious poets of belief.

# Private Interpretations: The Defense of Slavery, Nineteenth-Century Hermeneutics, and the Poetry of Frances E. W. Harper

*Katherine Clay Bassard*

In 1901, at the age of seventy-five, noted African American writer, speaker, and abolitionist Frances Ellen Watkins Harper published a slim volume of verse called *Idylls of the Bible*. It was self-published, judging from the address on the title page — "Philadelphia: 1006 Bainbridge Street," Harper's private residence since 1871. The small volume begins with a revision of an early poem, *Moses: A Story of the Nile*. Following a brief essay and two sentimental poems, however, the majority of the text is consumed with the passion, death, and resurrection of Jesus Christ: "Christ's Entry Into Jerusalem," "The Resurrection of Jesus," "Simon's Countrymen," and "Simon's Feast."[1]

That the baseline narrative of the life, death, and resurrection of Jesus — including his encounters with Mary and Simon, a woman and an African, during the course of events leading to his crucifixion — should loom so large in Frances E. W. Harper's poetic vision late in her life attests to the centrality of biblical narrative for any assessment of her writing, particularly her poetry. Since Frances Smith Foster's restoration of Harper to the African American and women's literary canon in 1990 with the publica-

---

1. The first of the two Simon poems features the African Simon of Cyrene who carried the cross after Jesus stumbled on the way to Gogotha, a scene related in all three of the Synoptic Gospels (Matthew 27:32; Mark 15:21; Luke 23:26). The second is set at the home of Simon the leper, another outcast figure in the Gospels (Matthew 26:6-13; Mark 14:3; John 11:1-2; 12:3), but features the prostitute Mary, who scandalously anoints Jesus' feet and wipes them with her hair.

tion of the anthology *A Brighter Coming Day,* the majority of criticism on Harper has been on her only novel, *Iola Leroy.* Harper's poetry has been treated most extensively by Foster, Melba Joyce Boyd, Maryemma Graham, and Carla Peterson, but only Boyd devotes an entire book to her poetic vision. Of her poetry, the long epic *Moses: A Story of the Nile* has received the most extensive commentary.[2] While the relative neglect of Harper's biblical poetry can be attributed to what Frances Smith Foster calls the triad of "gender, genre and vulgar secularism," the oversight is symptomatic of a more general displacement of the discussion of religious material into the social, political, and aesthetic domains. This chapter will focus on Harper's biblical poems in order to examine larger issues of religious subjectivity, sacred texts, and liberationist strategies.

We must begin, of course, with the plethora of challenges to biblical authority that characterized the nineteenth century. In *New England Literary Culture,* Lawrence Buell writes of the movement from a "religiocentric" American thought before 1865 to "the disappearance of belief" in the second half of the nineteenth century:

> The institutionalization of American belles lettres was accompanied and facilitated by a shift in biblical studies, led by New England scholars, from something like universal agreement among professing Christians that the canonical Scriptures were inspired, historically accurate writings to something like the present state of controversy, in which the traditional view had to contend against varying shades of liberalization, including the claim that the Bible was no more inspired than any other document.

Mediating what Buell calls the "literary liberation of the Bible," a shift from authoritative biblicism to liberated aestheticism was the rationalism

---

2. See Melba Joyce Boyd, *Discarded Legacy: Politics and Poetics in the Life of Frances E. W. Harper, 1825-1911* (Detroit: Wayne State University Press, 1994); Carla L. Peterson, *"Doers of the Word": African-American Women Speakers and Writers in the North (1830-1880)* (New York: Oxford University Press, 1995); Frances Smith Foster, ed., *A Brighter Coming Day: A Frances Ellen Watkins Harper Reader* (New York: Feminist Press, 1990) and *Written By Herself: Literary Production by African American Women, 1746-1892* (Bloomington: Indiana University Press, 1993); introduction to *Complete Poems of Frances E. W. Harper,* ed. Maryemma Graham (New York: Oxford University Press, 1988), pp. xxxiii-lviii.

that underlay the historical-critical methodology promoted by the German Higher Criticism.[3] A difficulty in Buell's account, however, arises from the underlying assumption that the liberationist reading is necessarily accompanied by and accomplished as a result of the decline of biblical authority. Embedded in a term like "literary liberation of the Bible" is an association of the appeal to scriptural authority with oppression.[4]

Frances Harper's late poetry poses a challenge to the predominant view of declining biblical influence in American literature. This consensus equates biblical authority with structures of oppression or oppressive subjectivities, and links rationalism, appeals to "common sense," to science, and to the arts, with social and psychical liberation. In this view, the only way to be free is to be free *from* the Bible. I am not out to "rescue" the Bible, because I do not believe it to be in need of rescuing; nor am I seeking to "unleash" some hidden meaning from the text, obscured by idiosyncratic misappropriations.[5] Instead, I wish to explore the range of hermeneutic possibilities available in nineteenth-century America for the purpose of locating writers, like Harper, whose use of biblical material does not fit the paradigm of radical revisionist reading strategies but points instead toward what Anthony Thiselton has called an "emancipatory hermeneutics." This hermeneutic does not separate the categories of textuality and sacredness, and it allows for a liberationist Christian subjectivity from within the sacred text.

I want first to set out some terms, and I can think of no better starting place that with the category "scripture," beginning with Paul Gutjahr's cultural history of Bible publishing and distribution from 1777,

---

3. Lawrence Buell, *New England Literary Culture: From Revolution through Renaissance* (New York: Cambridge University Press, 1986), pp. 166-67, 185.

4. The process that accomplished, in its final form, the separation of the Bible from history and historicity as well as from science simultaneously undermined any appeal to the Bible as the ground for constituting meaning and authority. See George Marsden, "Everyone One's Own Interpreter? The Bible, Science, and Authority in Mid-Nineteenth-Century America," in *The Bible in America: Essays in Cultural History*, ed. Nathan Hatch and Mark A. Noll (New York: Oxford University Press, 1982), p. 87.

5. See, for example, John Shelby Spong, *Rescuing the Bible from Fundamentalism: A Bishop Rethinks the Meaning of Scripture* (San Francisco: Harper, 1991), and Stanley Hauerwas, *Unleashing the Scripture: Freeing the Bible from Captivity to America* (Nashville: Abingdon, 1993).

the year of the appearance of the first American edition of an English language New Testament, to 1880, the year before the first widely accepted, one could say "authorized," revision of the Authorized Version (1611), The Revised Standard Version (1881). Gutjahr's use of textually marked boundaries follows from his conceptualization of the connection between the book as material artifact and its subsequent consumption/interpretation by readers. In *An American Bible,* Gutjahr writes that such attention to material textual history forces us to reconsider the Protestant notion of *sola scriptura:*

> This clarion call to foreground the words of Scripture frequently ignores the fact that God's word is never truly alone when it reaches its readers on a printed page. Even if not constrained by doctrine and clergy, Scripture is constrained by its own materiality: how it is set in type, formatted, commented upon in marginalia, illustrated, bound, and distributed. If the story of nineteenth-century publishing teaches us anything, it is that bible packaging, content, and distribution all inseparably work together to give the Book meaning. A book *is* judged by its cover. . . .[6]

Thus, for Gutjahr, the "scriptural nature" of the Protestant Bible is both reflected in and in turn constituted by certain material markers of difference, such as leather binding, size, and elaborate illustrations.

In "America's Bibles: Canon, Commentary, and Community," Stephen J. Stein connects the concept of scripture with definitions and delineations of readerly communities. He notes that "scripture is only scripture insofar as it is recognized and understood as such by a given community. Texts without such an interactive group are mere texts, ancient texts perhaps, or even modern texts, but not scripture."[7] Thus a "scripture" for Stein would survive as such only to the extent that a community which lends its support and consensus survives as well. A text that remains available yet has lost its consenting community may continue to be read but

6. Paul C. Gutjahr, *An American Bible: A History of the Good Book in the United States, 1777-1880* (Stanford: Stanford University Press, 1999), p. 178.

7. Stephen J. Stein, "America's Bibles: Canon, Commentary, and Community," *Church History* 64 (1995): 171.

loses its identity as scripture.[8] In particular, Stein draws attention to three "canons within the canon" that are important for my analysis here:

> Three different scriptures — Jefferson's personal bible, the African American conjurational canon, and *The Woman's Bible* — are each defined by a particular religious, social, or political agenda of an interactive community. The mode of expression in each varies — a private document, oral performances by singers and preachers, and a political manifesto. Yet in each case the essential elements of the scripturalizing process are present — canon, commentary, and community.[9]

However, these "three different scriptures" that Stein writes about betray a monolithic understanding of community-authorized textuality. Using Theophus Smith's term of an African American "conjurational canon," Stein collapses all African American hermeneutics under one framework, as if a "black Bible" exists that derives from a unitary individual consciousness like Jefferson's or Stanton's. From their earliest contact with the Christian Bible, African American readers have exhibited a wide range of approaches to biblical material and to the issue of the Bible's authority, from orthodox Christian readings to radical revisionist appropriations. It is helpful, therefore, to frame our discussion of nineteenth-century African American biblical interpretation(s) by first exploring the two documents known as Jefferson's "Bible" (*The Philosophy of Jesus* [1804] and *The Life and Morals of Jesus of Nazareth* [1819-1820?]) at the beginning of the nineteenth century and Stanton's *Woman's Bible* (1895) at the century's end.[10]

---

8. Stein points to several important American "bibles" published during the nineteenth century which reflect the presence and consensus of clear communities of readers: Joseph Smith's *The Book of Mormon* (1830), the Shaker text *Sacred and Divine Roll and Book* (1843), Mary Baker Eddy's Christian Science text *Science and Health* (1875), as well as two collections of excerpted Bible text of Thomas Jefferson's popularly called *Jefferson's Bible* (1804, 1819-1820), and Elizabeth Cady Stanton's *Woman's Bible* (1895). Following Theophus Smith's work, Stein posits a "Black Bible" that he calls a "canon within a canon." Stein, "America's Bibles," p. 179.

9. Stein, "America's Bibles," p. 182.

10. There are several editions of "Jefferson's Bible." I will primarily refer to the edition by Dickinson W. Adams, ed., *Jefferson's Extracts from the Gospels: "The Philosophy of Jesus" and "The Life and Morals of Jesus of Nazareth"* (Princeton: Princeton University Press, 1983).

Jefferson's extracts from the Gospels did not come to public attention until the mid-nineteenth century — the period when, according to Gutjahr, Bible publishing was at its peak. Jefferson's belief in a purely privatized religion made him reluctant to speak publicly about his own religious views. While Jefferson's views were personal, they were far from purely private, shaped as they were by Enlightenment demands for rationality and utility in religious institutions. Thus, ironically, Jefferson's very private biblical readings are shaped by larger public debates about rationalism and biblical accuracy posed by the German Higher Criticism that began to infiltrate American religion through liberal movements such as Unitarianism.

By all accounts, Jefferson experienced a "religious crisis" around the 1760s, stumbling over the doctrine of the Trinity, which he could not reconcile with the Bible's insistence on monotheism.[11] Out of that crisis, he began to piece together a "commonplace book consisting of extracts from the writings of various ancient and modern dramatists, philosophers, poets" around the 1760s and 1770s, a "literary Bible." Jefferson's highly privatized, even secretive, "commonplace book" stemmed from his demand for reasonableness and utility in religious institutions and texts. In fact, so skeptical was Jefferson of the historicity of the Bible's account of Creation that he was an early speculator of the theory of polygenesis, the "'suggestion' that blacks might have been originally created as a distinct race."[12] Like his Unitarian counterparts, Jefferson held to a "demystified" and "demythologized" form of Christianity.

Unlike Jefferson's "Bible," which was a work precipitated by a youthful spiritual crisis, Elizabeth Stanton's *Woman's Bible* was written soon after her eightieth birthday following a radical shift in her views about organized religion and scriptures. Earlier, Stanton had echoed the "positive, reform-minded biblical interpretation" of other women's rights activists

11. Much of this crisis was precipitated through reading the work of Joseph Priestley, *Institutes of Natural and Revealed Religion* (1772) and *An History of the Corruptions of Christianity* (1792). Jefferson called Priestley's work "the basis of my own faith." Quoted in David Robinson, *The Unitarians and the Universalists* (Westport, Conn.: Greenwood Press, 1985), p. 23.

12. Adams, *Jefferson's Extracts*, p. 11.

like Sarah Grimke and Lucretia Coffin Mott, but her views changed by the 1880s and 1890s:

> Rejecting the Bible as the Word of God, Stanton now defined the Bible as the foundation of women's oppression and the greatest stumbling block to women's complete emancipation. She also articulated a wholesale attack on organized religion. As an alternative, Stanton called for a more "rational" religion, much like such eighteenth-century Deists as Thomas Jefferson and Thomas Paine. Unlike the Deists, however, Stanton's theological revisionism aimed primarily to empower women.[13]

Lisa Strange's connection to the rationalism of Jefferson and Paine[14] points to the fact that there are wider social issues informing Stanton's biblical revisionism than allegiance to women's community or political activism, as Stein's community-based hermeneutics would maintain. Indeed, the invocation of Jefferson and Paine traces an ideological and interpretive legacy that has at its core the de-centering of biblical authority and contestations over new sources of authority for meaning and texts.

In *"Take, Read": Scripture, Textuality, and Cultural Practice,* Wesley A. Kort argues for the retention of the category of "scripture" as textual and cultural practice. For Kort, such a category needs to be "recovered and reconstructed" because of the breakdown in pre-Modern notions of the Bible as Scripture (as opposed to the Bible as literature or history). Thus, scripture "functions as a category in textural and cultural theory to designate the locations of persons, groups, and institutions on the textual field." In other words, scripture is not simply that constitution of texts as such because of materiality of form and distribution, as Gutjahr proposes, or community consensus, as Stein maintains, but "scriptures" exist as primary locations of identities. Scripture is, moreover, "a textual designation that stands somewhere between 'writing,' with its suggestion of

13. Lisa S. Strange, "Pragmatism and Radicalism in Elizabeth Cady Stanton's Feminist Advocacy: A Rhetorical Biography" (Ph.D. diss., Indiana University, 1998).

14. There is much debate whether "Deism" as a descriptive fits Jefferson's complicated and wavering religious allegiances. In his old age, Jefferson confessed, "I trust there is not a young man *now living* in the United States who will not die a Unitarian." Quoted in Robinson, *Unitarians and Universalists,* p. 23.

nonspecificity and dislocation, and 'canon,' with its suggestion of autonomy and transcendence."[15] As both a category of analysis and a reading strategy, then, scripture allows us to map the locations of various identities throughout a given textual field. In positing the Bible's status as scripture as a starting point for a survey of nineteenth-century hermeneutics, I am proposing a rubric for mapping the locations and displacements of African American identities.

The term "private interpretations" in my title is borrowed from the Authorized Version of the New Testament epistle of 2 Peter 1:20: "no prophecy of the Scripture is of any private interpretation." The Greek words translated "private" and "interpretation" are important because they stem from the words *idios* — meaning "individual," and the verb *luo*, which means "to loose." I point this out only to emphasize that the word translated "interpretation" is not the usual Greek word from which we derive the term "hermeneutics," signifying interpretation as a search for meaning. Instead, "to loose" implies an unraveling — or "undoing," we could say — that is more akin to our post-structuralist terminology of dismantling. This private interpretation, as demonstrated by both Jefferson and Stanton, in different eras and for different purposes, involves a two-step process: first, a selecting of certain passages around a common theme (moral philosophy or gender, in this case), which effects a "shrinking" of the canon and virtual "recanonization"; secondly, the addition of commentary (in Jefferson's case, the presence of other, non-biblical materials and literature), which effects a "recontextualization" of the material. Thus the private interpreter first shrinks the Bible to a select number of passages, and then proceeds to comment on those as though they served as a representation of the whole text. Moreover, upon close examination, this process always reveals an allegiance to a prior "scripture" which authorizes the privatized reading, even if the interpreter purports to appeal to no other authority than the Bible itself. As we will see, this is exactly the methodology of proslavery advocates.

In contrast to private interpretation, I would pose a category of pub-

---

15. Wesley A. Kort, *"Take, Read": Scripture, Textuality, and Cultural Practice* (University Park: Pennsylvania State University Press, 1996), p. 3. In referring to "writing" and "canon" Kort here echoes Derrida's designations of "writing" and "book" in *Of Grammatology*.

lic hermeneutics closely akin to what Hans W. Frei terms the *sensus literalis,* "the closest one can come to a consensus reading of the Bible as the sacred text in the Christian Church." Inquiring of the future of the literal reading in light of Ricoeur's phenomenology and deconstruction, Frei asks of a current, revised form of *sensus literalis,* "does it stretch or will it break?"[16] While some have argued that the category of the literal reading remains somewhat elusive and undefined in Frei,[17] it is predicated on the notion that it was "centrality of the story of Jesus that the Christian interpretive tradition in the West gradually assigned clear primacy to the literal sense in the reading of scripture." It is thus the commitment to the literal, baseline narrative of Jesus that legitimates other "legitimate" reading strategies, including tropological, allegorical, analogical, and others. These types of readings, especially when applied to what Christians call the Old Testament or Hebrew Bible, "could only be done because the story of Jesus itself was taken to have a literal or plain meaning," according to Frei. "He was the Messiah, and the fourfold storied depiction in the gospels, especially of his passion and resurrection, was the enacted form of his identity as Messiah." Moreover, the literal understanding of Jesus' narrative was not descriptive, but ascriptive:

> That "Jesus" — not someone else or nobody in particular — is the subject, the agent and patient of these stories is said to be their crucial point, and the descriptives of events, sayings, personal qualities, and so forth, become literal by being firmly predicated of him.[18]

An example of what I mean by private and public reading is discussed by Mark A. Noll in his essay "The Image of the United States as a Biblical Nation, 1776-1865." Noll contrasts the ministerial use of scripture to promote the idea of the United States as a "biblical nation" with the

16. Hans W. Frei, "The 'Literal Reading' of Biblical Narrative in the Christian Tradition: Does it Stretch or Will it Break?" in *The Bible and the Narrative Tradition,* ed. Frank McConnell (New York: Oxford University Press, 1986), p. 37.

17. See Anthony Thiselton's discussion of Frei's work in Roger Lundin, Clarence Walhout, and Anthony C. Thiselton, *The Promise of Hermeneutics* (Grand Rapids: Eerdmans, 1999), pp. 162-63. See also Hans W. Frei's *The Eclipse of Biblical Narrative: A Study in Eighteenth and Nineteenth Century Hermeneutics* (New Haven: Yale University Press, 1974).

18. Frei, "'Literal Reading,'" pp. 37, 42.

dissenting view of "enslaved Christians" whose approach to Scripture was hardly bound by the requirements of American nationalism:

> Ministers prepared and delivered sermons on a text of Scripture, but this text of Scripture became a gateway not for the proclamation of essentially biblical messages, but for the minister's social, political, or cultural convictions, which had been securely in place long before he had turned to the Bible.

For Christian slaves, on the other hand, "it was the Bible-as-story which captured the imagination."[19] Noll's insistence on the narrative quality of the Bible accords with Frei's promotion of the literal sense as essentially about its narrativity, grounded in the life, death, burial, and resurrection of Jesus Christ.


## Emancipatory Hermeneutics

In "New Testament Interpretation in Historical Perspective," Anthony C. Thiselton calls for an "emancipatory hermeneutics as neither a pull toward nor a flight from history as such, but as a call to renounce manipulative interpretation of all kinds."[20] When one thinks of "manipulative" hermeneutics and nineteenth-century America, one would be hard-pressed to find a better example than the debate over American slavery as it centered on appeal to biblical authority. While it is axiomatic that proslavery forces used the Bible to justify the enslavement of African and African American people, the question of what type of hermeneutical assumptions or theory of textuality authorized such racially oppressive use of scripture has gone unexamined. Even Riggins R. Earl's referral to such proslavery exegesis as "intentional misinterpretation" does not account for the theoretical, cultural, or textual ground

19. Mark Noll, "The Image of the United States as a Biblical Nation, 1776-1865," in Hatch and Noll, eds., *The Bible in America*, pp. 42, 49.

20. Anthony C. Thiselton, "New Testament Historical Interpretation in Historical Perspective," in *Hearing the New Testament: Strategies for Interpretation,* ed. Joel B. Green (Grand Rapids: Eerdmans, 1995), p. 36.

from which such a category as "misreading" must be constituted.[21] In a variety of cultural, historical, theological, and literary accounts of the nineteenth century, one repeatedly finds a link between proslavery exegesis and "literalism" — understood to mean a surface-level, face-value reading of the Bible — and anti-slavery or natural rights ideology and a "freer" reading of the Bible that ventures away from a simplistic, literal reading. Moreover, by "literal" reading, scholars always imply a simple faith in the authority of scripture. In his seminal account of the development of proslavery thought, for example, William Sumner Jenkins offers a representative account:

> The slaveholder's case based on the Bible stood until refuted. In order to rebut its conclusiveness and make out a contrary case, the anti-slavery moralist had to depart from a strict construction of the literal text. Applying liberal rules of textual criticism, the anti-slavery exegete denied the correctness of the slaveholder's conclusions, and by using the general principles of Christianity, he attempted to destroy the Bible defense.[22]

This link of authoritative biblicism with slavery and de-centered biblical authority with liberation has shaped much biblical and historical scholarship.

Wesley Kort traces a progression from John Calvin's sixteenth-century understanding of the Bible as scripture to the notion of nature, history, and finally literature as scripture in the nineteenth and twentieth centuries. Finally he locates in postmodernism the dismantling of the category of scripture altogether. Intertwined with this exchange of centers of authority is a secondary process in which the extrabiblical "scripture" (nature, history, literature respectively) is first understood as warranted by the Bible, then as competing with it, and finally as supplanting it:

> Reading an extrabiblical text as scripture begins as biblically warranted. It then becomes a competing practice requiring negotiations

21. See Riggins Renal Earl, *Dark Symbols, Obscure Signs: God, Self, and Community in the Slave Mind* (Maryknoll, N.Y.: Orbis, 1993).

22. William Sumner Jenkins, *Pro-Slavery Thought in the Old South* (Chapel Hill: University of North Carolina Press, 1935), pp. 218-19.

of differences from and conflicts with reading the Bible. Finally, it usurps dominance, overshadowing and setting the terms for reading the Bible.[23]

In an almost ironic twist, the new "scripture," originally justified as biblically mandated, becomes now the ground of authority from which the Bible must be read. Interpretations of the Bible, therefore, must give account to the new "scripture" now viewed as the authority of not simply biblical meaning but meaning itself.

For example, in tracing the progression from biblical to natural authority, Kort locates the beginning of the concept of nature as a "Book" to be read in Old Testament wisdom writings, which urge readers to move from the Bible (text) to world (nature and society) as a way of living out in an activist sense their belief in God (becoming "doers of the word"). He traces the inversion of Calvin's idea that the saving knowledge of God prepares one to gain a renewed (hence truer) reading of nature to Bacon's view that the reading of nature is preparatory to reading the Bible. Yet it is Locke's Deism that proved the pivotal approach for the de-centering of biblical authority and the authorizing of nature. For Kort, Locke's belief that "knowledge received from reading nature can be trusted absolutely" betrays as much a faith in the certainty of observable natural phenomenon as a distrust of language and textuality.[24] Ultimately it is Thomas Paine, in Kort's account, who takes the next step to supplant the Bible with nature.[25] This "usurpation" of authority, to borrow Kort's terminology, is founded on Paine's (and Locke's and possibly Jefferson's) quest for certainty, the quest that will now become the precondition for reading the Bible during the Enlightenment, which in turn sets the tone for the rationalistic underpinnings of nineteenth-century American biblical hermeneutics.

In "Everyone One's Own Interpreter? The Bible, Science, and Authority in Mid-Nineteenth-Century America," George Marsden notes a similar complicity between Enlightenment ideology and biblical textuality:

23. Kort, *"Take, Read,"* p. 41.
24. Kort, *"Take, Read,"* p. 45.
25. Kort, *"Take, Read,"* p. 49.

By and large, mid-nineteenth century American theologians were champions of scientific reasoning and scientific advance. Their own work was modeled on that of the natural scientists, and they had full confidence in the capacities of the scientific method for discovering truth exactly and objectively.

This trust in rationality and objectivity came together with nineteenth-century "popular Romanticism," which, "despite its subjective tendencies, was not necessarily at odds with the scientific objectivism that dominated the Protestant intellectual community." Dubbed the "common sense" approach, such a hermeneutic depended on the belief that

> The God of science was after all the God of Scripture. It should not be difficult to demonstrate, therefore, that what he revealed in one realm perfectly harmonized with what he revealed in the other. The perspicuity of nature should confirm the perspicuity of scripture.[26]

I'd like to suggest that this belief in the harmony of scripture and nature is behind the use of scripture in the debate over the enslavement of Africans in America that comes to a peak in the nineteenth century — a debate of great interest to African Americans and which profoundly shaped African American readings of the Bible and their subsequent use of the Bible in their writings. Moreover, when we examine these debates in light of textuality and hermeneutical practice, it becomes clear that the prevailing understanding of the "nature of the Negro" as inherently and biologically inferior to whites constitutes the real ground of authority for proslavery readings of the Bible. Thus, proslavery advocates often did not derive their belief in black inferiority *from* the Bible, as they claimed, but from empirical "evidences" of science and experience. Standing on the high ground of experience, "common sense" reasoning and often developments within natural science and natural philosophy, the proslavery camp invented a hermeneutic that shackled the biblical text in either a hyper-literalistic or, just as often, a fancifully allegorical recontextualization. What is evacuated between these two poles, however, is the possibility of a literal reading that carries with it the assump-

26. Marsden, "Everyone One's Own Interpreter?" p. 86.

tion of biblical authority and historicity and provides the ground for a black/anti-slavery emancipatory hermeneutic practice.[27]

To return to Hans Frei's terminology, the breaking point of a presumed literal reading is evidenced in the contradiction inhering in the biblical defense of slavery. Slaveholders' commitment to a prior "scripture" of black racial inferiority ultimately participated in the dismantling of the authority of the very Bible upon which they claimed to stand. Indeed, I regard the turn to scientific racism in the 1850s as necessitated by the fact that the proslavery biblical argument helped to undermine the appeal to biblical authority and contributed to the rise of science as the new ground of authority. On the other hand, the *sensus literalis,* especially with its grounding in the literal narrative of Jesus, stretched to fit the emancipatory ideals of many African American readers and writers, of whom Frances E. W. Harper is a notable and paradigmatic example. Before turning directly to Harper's poetry, however, I will trace the development and dissemination of the proslavery hermeneutic in order to locate African Americans within the textual field of racial "scriptures" in the nineteenth century.

According to Jenkins, the authority of the biblical text was often secondary to the allegiance to a prior discourse of racial inferiority. Jenkins traces proslavery thought from its beginnings in 1701 with John Saffin's *A Brief and Candid Answer to a Late Printed Sheet, Entitled The Selling of Joseph* through its engagement with natural rights philosophy during the American Revolution and the moral philosophy and ethnological debates in the middle and parts of the nineteenth century, right up until the Civil War. Noting that proslavery thought is "characteristically defensive in nature," Jenkins observes that in its early incarnations, proslavery thought "denied general principles of natural equality of men and argued that divine revelation showed inequality to be the natural order of the universe." Yet throughout the first third of the eighteenth century, Jenkins notes, "the slaveholder relied upon the historical sanction, that slavery was a natural phenomenon of society, which had existed in all ages."[28] It

---

27. See Hans W. Frei, *Eclipse of Biblical Narrative* and "'Literal Reading.'" See also Kevin J. Vanhoozer, *Is There a Meaning in This Text? The Bible, the Reader, and the Morality of Literary Knowledge* (Grand Rapids: Zondervan, 1998).

28. Jenkins, *Pro-Slavery Thought,* pp. 39-40.

is from this historical sanction of slavery as "natural," I would contend, that slaveholders derived "the Biblical sanction" for African enslavement.

The assumption of a normative whiteness led to a feverish rush to account for the blackness of African skin color as early as the age of exploration. In his definitive study *White Over Black*, Winthrop D. Jordan writes that the range of possible answers to account for the blackness of Africans was "rigidly restricted . . . by the virtually universal assumption, dictated by church and Scripture, that all mankind stemmed from a single source." This "universalist strain" in Christian thought militated against an overdetermined doctrine of essential difference, while maintaining theological categories of "Christian" and "heathen" as categories of distinction. Jordan argues that explorations into biblical conceptualizations of blackness arose from "a feeling that blackness could scarcely be anything *but* a curse and by the common need to confirm the facts of nature by specific reference to Scripture."[29] By the seventeenth century, these "facts of nature" (the "feeling" that black skin color constituted a "curse") had become a competing discourse — a "scripture," if you will, that would ultimately, two centuries later, supplant the Bible and hold it accountable to this new discourse. Thus a specifically racialized hermeneutic developed for the purpose of the oppression and exploitation of peoples of African descent. If the "Book of Nature" came to compete with the "Book of Books" as the center for authority and meaning, the text of color difference constituted at least a chapter that marked Africans and their descendants as inherently and naturally inferior. The belief in African inferiority as evidenced by black skin color became so widespread an assumption as to constitute a kind of subconscious marginalia to the reading of the Bible itself.

As Jordan writes of the attempts to use the so-called curse of Ham text of Genesis 9, "the difficulty with the story of Ham's indiscretion was that extraordinarily strenuous exegesis was required in order to bring it to bear on the Negro's black skin."[30] This "extraordinarily strenuous exegesis," I might add, operated in two directions: extremely literalistic (as

---

29. Winthrop D. Jordan, *White over Black: American Attitudes toward the Negro, 1550-1812* (Chapel Hill: University of North Carolina Press, 1968), pp. 12, 22, 19.

30. Jordan, *White over Black*, p. 19.

opposed to literal) and allegorical. The Bible anticipates both exegetical extremes in the Book of Revelation:

> For I testify unto every man that heareth the words of the prophecy of this book, If any man shall add unto these things, God shall add unto him the plagues that are written in this book: And if any man shall take away from the words of the book of this prophecy, God shall take away his part out of the book of life, and out of the holy city, and from the things which are written in this book.[31]

What I would call allegorical readings could be loosely called "adding to" scripture, that is, supplying a context that is extrabiblical. What I call literalistic would be "taking away from" — that is, clearly ignoring the historical, literary, rhetorical and linguistic context of the biblical passage. Kevin J. Vanhoozer describes a literalistic reading as "one that insisted on staying on the level of ordinary usage, even when another level is intended." Thus it is that the "literalistic reading is less than fully 'literal' — that is, insufficiently and only thinly literal":

> It is most important to distinguish literalistic from literal interpretation. The former generates an unlettered, ultimately *illiterate* reading — one that is incapable of recognizing less obvious uses of language such as metaphor, satire, and so forth. . . . Literal interpretation, on the other hand, is more like a translation that strives for dynamic equivalence and yields the literary sense. The distinction, then, is between "empirically minded" interpreters, who, in their zeal for factual correspondence, take an unimaginative, almost positivist, view of things, and "literate-minded" readers, who are sensitive to context and familiar with how literary texts work.

When most scholars equate the oppressive, manipulative use of the Bible with "literalism," they are usually thinking of wooden, literalistic interpretations. Vanhoozer also maintains a distinction between the literal, the literalistic, and the allegorical when he notes that "interpreters err either when they allegorize discourse that is intended to be taken

---

31. Revelation 22:18-19 (KJV).

literally or when they 'literalize' discourse that is intended to be taken figuratively."[32]

A literalistic reading, for example, occurred in a pamphlet by Alexander McCaine, *Slavery Defended from Scripture, Against the Attacks of the Abolitionists,* in the Methodist Protestant Church in Baltimore 1842. Writing of Noah's drunken proclamation, "Cursed be Canaan; a slave of slaves shall he be to his brothers [Shem and Japheth]" (Gen. 9:25), McCaine asserts that Noah "spoke under the impulse and diction of Heaven. His words were the words of God himself, and by them was slavery ordained. This was an early arrangement of the Almighty, to be perpetuated through all time."[33] McCaine clearly reads past the mediation of Noah as the protagonist of the narrative — a practice that popular Bible commentators such as Adam Clarke, a favorite cited authority of slaveholders, helped set in motion. On the text of Genesis 9:22-24, for example, Clarke writes,

> Had Noah not been innocent, as my exposition supposes him, God would not have endued him with the spirit of prophecy on this occasion, and testified such marked disapprobation of their conduct. . . . On the one the spirit of prophecy (not the incensed father) pronounces a curse: on the others the same spirit (not parental tenderness) pronounces a blessing.[34]

This attribution to Noah of "prophetic" ("thus saith the Lord") speech emanates not from the text but from Clarke's "supposition" about Noah's innocence. Upon the reading of Noah's speech as unmediated divine discourse, then, depends the "cursing" of Ham's/Canaan's (read: Africa's) progeny and the "blessing" of Japheth's (Europe's) descendants. This "curse," according to Jenkins, was "the ultimate basis on which the religious element in the South justified slavery."[35] As abolitionist Theo-

32. Vanhoozer, *Is There a Meaning?* pp. 117, 311.

33. Alexander McCaine, quoted in H. Shelton Smith, *In His Image, but . . . : Racism in Southern Religion, 1780-1910* (Durham: Duke University Press, 1972), p. 130.

34. Adam Clarke, *The Holy Bible Containing the Old and New Testaments, the Text Printed from the Most Correct Copies of the Present Authorized Translation Including the Marginal Readings and Parallel Texts, with a Commentary and Critical Notes Designed as a Help to a Better Understanding of the Sacred Writings,* vol. 1 (New York, 1832), p. 130.

35. Jenkins, *Pro-Slavery Thought,* p. 204.

dore Weld put it, "the prophecy of Noah is the *vide mecum* of slaveholders, and they never venture abroad without it."[36]

An allegorical reading, by contrast, involves supplying context that is blatantly extrabiblical. In Northrop Frye's classic sense of the word, allegory involves "an 'abstract' approach which begins with the idea and then tries to find a concrete image to represent it."[37] Yet another example involves the Book of Genesis via the commentary of Adam Clarke. Here Samuel A. Cartwright enters the 1850s debate over the origins of black peoples:

> Fifty years ago, Dr. Adam Clark [sic], the learned commentator of the Bible, from deep reading in the Hebrew, Aramaic, and Coptic languages, was forced to the conclusion that the creature which beguiled Eve was an animal formed like a man, walked erect, and had the gift of speech and reason. He believed it was an ourang-outang and not a serpent. If he had lived in Louisiana, instead of England, he would have recognized the *negro gardener*.[38]

As laughable as Cartwright's unmasking of the real identity of the serpent as a black gardener may be, he bases his remarks on Clarke's commentary, which is authoritative because of Clarke's supposed "deep reading in the Hebrew, Aramaic, and Coptic languages." That such an unreasonable reading could come from an assumed basis in linguistic evidence should give us pause. Clarke's comment on a small snippet of Genesis 3:1, "Now the serpent," is extensive indeed, running a full six pages (pp. 51-57) and turning on his explication of the Hebrew word for serpent, *Nachash*. Yet Cartwright goes beyond even Clarke's fanciful linguistic gymnastics (which he confesses is based on an Arabic word and not actually on the Hebrew) in insisting that the Hebrew word *Nachash* should be translated "negro." As Frye and others have observed, mixed metaphors often produce naïve allegories.

---

36. Theodore Weld, quoted in Smith, *In His Image, but . . .* , p. 130.

37. Northrop Frye, "Ethical Criticism: Theory of Symbols," *The Anatomy of Criticism* (Princeton: Princeton University Press, 1957); reprinted in *Critical Theory Since Plato*, ed. Hazard Adams (New York: Harcourt, 1971), p. 1128.

38. Samuel A. Cartwright, quoted in Jenkins, *Pro-Slavery Thought*, p. 254.

The other popular choice among slaveholders anxious to find concrete biblical imagery for the abstraction of black inferiority was the text of Genesis 9 referenced earlier, the so-called "curse of Ham." Interpretations designed to connect Ham linguistically with denotations of "blackness" and African physiological and geographical origins included the belief that Ham had copulated on the ark and that he committed miscegenation.

## Harper and the Hermeneutics of Restoration

Hans W. Frei's description of the *sensus literalis* will serve well as a theoretical point of departure in an assessment of Frances Harper's biblical poems. Frei notes that the literal reading of scripture, beginning with the literal ascription to Jesus of the events of the Gospel narratives, especially his passion and resurrection, constitutes the consensus reading of the Christian church at least since the Protestant Reformation. Situating the literal reading "between disclosure and appropriation," between "naive literalism" and "theories of suspicion," Frei coins the term "hermeneutics of restoration" or retrieval, to designate a post-critical recovery of *sensus literalis:*

> If the general theory of hermeneutics is to stand, it must persuade us that its appeal to a second naiveté and to a hermeneutics of restoration constitutes a genuine option between reading with first naiveté on the one hand and on the other reading with that 'suspicion' which regards the linguistic 'world,' which text and reader may share, as a mere ideological or psychological superstructure reducible to real or true infrastructure, which must be critically or scientifically reduced.[39]

This type of "hermeneutics of reconstruction" seems to be at work in Harper's biblical poetry. I use the word "reconstruction" not only in Frei's sense, but to signal the historical dimension of Harper's poetry, which began to be published in the pre-emancipation period and extends beyond Reconstruction. Thus terms like "emancipatory hermeneutic" (Thiselton)

39. Frei, "Literal Reading," pp. 55, 51.

and "hermeneutics of reconstruction" (Frei) are not merely theoretical in Harper's biblico-poetics but grounded in the lived history of African Americans seeking liberation from physical, political, and ideological bondage, especially as such bondage is tied up with nineteenth-century notions about the authority of the Bible.

Harper was born free in Baltimore in 1825. She was orphaned at three years of age and raised by her maternal uncle, William Watkins, who ran an academy for Negro youth. The rigorous curriculum for the academy included "daily study of the bible . . . History, Geography, Mathematics, English, Natural Philosophy, Greek, Latin, Music, and Rhetoric." William Watkins was very active in antislavery causes, and his son, William J. Watkins, assisted Frederick Douglass with his abolitionist paper, *The North Star*.[40] In 1850-52, Harper held teaching positions at Union Seminary in Wilberforce, Ohio, and Little York, Pennsylvania. In 1854 *Poems* was published in Boston, and Harper began a long career as a speaker as she joined the antislavery lecture circuit. She married Fenton Harper in 1860, and their one daughter, Mary, was born in 1862 (Fenton Harper had three other children from a previous marriage). They settled on a farm in Columbus, Ohio, until Frances was widowed in 1864 and returned to Baltimore the following year. Two Reconstruction lecture tours, 1867-1869 and 1869-1871, took Harper to Georgia, Florida, Alabama, Mississippi, Louisiana, North Carolina, Virginia, Kentucky, Tennessee, Missouri, Delaware, and Maryland. Harper drew heavily on her experiences during these travels in her only novel, *Iola Leroy, or Shadows Uplifted*. In 1871 Harper settled in Pennsylvania with her daughter, Mary, who preceded her in death in 1909. Harper died in Pennsylvania in 1911.

The public debate format, in both oral and published form, was probably the vehicle through which Frances E. W. Harper learned of, according to the title of one of her poems, "The Bible Defence of Slavery."[41] It is this poem as well as another, "The Dismissal of Tyng," which

40. Boyd, *Discarded Legacy*, pp. 36, 37.

41. Melba Joyce Boyd remarks that this poem shares a title with a published anti- and pro-slavery debate in Louisville, Kentucky, in 1851. While the title may be coincidental, Harper would definitely have been exposed to debates like the 1845 debate between Rice and Blanchard discussed above. The Midwestern and Border States, both north and south, seem to have served often as venues for such rhetorical contests.

reports a church's disfellowshipping of a congregant who makes pro-slavery statements during a worship service, that demonstrates Harper's acute awareness of the use of the Bible for proslavery arguments.[42] Taken together, these poems situate Harper's biblico-poetics within the debate over proslavery biblical justifications and the vexed issue of the relationship between slavery and Christianity in general. The poems are linked verbally by the repetition of a key phrase:

> Remember Slavery's cruel hands
> Make heathens at your door! ("Bible Defence of Slavery," ll. 23-24)

and,

> 'Tis right to plead for heathen lands,
> To send the Bible to their shores,
> and then to make, for power and pelf,
> A race of heathen at our door. ("The Dismissal of Tyng," ll. 13-16)

The celebration of Tyng's dismissal from a local church may have been based on an actual incident. In any event, it represents Harper's affirmative answer to the classic debate question rendered as a subtitle to the 1846 volume *A Debate on Slavery*: "Is slave-holding in itself sinful, and the relation between master and slave, a sinful relation?"[43] The debate, which occurred in Cincinnati in 1845 between Jonathan Blanchard and Nathan L. Rice, included a discussion on the denial of Christian fellowship to slaveholders, a topic hotly debated in a number of Christian denominations and local churches. Rice, taking the proslavery side of the question, argues,

> I maintain, that the Methodist church never has excluded men from the church, simply because they were slave-holders. Although that church has been divided by the question of slavery, even the northern

---

42. Note that Melba Joyce Boyd assumes the poem "The Bible Defence of Slavery" is taken from a published debate by the same title that took place in Louisville, Kentucky, in 1851. These volumes of published debates were quite common, especially in the Midwest and Border States. Harper could have based the poem on any such event, not necessarily the one from Kentucky.

43. See Jonathan Blanchard, *A Debate on Slavery: Held in the City of Cincinnati, on the First, Second, Third, and Sixth Days of October, 1845* (Cincinnati, 1846).

division of it has not yet made slave-holding a bar to Christian fellowship. And the same may be said of every denomination of Christians of respectable size in our country. Some small churches have excluded slave-holders from their communion; but their numbers in the slave States are extremely small. And this fact shows the tendency of abolitionism even in its mildest form to take the gospel from both masters and slaves.[44]

In Harper's poem, the equation of Christian/heathen with white/black is a function of the system of slavery; by withholding Bibles and Christianity from enslaved peoples, Harper suggests, one renders them permanently "heathens" and outsiders. This is significant because Harper's biblical poems will most often feature a character who is a social outcast but, in coming to Christ, is brought near and accepted as an insider to God's economy of grace.

In Harper's poetic canon, twenty-two poems are based on direct exegesis of a sustained passage from the Bible. Another ten have biblical titles but are not direct interpretations of a text. Of the twenty-two biblical poems, fourteen are from New Testament passages, all of which feature Jesus and are based specifically on the Gospel narratives. This problematizes the general view that African Americans are an "Old Testament people," with the Exodus motif as the central and dominant point of biblical engagement.[45] Moreover, Harper's New Testament emphasis is centered on the Gospels and the person of Jesus. This is an implicit corrective to the proslavery canon, which emphasizes select portions of Genesis and the Pauline epistles. The only proslavery argument involving Jesus declared that Jesus did not explicitly talk about slavery and thus must not have been against it.[46] It is also significant that the most serious

---

44. Blanchard, *Debate on Slavery*, pp. 400-401.

45. Here I agree with Cain Hope Felder in the corrective to take seriously African American understandings of the Bible as proceeding from a New Testament perspective (see Felder, *Troubling Biblical Waters: Race, Class, and Family* [Maryknoll, N.Y.: Orbis, 1989]). On the Exodus typology see Theophus Smith, *Conjuring Culture: Biblical Formations of Black America* (New York: Oxford University Press, 1994). Harper's longest poem, *Moses: A Story of the Nile*, has been treated extensively by Melba Joyce Boyd in *Discarded Legacy*. For this analysis, I will focus on the other biblical poems in Harper's canon.

46. See Jonathan Blanchard, *Debate on Slavery*, and Albert Barnes, *An Inquiry into the*

biblical stumbling block for slaveholding biblicists from the late eighteenth century on proved to be Jesus' teaching of the Golden Rule, a passage quoted in every antislavery biblical argument. Thus Harper's invocation of Jesus is neither arbitrary nor gratuitous, but a purposeful refutation of the logic of proslavery biblical discourse.

Yet though Harper's choice of biblical subject restates the abolitionist biblical argument, she evidences a more comprehensive Christology and biblical vision than antislavery debaters who tended to rely on stock arguments and texts. Thus Harper's biblical poems are not simply versified antislavery speeches but exhibit an intimacy in the portrayal of Jesus that exceeds the desire to appropriate the Bible for political ends. On the other hand, Harper does not simply retell the Bible stories but makes choices of detail and structure designed to lift the text off the page and into the imagination, hearts, and minds of readers. First, I want to situate Harper's Bible poems in the context of other black women poets of the nineteenth and early twentieth century, a contextualization that has been overlooked in most treatments of Harper's poetry. Then, I will look at two of her early poems from an 1854 volume whose title deliberately recalls literary predecessor Phillis Wheatley: *Poems on Miscellaneous Subjects*.[47] While "Bible Defence of Slavery" and "The Dismissal of Tyng" show Harper's familiarity with proslavery hermeneutics, Harper's undoing of racial hermeneutics is accomplished through her own poems on

---

*Scriptural Views of Slavery* (Philadelphia, 1846). Blanchard cites N. L. Rice's proslavery argument that "Christ and his apostles did not denounce slave-holding, in so many words, or forbid it" as evidence that Jesus approved of slavery (p. 427). Barnes refutes this same view, noting "nothing then can be inferred from the silence of the Savior on the subject" (p. 244). Blanchard's point that "the Bible also denounces slavery, whenever it denounces *oppression*" is well taken (p. 429) and echoed in Barnes's statement that "there is almost nothing which is more frequently adverted to in the Bible, than *oppression*" (p. 358). Barnes also points out that Jesus himself, as a Jew under Roman rule, was an oppressed person.

47. *Poems on Miscellaneous Subjects* was published in Boston. The 1854 edition is apparently the second edition of the volume, which went to twenty editions, with seven new poems added to the twentieth edition published in Philadelphia in 1874. I am referring here to the textual history information compiled by Susana Dietzel as the Appendix for the Schomberg Library volume of Harper's poetry. All citations of the poetry will be taken from *Complete Poems of Frances E. W. Harper*, ed. Maryemma Graham. Harper's title for the 1854 volume signifies on Phillis Wheatley's *Poems on Various Subjects, Religious and Moral* (London, 1773).

Bible stories and characters. "The Syrophenician Woman" and "Saved by Faith," two poems that depict women's encounter with Jesus, demonstrate Harper's own brilliant readings of biblical material and display a familiarity with and insight into the texts consistent with a literal reading of the text.

Harper's uncle, who so heavily influenced her early life, was a member of the newly formed African Methodist Episcopal Church, incorporated in 1816. Despite these early roots in the AME denomination and Harper's continued presence in AME publications and as a speaker in AME Churches and Sunday Schools,[48] Harper's funeral took place in the First Unitarian Church on Chestnut Street in Philadelphia. This has led biographers to assume that Harper embraced Unitarian philosophy and theology. Carla Peterson writes, "Evangelical Unitarianism enabled Watkins Harper to envision herself as a poet-preacher whose faith in the particular figure of Christ empowered her to promote social engagement in order to achieve the goal of universal harmony." Peterson notes that Unitarianism promoted a faith which must be "rationalized, assented to on the basis of intellectual reasoning."[49] Joan Sherman goes so far as to call the AME denomination Harper's "adopted" faith, stating unequivocally "she was a Unitarian."[50]

I want to suggest that while Unitarianism may have been attractive to Harper for a number of reasons, its doctrine did not have a significant impact on Harper's poetry. In particular, her use of biblical texts is inconsistent with the debate over biblical authority that infiltrated especially New England Unitarianism in the nineteenth century.[51] One of the great

48. For an excellent treatment of Harper's long publishing history with the AME Church and the Afro-Protestant Press, see Frances Smith Foster's essay "Gender, Genre and Vulgar Secularism: The Case of Frances Ellen Watkins Harper and the AME Press," in Dolan Hubbard, ed., *Recovered Writers/Recovered Texts: Race, Class, and Gender in Black Women's Literature* (Knoxville: University of Tennessee Press, 1997), pp. 46-59.

49. Peterson, *Doers of the Word*, p. 125.

50. Joan R. Sherman, *Invisible Poets: Afro-Americans of the Nineteenth Century* (Urbana: University of Illinois Press, 1974), p. 65.

51. See Robinson, *Unitarians and Universalists*. While not all Unitarians were as unorthodox as what became the Transcendentalists, Robinson reports that by the early nineteenth century the drift in Unitarian belief was clearly "away from biblicism and the divinity of Jesus" (p. 5).

ironies is that while Unitarians were so clearly outspoken antislavery advocates and liberal in their political leaning, the denomination attracted very few African American worshippers. Mark Morrison-Reed in *Black Pioneers in a White Denomination* conjectures that the downplaying of the Bible is the chief reason Unitarianism failed to draw a sizeable African American following:

> It is no wonder then that while there are intellectual concepts, Unitarianism lacks imagery. Finding little justification within the Bible (the deuteronomic writers were wholly intolerant of other religions), the concept of tolerance was articulated in philosophical and legal terms, as in the statute of Virginia for Religious Freedom, written by Thomas Jefferson. Religious freedom was part and parcel of the freedom of the mind the Enlightenment had glorified.[52]

Given this allegiance to Enlightenment rationalism, Unitarianism was one of the main denominations impacted by German Higher Criticism and the undoing of literal biblical authority by thinkers like William Ellery Channing, for whom "complete intellectual freedom" consisted of "'resisting the bondage' of biblical literalism":

> The call for intellectual freedom is simply not the central message of the Bible; it is at best found implicitly. . . . The typology of freedom — spiritual, political, and intellectual — that we found in black religion is reversed in the Unitarian faith. Intellectual freedom is foremost.[53]

While intellectual freedom was important to Harper and she is rightly regarded, by Peterson and others, as an intellectual, her ideas of freedom resemble the Christian paradigm that spiritual freedom, found in a relationship with Jesus Christ, is the central longing of humanity and the freedom from which all other liberations spring and derive meaning. This Christocentric view of human liberation stems from the enormous value Harper places on the Bible as not only a resource for language and imagery but as the authority over the individual life and character. In her

---

52. Mark Morrison-Reed, *Black Pioneers in a White Denomination* (Boston: Beacon, 1984), p. 20.

53. Morrison-Reed, *Black Pioneers*, p. 21.

essay "Christianity," for example, which was published in the 1854 volume of *Poems,* Harper writes of the Bible:

> Amid ancient lore the Word of God stands unique and pre-eminent. Wonderful in its construction, admirable in its adaptation, it contains truths that a child may comprehend, and mysteries into which angels desire to look. It is in harmony with that adaptation of means to ends which pervades creation, from the polypus tribes, elaborating their coral homes, to man, the wondrous work of God. It forms the brightest link of that glorious chain which unites the humblest work of creation with the throne of the infinite and eternal Jehovah. As light, with its infinite particles and curiously-blended colors, is suited to an eye prepared for the alternations of day; as air, with its subtle and invisible essence, is fitted for the delicate organs of respiration; and, in a word, as this material is adapted to man's physical nature; so the word of eternal truth is adapted to his moral nature and mental constitution.[54]

Furthermore, Harper's Christology is distinct from the "humanized Christology" of Unitarianism. Although Harper's Jesus is approachable and immanently present in her poems, he is clearly consistent with a trinitarian belief in the divinity of Jesus.[55] At the end of the essay "Christianity," in fact, Harper clearly espouses a trinitarian view of God:

> It [the Bible] unveils the unseen world, and reveals Him who is the light of creation, and the joy of the universe, reconciled through the death of His Son. It promises the faithful a blessed reunion in a land undimmed with tears, undarkened by sorrow. It affords a truth for the

54. Harper, in Foster, ed., *Brighter Coming Day,* p. 98.

55. Prescott Browning Wintersteen notes, for example, that Unitarians are "not biblical literalists" and therefore do not accept the virgin birth of Jesus. Moreover, though they acknowledge that Jesus is "human, yet more than human," his "humanness is the ground of his appeal." Rather than divine in his own right, Jesus is seen as "God's spokesman." Finally, his miracles, including the resurrection, "can be accepted or denied according to personal preference." *Christology in American Unitarianism: An Anthology of Outstanding Nineteenth- and Twentieth-Century Unitarian Theologians, with Commentary and Historical Background* (Boston: Unitarian Universalist Christian Fellowship, 1977), pp. 137-38.

living and a refuge for the dying. Aided by the Holy Spirit, it guides us through life, points out the shoals, the quicksands and hidden rocks which endanger our path, and at last leaves us with the eternal God for our refuge, and his everlasting arms for our protection.[56]

If some scholars have seemed to overplay Harper's connection to Unitarianism, others have insisted on portraying her as a more radical Afro-Christian revisionist. In her essay "Gender, Genre and Vulgar Secularism," Frances Smith Foster documents the extensive publication record of Harper with Afro-Protestant publishers and presses, notably *The African Methodist Episcopal Church Magazine, Repository of Religion and Literature and of Science and Art,* and the widely-circulated and influential *Christian Recorder.* Foster writes, "Frances Harper, for example, was part of the same Christianity that produced Nat Turner and John Brown. Harper was a church militant whose congregation included several radicals named Moses." Writing of Harper's essay "Christianity," Foster concludes that Harper subordinated literature "to serve a militant religion that she called Christianity."[57] Yet Harper's use of the Bible in no way resembles Turner's radical racial hermeneutics. In fact, the first line of the essay "Christianity" (which Foster cites), "Christianity is a system claiming God for its author, and the welfare of man for its object" is a subtle echo of a New Hampshire Baptist confession of the authority of scripture adopted in 1833 as a response to challenges by Transcendental Unitarianism and other movements:

> We believe that the Holy Bible was written by men divinely inspired, and is a perfect treasure of heavenly instruction; that it has God for its author, salvation for its end, and truth, without any mixture of error, for its matter.[58]

More specifically, Turner and Walker rely mostly on the Old Testament prophetic discourse and on the New Testament Apocalypse for their visions, eliding the person of Christ. In this way, ironically, they repeat the

56. Harper, in Foster, ed., *Brighter Coming Day,* p. 99.

57. Foster, "Gender, Genre and Vulgar Secularism," pp. 54, 55.

58. New Hampshire Baptist Confession, quoted in Marsden, "Everyone One's Own Interpreter?" p. 88.

pattern of proslavery biblicists. This is more than preference or a difference of emphasis; it constitutes the ground for a distinct hermeneutic.

What is missing in the critical assessment of Harper's biblical poetry is a close comparison of Harper's biblical poetry with its corresponding Bible texts. Such an analysis reveals that, allowing for poetic license of character development and voice, Harper held to a literal reading of the Bible. Such a literal reading, however, was readily applied to her situation as an African American reader and to the social and political situation of the times. Yet Harper's emancipatory hermeneutics (Thiselton) did not evolve into a private interpretation that dismantled biblical authority. In Thiselton's words, her reading strategy became a poetics that was "neither a pull toward nor a flight from history as such."[59]

Hans Frei writes of the need for a hermeneutics which allows for "the absolute centrality of the link between disclosure through text and the world to which it refers and the temporally present event of understanding."[60] Such a reading "between disclosure and appropriation" is what Harper manages to accomplish in her biblical poetry. This "simultaneity," in which "the language of the text in opening up a world is simultaneously opened up by it," is achieved through Harper's choice of pericopes that are themselves situated along borders of inside/outside, clean/unclean, near/distanced subjectivities. In this way, Harper first accomplishes a centripetal reading (Kort) that divests the readerly subject of its tendency toward "illusory self-projection."[61] Yet this centripetal reading experience is always applied via a centrifugal alignment of the biblical text's emancipatory potential to the situation of African American women in nineteenth-century America. Both "The Syrophenician Woman" and "Saved by Faith" involve women characters within an economy of larger issues of difference.

Centering on her religious poems, usually regarded as important yet subordinate to more political expressions, one cannot help but notice the intimacy of her depictions of Jesus, especially in the poetry involving women subjects. Jesus is bodily present in her poetry. One critic describes

---

59. Thiselton, "New Testament Interpretation," p. 36.
60. Frei, "Literal Reading," p. 53.
61. Frei, "Literal Reading," p. 53.

Harper's Jesus as "a soothing source of peace and transcendence," yet the Jesus of Harper's religious poems is incredibly immanent, as evidenced by the predominance of language of touch in the poems.[62] In this regard, I want to turn to the opening poem in the 1854 *Poems on Miscellaneous Subjects,* "The Syrophenecian Woman," which recounts the Canaanite woman's persistent petition for her daughter's deliverance, and "Saved by Faith," which retells the pericope of the Woman with the Issue of Blood from the synoptic Gospels.[63]

The women in both of these stories transgress boundaries of gender that would limit women's conversation with men in public, let alone touch. Moreover, both pericopes are embedded in first-century animosities between Jew and Gentile, the main "racial" division and marker of difference in the Gospels. Jesus thus refers to the woman with the issue of blood as "Daughter," indicating her Jewishness, and the Gentile woman simply as "woman." The Syrophenician woman, as a Gentile, is doubly "other" by virtue of both race and gender. In the other story, however, the woman is referred to as "diseased" (Matt. 9:20) and would be in a religious context doubly unclean and thus also untouchable. Both women, then, represent extreme marginalization and social alienation.

Harper makes excellent dramatic use of this context as she emphasizes, in both poems, Jesus' nearness and availability to the most socially marginalized. In "The Syrophenician Woman," for example, twice in the first two stanzas, presumably from the woman's first person perspective, we are told that "Judea's prophet draweth near!" (l. 2) and "Now the prophet draweth near" (l. 7). Having set up the expectation of deliverance, however, the anguished appeal of the woman is met with silence: "Jesus answered not a word" (l. 12). It is at this point that the woman as-

---

62. Boyd, *Discarded Legacy,* p. 71.

63. Melba Joyce Boyd claims that the poem, along with Harper's other religious poetry, represents "more modern interpretation" of the Bible account. Carla Peterson reads the poem in light of the "sentimental discourse" of nineteenth-century women's literature. Yet neither Boyd nor Peterson analyzes closely the Bible passage from which the poem is drawn in their brief readings. Both women assume the pericope is from Mark 7 (verses 24-30), but on closer inspection, Harper is probably drawing on a composite portrait from both Mark and Matthew, drawing most heavily on the account in Matthew 15:21-28.

sumes a posture that would have been recognizable to virtually every nineteenth-century reader of this poem:

> With a purpose naught could move,
> And the seal of woman's love,
> Down she knelt in anguish wild —
> "Master! save, Oh! save my child!" (ll. 13-16)

Jean Fagan Yellin has written at length about the prominence of the antislavery emblem "Am I Not a Man and a Brother" and its female counterpart "Am I Not a Woman and a Sister" that depicts a kneeling bondman or bondwoman with hands outstretched in a petition for freedom.[64] Here, in the centermost stanza of a seven-stanza poem, Harper references the iconography of the female antislavery emblem. In the original texts, we are told that the woman "worshipped him" (Matt. 15:25) and "fell at his feet" (Mark 7:25) but Harper's careful description — even using the terminology "the seal of woman's love" — would have been blatant to any contemporary reader.

Yet Harper's application of the story to contemporary abolitionism stops short of de-authorizing the biblical account in that, rather than read "against the grain" of the original pericope, she simply exposes to view the subversiveness inherent in its textuality. Jesus explains to the woman that his primary mission is to "Israel's lost and scattered sheep," which seems to reify the racial/cultural hierarchy of Jew over Gentile. Harper is not inverting the biblical story here; the very inversion and transgression she is trying to promote are already present in the biblical narrative. The Syrophenician woman's subversion of the social discourse of hierarchy takes place in her witty punning off of Jesus' metaphorical reference to "the children's bread" (l. 18; see also Matt. 15:26 and Mark 7:27). Jesus' use of the word "dog" is both metaphorical and literal as he mimics (for didactic purposes to his disciples) the discourse of othering that referred to women and Gentiles as "dogs." The woman's witty retort — revoicing even her own outside position by laying claim, ironically, to the word "dogs" — renames her petition for help as a seeking after "crumbs."

---

64. Jean Fagan Yellin, *Women and Sisters: The Anti-slavery Feminists in American Culture* (New Haven: Yale University Press, 1989).

Yet it is Harper's portrayal of Jesus as the site of miraculous deliverance and power that invests this poem with biblical authority; the woman seeks Jesus because "sickness and sorrow before him depart" (l. 4). Even after the overlaying of the antislavery icon, the woman continues to appeal to Christ because "True and faithful is thy word" (l. 22). Having proclaimed the authority of Jesus' word, the woman's "but" in line 23 simply opens a space for inclusiveness: "But the humblest, meanest, may / Eat the crumbs they cast away" (ll. 23-24). Jesus' response, however, exceeds her expectations. Not only does he promise the granting of her petition, but exclaims, "be it even as thy word!" (l. 26), investing her words with power. The power of the Gentile woman's words "Thou hast ask'd, and shall prevail" (l. 28) derives from her acknowledgment that Jesus' words are "true and faithful."

# Mark Twain's Lincoln as "Man of the Border": Religion, Free Thinking, and the Civil War

*Harold K. Bush, Jr.*

I N 1879, Mark Twain participated in a week-long reunion of the Army of the Tennessee in Chicago, at which General Ulysses S. Grant acted as guest of honor. Twain had great admiration for many other Union figures, but none more than the quintessential Union war hero and former President Grant, who became one of the passions of Twain's major period. Twain's love for Grant was nearly a form of hero worship: "Grant embodied a laissez faire serenity and power that made him the prime exemplar for America after the Civil War."[1] Twain's high regard for Grant, combined with his deep sympathy for him and his family, who faced huge financial difficulties after being swindled out of most of their assets by a business partner, resulted in his contracting to have Grant's *Personal Memoirs* published with Twain's own American Publishing Company. The result was the largest single royalty payment in America up to that time, which Twain proudly presented to Grant's widow Julia after the former President's painful death from throat cancer. If one writer exaggerates a bit when he claims that Twain "regarded publishing Grant's memoirs as the most significant achievement of his life" we can forgive him, since at the time it was probably close to the truth.[2] All of his involvement with the Grant family commenced with the heady environ-

---

1. Andrew Hoffman, *Inventing Mark Twain: The Lives of Samuel Langhorne Clemens* (New York: Morrow, 1997), p. 282. Hoffman provides a thorough discussion of the Twain-Grant relationship on pp. 323-29.

2. Hoffman, *Inventing Mark Twain*, p. 326.

ment of war heroes and Union victory that he encountered in Chicago. It is not too much to claim that the reunion of the Army of the Tennessee was for Mark Twain one of his most glorious moments. He even said at the time to his wife, Livy, "I guess this was the memorable night of my life."[3]

In some ways Twain identified very closely with Grant — "Both were poor boys, unlikely successes, with hard-drinking pasts, who succeeded through a combination of genius and hard work."[4] They were middle western boys of the frontier who had made names for themselves back east. Both were men of the Border States at the outbreak of the war, and thus able to sympathize with Americans on both sides. Grant was, like Mark Twain himself, a living embodiment of the American dream: he was, as one writer fancifully put it, "touched by history and the Holy Ghost and achieved greatness."[5] More concretely, Grant represented the victory of the Union, along with its northern civil religion, over the fallen and corrupt ideology of the confederacy. Thus, Grant's symbolic payload included some aspects of a religious symbolism for Mark Twain. And not just Twain: "even [General William T.] Sherman, a nonbeliever, said that he fought under Grant 'with the faith a Christian has in his Saviour.' To the North, during the war years, Grant seemed God's tool." Elsewhere, General Sherman said in an 1885 speech: "Grant more nearly impersonated the American character of 1861-65 than any other living man. Therefore he will stand as the typical hero of the great Civil War in America."[6] Putting these two quotes together brings the realization that Grant, the typical Civil War hero of the North, embodied some elements that fostered among his men a kind of veneration usually reserved for religious or spiritual leaders. Grant became for Twain a religious figure at least in the sense of religion as outlined by Clifford Geertz: "(1) a system of symbols which acts to (2) establish powerful, per-

3. Orvin Larson, *American Infidel: Robert G. Ingersoll, A Biography* (New York: Citadel, 1962), p. 235.

4. Hoffman, *Inventing Mark Twain*, p. 325.

5. Justin Kaplan, *Mr. Clemens and Mark Twain: A Biography* (New York: Simon, 1966), p. 224.

6. Quoted in Lloyd Lewis, *Sherman, Fighting Prophet* (New York: Harcourt, 1958), p. 639.

vasive, and long-lasting moods and motivations in men by (3) formulating conceptions of a general order of existence and (4) clothing those concepts with such an aura of factuality that (5) the moods and motivations seem uniquely real."[7] And the Chicago reunion of 1879, according to this definition, constituted for Mark Twain a "religious" event, insofar as it did establish "powerful, pervasive, and long-lasting moods and motivations" in Twain's life — business and personal — for many years to come.

## Twain, Freethinking, and the Ideal of America

But Grant was not the only "religious" figure to appear at the great reunion in Chicago. At the final banquet at the Palmer House, Twain wrote home to his wife that he was "transfigured by oratory" as he listened to the patriotic rhetoric throughout the evening.[8] In particular, Twain was moved by the eloquence of one speaker: Colonel Robert G. Ingersoll, a former cavalry officer for the Union who later became the nation's most famous orator during the golden age of freethought. Twain's reaction to Ingersoll's impassioned speech that evening was rapturous: "[Ingersoll is] the most beautiful human creature that ever lived." He wrote later to William Dean Howells, "I doubt if America has ever seen anything quite equal to it. . . . how radiant, how full of color, how blinding they were in the delivery! . . . [Ingersoll's speech was] the supremest combination of English words that was ever put together since the world began."[9] Besides the sheer power of Ingersoll's famous delivery and command as a speaker, Twain obviously resonated with a number of his themes. Among the most important was Ingersoll's longstanding critique of any idea, belief, or superstition which effectively enslaved human beings. Opposed to such slavery of the mind was freethinking, a term identifying the movement as one that questioned religious authority and the certainties of church dogma.

7. Clifford Geertz, *The Interpretation of Cultures: Selected Essays* (New York: Basic Books, 1973), p. 90.

8. Kaplan, *Mr. Clemens and Mark Twain*, p. 226.

9. Kaplan, *Mr. Clemens and Mark Twain*, pp. 225-26.

And yet, ironically, Twain also resonated with Ingersoll's highly idealistic vision of the meaning and purpose of America. Although "free-thought" is generally considered to have been the equivalent of agnosticism or even atheism, in its antebellum and later nineteenth-century forms it need not have been so understood. Rather, freethought was "a phenomenon running the gamut from the truly antireligious — those who regarded all religion as a form of superstition and wished to reduce its influence in every aspect of society — to those who adhered to a private, unconventional faith revering some form of God or Providence but at odds with orthodox religious authority."[10] Along this spectrum of free-thinking, the former version emphasizing anti-religious zeal generally came after the onslaught of the Civil War and the onslaught of science. And Robert Ingersoll was its primary prophet, becoming known nation-wide as the "American infidel" for his explosive denunciations of religious hypocrisy, irrational beliefs and superstitions, and even of such specific religious habits as keeping the Sabbath holy — an activity that he detested from his strict Presbyterian youth.

Colonel Robert Ingersoll would have great influence upon Mark Twain, and without question was the preeminent "freethinker" of the century, but an earlier and somewhat milder form of freethinking had been surprisingly rampant in many parts of frontier America, including the Missouri of Twain's youth. Twain's father, John Clemens, exemplified this earlier form — asserting the reality of God but questioning the authority of earthly institutions claiming to speak for that God. John Clemens's milder form of freethought made its most significant American appearance in the writings of Thomas Paine, especially *The Age of Reason,* a book that Twain swallowed whole and nearly memorized in about 1857.

While the movement is typically remembered as having been peopled with atheists or agnostics, this is a bit of a distortion. Many free-thinkers, including Paine, were deists who believed in a watchmaker God but did not believe that he had any dealings with Earth after the initial acts of creation. Some of Paine's deistic beliefs were embraced by Twain's father John, and by his favorite uncle John Quarles, but Twain

---

10. Susan Jacoby, *Freethinkers: A History of American Secularism* (New York: Metropolitan, 2004), p. 4.

later claimed to read Paine only when he was a cub-pilot. He remembered reading *The Age of Reason* "with fear and hesitation, but marveling at its fearlessness and wonderful power."[11] Arguably it was of all books the one most definitive in forming the philosophy of the mature Mark Twain, although perhaps in an unconscious way that remains hard to document. Nevertheless, Sherwood Cummings has shown the very close connections between Mark Twain's written declarations of faith and Paine's *The Age of Reason,* arguing that perhaps these close paraphrases resulted from "unconscious memory."[12] And yet Paine's influence was probably more about an approach to religious issues than about providing answers. The deism of Paine and others was more a critical movement emphasizing enlightened and open thinking than it was some set of doctrines or religious practice. Deism's original contribution was in its desire to adapt Christianity to the many changes it would be forced to face with the sudden emergence of a modern, scientific world.

Freethinking welcomed multiple viewpoints, skeptical approaches to tradition, and above all ready attacks on dogmatic certainty. This iconoclastic version of religious skepticism was surprisingly prominent on the middle western frontier, in such locations as the Missouri of the Clemens family as well as the Illinois where Ingersoll was born and raised. Historians Fred Whitehead and Verle Muhrer have also shown that several other states, particularly Iowa, Kansas, and Texas, were hotbeds of American freethought during the decades that Twain and Ingersoll came of age. These locations attracted tens of thousands of antireligious refugees, most from central Europe, especially after the failed democratic revolutions of 1848. Despite the satirical treatment of legalistic religious uniformity in the middle west by such later writers as Sinclair Lewis, states like Illinois and Missouri featured many thousands of vigorous and outspoken religious skeptics who dramatically shaped the secularization of American mainstream Protestantism.[13] Twain utilized the theme of

11. Albert Bigelow Paine, *Mark Twain: A Biography; The Personal and Literary Life of Samuel Langhorne Clemens* (New York: Harper, 1912), p. 1445.

12. Sherwood Cummings, *Mark Twain and Science: Adventures of a Mind* (Baton Rouge: Louisiana State University Press, 1988), pp. 20-21.

13. See Fred Whitehead and Verle Muhrer, *Free-Thought on the American Frontier* (Buffalo: Prometheus, 1992), esp. pp. 15-36.

freethinking most explicitly in *Pudd'nhead Wilson,* in which the title character and Judge Driscoll are the only two members of the "Free-Thinker's Society" of Dawson's Landing. As such, he distorts somewhat the movement's apparently widespread and geographically diverse elements as described by Whitehead and Muhrer.

Although they may have disliked the grand pronouncements of the church, nineteenth-century freethinkers were not by definition opposed to presenting their own grand and idealistic visions of the American nation. Thus it may seem ironic, given Ingersoll's status as America's leading freethinker and agnostic (which ostensibly means one who holds that ultimate reality is unknowable), that in his speech in Chicago at the Army reunion he made broad, metaphysical assertions about the meaning and purpose of the Civil War. The agnosticism of our present day typically resists similar gestures toward totalization or American empire with a vengeance. However, "Freethinkers did not hesitate to describe atheism and agnosticism as faiths like any other, often using the term religion in a secular sense to define an ethical and metaphysical system grounded in the search for truth rather than in the conviction of having found the truth."[14] It is significant that nineteenth-century intellectuals understood what many seem to forget today: that any ideological system embraced with passion can be perceived as religious in nature, as defined by such theorists as Clifford Geertz and others. Ingersoll's speech in Chicago did in fact present a religious view of America and the war, insofar as it advocated an "ethical and metaphysical system." Indeed, in terms of America's civil religion, Ingersoll's speech that evening before General Grant and his victorious troops must be considered nothing less than a sermon on the gospel of America:

> [The soldiers of the republic] fought to preserve the homestead of liberty, that their children might have peace. They were the defenders of humanity, the destroyers of prejudice, the breakers of chains, and in the name of the future they saluted the monsters of their time. They finished what the soldiers of the revolution commenced. They relighted the torch that fell from those august hands and filled the world again

14. Susan Jacoby, *Freethinkers,* p. 148. The previous quotation is an adaptation of the title of chapter 6 from this same book, p. 149.

with light. . . . They broke the shackles from the limbs of slaves, from the souls of masters, and from the Northern brain. They kept our country on the map of the world and our flag in heaven. They rolled the stone from the sepulcher of progress, and found therein two angels clad in shining garments — nationality and liberty.[15]

Much of this rhetoric sounds vaguely familiar to themes that have emanated regularly from the Bush administration after 9/11 (generating great public concern about the threat and arrogance of an "American empire"), but in the aftermath of the Civil War these tropes and biblical allusions were widely applauded by almost all Americans of the North. The Civil War, says Ingersoll, completes the work of the Revolution. The Union is the defender of all humanity, not just America. And the wartime victory succeeded in rolling away the stone that had sealed the tomb of the sacred and Christlike Union. The two angels within the tomb indicate the secularizing trends of postwar civil religion: they are clad in "nationality and liberty," with no reference to God or the Bible.

Ingersoll's speech ended with a toast to the great victors of the war. Significantly, it also included a chastisement of the South's errors, particularly slavery, and emphasized the cultural work of the war as including a grand liberation of mind:

> The soldiers were the saviors of the nation. They were the liberators of man. In writing the proclamation of emancipation, Lincoln, greatest of our mighty dead, whose memory is as gentle as the summer air when reapers sing 'mid gathered sheaves, copied with the pen what Grant and his brave comrades wrote with swords. . . . The Southern people must submit, not to the dictation of the North but to the nation's will and to the verdict of mankind. They were wrong, and the time will come when they say that they are victors who have been vanquished by the right. Freedom conquered them, and freedom will cultivate their feelings, educate their children, weave for them the robes of wealth, execute their laws, and fill their land with happy homes. . . . The soldiers of the Union saved the South as well as the North. They

15. Robert G. Ingersoll, *Complete Lectures of Col. R. G. Ingersoll* (Chicago: Regan, 1926), pp. 131-32.

made us a nation. Their victories made us free and rendered tyranny in every other land as insecure as snow upon volcanoes' lips.[16]

Again, Ingersoll's claim that the South has been "vanquished by the right" assumes a version of a metaphysical justice. Thus, although Ingersoll is remembered as the nation's leading agnostic of the period, these lines reverberate with a sense of the cosmic meaning and destiny of the American republic. It is a republic whose implications are world-wide, says Ingersoll: "tyranny in every other land" has now been made permanently "insecure." Finally, the notion of the salvation of the South along with the North, as a result of the sacrifices of the soldiers, places the cultural effect of the war within another traditional metaphor of Christianity. And yet the redemptive force, again, is no longer Jesus, God, or the Bible; it is now the abstraction "Freedom," which is the agent of many verbs for Ingersoll. According to Ingersoll, freedom conquers, cultivates, educates, weaves, executes laws, and fills the land with happiness.

## Civil War, Civil Religion

Ingersoll's vision here is a symptom of the period of American thought in which the object of faith is passing subtly away from God and the Bible, and becoming more focused on an impersonal, nationalistic faith in America itself. The crucial point in all of this, however, is to realize that Ingersoll, despite his insistence on the one hand that Americans not become enslaved to any particular system of thought, was himself presenting a very particular "gospel" of the meaning and purpose of America. The main goal of his career is expressed in perhaps his most famous speech, "The Gods": "We are laying the foundations of the grand temple of the future — not the temple of all the gods, but of all the people — wherein, with appropriate rites, will be celebrated the religion of Humanity."[17] But curiously, this religion drew heavily upon a fairly conven-

16. Ingersoll, *Complete Lectures*, pp. 131-32.
17. Quoted in Jacoby, *Freethinkers*, p. 172.

tional rendering of the meaning and purpose of the Civil War. Ingersoll's analysis was highly indebted to the standard American perception of the time that the Civil War was very much a religious event.

Of course, Americans of the early twenty-first century do not generally consider the American Civil War to have been largely, if not primarily, a religious war. Many reasons exist for this cultural amnesia, including perhaps most notably the secularization of culture and society, the privatization of belief, and possibly for some the embarrassment in believing that Americans of the past would be motivated by sacred belief in prosecuting a bloody war. Perhaps in our own day of global terrorism, we are prone to consider religious fanaticism in the context of violence as decidedly anti-modern, even anti-American. We find religious ideology in the business of systematic atrocity to be beyond the pale of modern society. But the Civil War was very much a clash of religious worldviews. One group of eminent historians has claimed that in fact "surprisingly little attention has been devoted to the war as a religious experience and event. . . . [but] the findings [are] substantial. God was truly alive and very much at the center of this nation's defining moment. . . . it is now clear how, in fundamental respects, religion stood at the center of the American Civil War experience."[18] As several prominent historians have shown recently, our understanding of the war and its long aftermath is clarified when we realize that the Confederacy created its own distinct "civil religion" that not only motivated southerners during the war but also played a crucial role in its development for decades afterward:

> The Southern public faith involved a nation — a dead one, which was perhaps the unique quality of this phenomenon. One of the central issues of American faith has been the relationship between church and state, but since the Confederate quest for political nationhood failed, the Southern faith has been less concerned with such political issues than with the cultural question of identity. . . . Because of its origins in Confederate defeat, the southern civil religion offered confused and

18. Randall M. Miller, Harry S. Stout, and Charles Reagan Wilson, "Introduction," in Randall Miller et al., eds., *Religion and the American Civil War* (New York: Oxford University Press, 1998), pp. 3-4.

suffering Southerners a sense of meaning, an identity in a precarious but distinct culture.[19]

Staggering documentary evidence from the years immediately after Appomattox in 1865 shows that Americans both North and South made sense out of the war experience through religious means. Civil War memory, in other words, was heavily invested in religious terms and images. The greatest rhetorical expressions of the meaning of the war, Abraham Lincoln's Gettysburg Address and Second Inaugural Address, are brimming with biblical images and theological belief. The death and apotheosis of Lincoln, to take one of the weightiest incidents, was steeped in Christian symbolism and the topic of virtually all northern sermons in the weeks following the assassination.[20] Famous northern clergymen, such as Henry Ward Beecher and Horace Bushnell, gladly participated in the construction of the Union as holy political entity, and the war as sacred national cleansing.

Beecher was the featured speaker at the highly symbolic raising of the Union flag in Charleston harbor on April 14, 1865, at war's end. Bushnell's theological treatises were among the most influential statements regarding the metaphysical meanings of the war. His 1866 volume *The Vicarious Sacrifice* explored in great depth the spiritual work carried out by soldiers of both sides as somehow being crucial to the redemption of the nation as a whole. This work developed a new approach to the atoning work of suffering as it shifted emphasis from the work of Jesus Christ on the cross to the sacrificial work of each individual American in the redemption of others. This idea became prominent at the same time that many "children abandoned by their fathers . . . turned to the ways of their mothers and took Christianity out of the home to save the world." The preeminent social gospel figure Walter Rauschenbusch is one of many raised by his mother in such a religious milieu. As Phillip Shaw Paludan has suggested, there is a strong connection between the emerging theologies of the North, as typified by Bushnell, and the postwar rise

19. Charles Reagan Wilson, *Baptized in Blood: The Religion of the Lost Cause, 1865-1920* (Athens: University of Georgia Press, 1980), p. 13.

20. I have told part of this story in Harold K. Bush, *American Declarations* (Urbana: University of Illinois Press, 1999), pp. 90-106.

of the Social Gospel, often described as an ongoing war or crusade. As Paludan points out, "Social Gospel thinkers emphasized not a distant God but a more nurturing, more human divinity. And they adopted values of nurture and self-sacrifice to modify or in some cases reject the extreme individualism of their fathers."[21]

The connection between theological understandings of the war and the emerging religious ethos of the North, as typified by Union Republicanism, Social Christianity, the Social Gospel, and Christian manhood, has not been commonly explored in literary studies. And yet these religious themes permeated thinking about the nation in the aftermath of the Civil War. In fact, the manifestation of a unified religious and moral nation was considered by some to have become the primary effect of the war experience, as in Bushnell's statement: "These United States, having dissolved the intractable matter of so many infallible theories and bones of contention in the dreadful menstruum of their blood are to settle into a fixed unity and finally into a nearly homogeneous life."[22] The Rev. Joseph Twichell, one of Bushnell's protégés and the man known in his lifetime as "Mark Twain's Pastor," made these themes central to his ministry. And by extension, they had a lasting effect upon the thinking and writing of Mark Twain.

## Twain and the "Lost Cause"

Perhaps much less well known is the manner in which southern apologists created and deployed their own version of the religious analysis of the war experience, a version that became known as the myth of the Lost Cause. While there have been many excellent historical accounts of the emergence and the ideological content of the Lost Cause mentality, almost no literary analysis has drawn upon these histories; and further, few studies of Mark Twain have made use of these materials, or even shown any interest in or knowledge of the Lost Cause as a social and cultural

21. Phillip Shaw Paludan, "Religion and the American Civil War," in Miller et al., eds., *Religion and the American Civil War*, p. 35. See also William Clebsch, "Christian Interpretations of the Civil War," *Church History* 30 (1961): 212-22.

22. Horace Bushnell, quoted in Paludan, "Religion and the American Civil War," p. 28.

phenomenon.[23] This is particularly surprising given the fact that Twain's writings can so easily be understood in the context of Civil War memory, and the obvious fact that he was a southerner merging into northern culture, and thus highly conscious of his outsider status among gentrified Yankees. Generally, critics have given short shrift to Twain's complicated response to the rapid embrace of the myth of the Lost Cause among Americans both North and South. This is unfortunate, since he provided extensive insider knowledge of that myth, a knowledge that he chose on many occasions to share with his reading and listening audiences. In fact, Twain did respond fully to the Lost Cause ideology — and in doing so, provided his own religious interpretation of the Civil War. Attempts to outline Twain's heavy involvement in the cultural memory of the war are complicated and require a contextualized discussion of many aspects of postbellum northern ideology. But a description of the religious and moral lenses through which Americans viewed the war, and subsequently tried to make sense out of the traumatic experience of the war, shows that many of Twain's views were characteristic of his time and social position.

The precise origin of the term "Lost Cause" is hard to pin down, but the concept and arguments that we now associate with it were featured prominently with the volume entitled *The Lost Cause,* published in 1866 by the wartime editor of the *Richmond Examiner,* Edward A. Pollard. There, Pollard called for a "war of ideas" to continue indefinitely after the military defeat. Tellingly, Pollard's manifesto stated unequivocally that the Civil War might have decided the "restoration of the union and the excision of slavery, but the war did not decide Negro equality."[24] The character of Pollard's insights may be judged from a quotation from another of his books, *Southern History of the War,* published in 1866, in which he wrote, "The occasion of that conflict was what the Yankees called — by one of their convenient libels in political nomenclature —

23. Historical accounts of the Lost Cause are numerous; most valuable for my work here have been Miller et al., eds., *Religion and the American Civil War;* Wilson, *Baptized in Blood;* David W. Blight, *Race and Reunion: The Civil War in American Memory* (Cambridge: Belknap Press of Harvard University Press, 2001); and Gary W. Gallagher and Alan T. Nolan, eds., *The Myth of the Lost Cause and Civil War* (Bloomington: Indiana University Press, 2000).

24. Edward Pollard, quoted in Blight, *Race and Reunion,* p. 32.

slavery; but what was in fact nothing more than a system of Negro servitude in the South . . . one of the mildest and most beneficent systems of servitude in the world."[25] Thus, it is important to notice that even in its infancy, the myth of the Lost Cause clearly foregrounded a proslavery, racist agenda. To say it another way, the Lost Cause mentality generally failed to admit to the evil of slavery or of racial prejudice.

More generally, the myth of the Lost Cause constituted the means by which southerners and their sympathizers (including, as the decades ensued, many in the North) would choose to remember the war. As Gary W. Gallagher defines it: "During the decades following the surrender at Appomattox, [ex-Confederates] nurtured a public memory of the Confederacy that placed their wartime sacrifice and shattering defeat in the best possible light. This interpretation addressed the nature of antebellum Southern society and the institution of slavery, the constitutionality of secession, the causes of the Civil War, the characteristics of their wartime society, and the reasons for their defeat." Gallagher has outlined the two primary motives that caused Confederates to create such a memory: 1) to justify their own actions and allow themselves and other former Confederates to find something positive in all-encompassing failure; and 2) to provide their children and future generations of white southerners with a "correct" narrative of the war.[26] His co-editor Alan T. Nolan has provided "The Claims of the Legend," a succinct version of what almost all Confederates and many northerners believed for decades after Appomattox.[27]

The most striking feature of Nolan's fine outline of the ideology of the Lost Cause is the doctrinal quality of its precepts — a quality bespeaking the quasi-religious nature of the myth itself. If we are willing to

---

25. Edward Pollard, *Southern History of the War* (New York, 1866), p. 13.

26. Gallagher, "Introduction" to Gallagher and Nolan, eds., *Myth of the Lost Cause,* pp. 1-2.

27. See Alan T. Nolan's exposition of the content of the myth in "The Anatomy of the Myth," in Gallagher and Nolan, eds., *Myth of the Lost Cause,* pp. 11-34. In particular, for Nolan's version of the claims of the legend, see pp. 15-19. For Nolan's excellent refutation of these claims, see pp. 19-29. Together with Gallagher's "Introduction" to the same volume, my outline here is heavily indebted to these two essays, which comprise the best and most thorough introduction to the concepts of the Lost Cause.

accept a description of religion such as Clifford Geertz's — religion is a "system of symbols which acts to . . . establish powerful, pervasive, and long-lasting moods"[28] — then it is reasonable to consider the myth of the Lost Cause, as well as Unionist discourse after the war, as more than mere sets of historical suppositions. Instead these detailed assertions comprise the heart of the southern and northern civil religions as they had developed by the beginning of the war, and as they continued to motivate people for many decades afterwards. Indeed, these are claims which many Americans still appear to believe today, as illustrated powerfully in Civil War reenactments or at screenings of films like *Gods and Generals* filled with viewers proudly wearing Confederate uniforms.[29] Geertz's fine definition emphasizes the important fact, missed by so many Americans these days, that in a certain sense every one of us is a profoundly religious being. And certainly it goes without saying that the civil religions of North and South both established "powerful, pervasive, and long-lasting moods" among those who subscribed to them. In this sense was the Civil War America's religious war.

This insight was certainly not lost on Mark Twain. The commencement of his own serious exploration of the meaning and effects of the war can be dated fairly precisely. In 1882, Twain set out for an extensive tour of the Mississippi River Valley as a means of gathering information and impressions for the revision of his "Old Times" sketches into the volume that would become *Life on the Mississippi*. It was the first return to the river scenes of his triumphant steamboat piloting years since the Civil War, and included stops in Hannibal, St. Louis, Vicksburg, and New Orleans, where he had friendly visits with George Washington Cable and Joel Chandler Harris, author of the Uncle Remus tales. The journey featured long days aboard a riverboat called the *Gold Dust*, headed for New Orleans. As the ship moved downstream, Twain experienced the "psychological and cultural regression of the slow, easy, lazy drift into a backward and defeated civilization."[30] But he also was required to do some

28. Clifford Geertz, *The Interpretation of Cultures*, p. 90.

29. For contemporary obsessions with Civil War memory, see Tony Horwitz, *Confederates in the Attic: Dispatches from the Unfinished Civil War* (New York: Pantheon, 1998).

30. James Cox, "Introduction" to Mark Twain, *Life on the Mississippi* (New York: Penguin, 1986), p. 16.

hard work. The purpose of the trip was to gather interviews, anecdotes, and news accounts of the region: its history, geography, and the social and cultural conditions after the war. But what he ultimately learned about the present state of his beloved river country was the climax of a lengthy period of sustained reflection on the meaning, purpose, and effects of the Civil War — a period that would result in what one critic has called the "classic texts in Mark Twain's Civil War writings": *Life on the Mississippi, Huckleberry Finn,* and "A Private History of a Campaign that Failed."[31]

Although these works treat many other topics, especially the first two, they go together well because of their common examination of America's religious war — and particularly the myths and ideologies of the southern cause. They also provide inspired analysis of the changes that had taken hold in the South in the aftermath of the war, which contrasted so significantly with growth and progress in the North, especially New England and New York. These regional changes were even more striking than he could have imagined, so that he was both delighted and dismayed by what he found. He wrote to Livy, "That world which I knew in its blossoming youth is old and bowed and melancholy, now; its soft cheeks are leathery and wrinkled, the fire is gone out in its eyes, and the spring from its step."[32] The bottom of the river south of St. Louis was littered with the buried hulks of sunken steamboats — a ghostly legacy of both the river's untamable natural powers and the war years, as well as a poignant reminder of his heroic days as a pilot. This image of the wrecked steamboats would become an important image in *Huckleberry Finn:* the *Walter Scott,* on which was found the corpse of Huck's despicable father. And the memories of actual survivors of battles in such locations as Vicksburg brought Twain face to face with of some of the most brutal tales of the war. Those tales are recalled in Chapter 35 of *Life on the Mississippi,* entitled "Vicksburg during the Trouble." The frequent bombardment of the city would result in "frantic women and children scurry-

31. Neil Schmitz, "Mark Twain's Civil War: Humor's Reconstructive Writing," in *The Cambridge Companion to Mark Twain,* ed. Forrest G. Robinson (Cambridge: Cambridge University Press, 1995), p. 79. Schmitz also includes in this grouping "A True Story," which appeared in 1874.

32. *Mark Twain's Letters,* 2 vols., ed. Albert B. Paine (New York: Harper, 1917), 1:419.

ing from home and bed toward the cave dungeons — encouraged by the humorous grim soldiery, who shout 'Rats, to your holes!' and laugh."[33]

It is not surprising that this nostalgic trip would jar Twain's imagination back to the days when he, if ever so briefly, had his own personal contact with the Civil War. Young Sam had been working the river, and was in New Orleans in January 1861 when the state of Louisiana officially seceded from the Union; he was also there in April when Fort Sumter was fired upon, officially beginning the war. Almost immediately, his work on the river came to an end, at which time he headed back to Missouri. There, while in Marion County in June 1861, Sam Clemens joined briefly with fourteen other young men to form a militia unit of the Missouri State Guard. They called themselves the Marion Rangers. During two weeks in the stifling summer heat, they marched, trained, slept out under the stars, and generally tried to act like actual infantry volunteers. For reasons that are not entirely clear, Sam left the Marion Rangers after those two weeks to join his brother Orion on a journey out west, where he would act as assistant to his big brother, recently appointed secretary of the territorial government of Nevada. Twain never said much about this brief experience in the Missouri State Guard, whose ostensible goal was to protect the state from the threat of invasion. Perhaps he was hesitant to speak openly about it because of the possibility of being charged as a deserter, or as simply a coward. But the trip out to the Mississippi in 1882, over twenty years later, was a catalyst in bringing back the stories from that period.

Although various versions of his tale of service were published as narratives or presented as speeches over the course of his career, the most famous was the "Private History of a Campaign that Failed," where Twain claims that "I was in the Confederate army."[34] Twain's analysis of the Civil War and the Lost Cause myth was undertaken by one who often announced his initial allegiance with the southern

33. Twain, *Life on the Mississippi*, p. 258.

34. "A Private History of a Campaign that Failed," in *Great Short Works of Mark Twain*, ed. Justin Kaplan (San Francisco: Harper, 1967), p. 145. See John Gerber, "Mark Twain's Private Campaign," *Civil War History* 1 (1955): 37-39, for the various manifestations of this tale; Gerber counts eight, including Absalom Grimes's account in his book published over sixty-five years after the war's inception.

cause: "I was born and reared in a slave state; my father was a slave owner; and in the Civil War I was a second lieutenant in the Confederate service."[35] Here we see a familiar pattern of Twain's somewhat enlarged version of his actual military involvement. However, it is not accurate to use the term "confederate" to describe the outfit in which Twain briefly served (although numerous critics have often used "Confederate" to describe Twain).[36] It is more accurate to call him a member of the Missouri State Guard at a time of high tensions, as the state tried to determine its loyalties; his oath of allegiance upon entering the Guard was to the state of Missouri, not the Confederacy. More generally, Twain's ambivalence at the outbreak of war reflected the general confusion, yet largely Unionist sentiments, of Hannibal and the state of Missouri from St. Louis northward. Terrell Dempsey notes, "The people of Hannibal and Marion County simply did not want to leave the Union. There were pro-secessionists, but they had little support in the community. When a secession rally was held at the county seat in Palmyra on November 14, 1861, only a dozen people attended. . . . Seventy-two percent of the voters of Marion County voted for pro-Union candidates." According to Dempsey, by February of 1861, even after the newly elected pro-South Governor of Missouri, Claiborne Fox Jackson, had tried to turn the public sentiment toward the Confederacy, "the issue of secession was dead in Missouri and Hannibal. It would stay that way after the shooting started."[37] Annie Moffett, Twain's niece, remembered the mixed emotions that everyone in St. Louis felt at the time; she also recalled that on one occasion, Twain "helped some boys make Confederate cockades and only shortly afterward became furiously angry with the same boys when they burned the Union flag."[38] Moffett believed that "[Twain] would gladly have given his life for his country, but he was a Southerner, his friends were

35. Paul Fatout, ed., *Mark Twain Speaking* (Iowa City: University of Iowa Press, 1976), p. 229.

36. See Terrell Dempsey, "Why Sam Clemens was never a Confederate . . . and a few other things you should know about Hannibal in 1860 and 1861," Mark Twain Forum (2001), www.yorku.ca/twainweb/filelist/1861.html.

37. Dempsey, "Why Sam Clemens was never a Confederate. . . ."

38. Gerber, "Mark Twain's Private Campaign," p. 39, n. 7.

all Southern, his sympathies were with the South."[39] Dempsey states, "There were Missouri Confederates, but the fact is that 75% of the Missourians who took up arms during the Civil War did so on the Union side." Twain reported that when news of the first secession broke in December 1860 while he was piloting on the Mississippi, "My pilot mate was a New Yorker. He was strong for the Union; so was I."[40]

And yet we see time and again that Mark Twain would claim to have been once a Confederate soldier, and even a soldier of the Lost Cause. One overt example of his occasional embrace of the Lost Cause mythos is in a speech in 1901, when he describes himself as one of the "soldiers of the Lost Cause and foes of your great and good leader."[41] Here Twain names directly the Lost Cause as his former allegiance. And so an analysis of Twain's repugnance for and critical appraisal of the cause's mentality must also take into account that on some occasions he was willing to embrace it and even treat it as sacred — a feat common in much post–Civil War discourse of reunion. A major reason for his insistence that he was once a Confederate regular may be the necessity of assuring his audience that his ultimate rejection and critique of southern ideology comes from one who was previously a full participant, an acolyte of the myth of the Lost Cause. His critique becomes most powerful from the vantage point of someone who was once an insider, one who was fully steeped in its intricacies and grandeur. And yet Twain made more conscious efforts to reject and even satirize the remnants of Lost Cause ideology. He did this by responding, in effect, to many of the claims of the legend.

Mark Twain even invented his own nomenclature for the myth of the Lost Cause, a set of terms he deployed more generally to signify the entrenched and ossified ideology of the South. The best-known term was "the Walter Scott Disease," most famously described in *Life on the Mississippi*. Significantly, Twain named the sinking steamboat in *Adventures of Huckleberry Finn* after Walter Scott. In the context of any discussion of the Lost Cause, we must recall that the term historically derives from Scotland's attempts at independence from Britain. Scotland's travails were me-

39. Quoted in *Mark Twain, Business Man*, ed. Samuel Charles Webster (Boston: Little, Brown and Company, 1946). p. 62.

40. "A Private History," p. 144.

41. Fatout, ed., *Mark Twain Speaking*, p. 231.

morialized in many of the works of Walter Scott, especially his Waverly novels. Twain read many of these novels, some of them almost obsessively at times. As Thomas Connelly and Barbara Bellows put it, southerners "thrived upon Sir Walter Scott's accounts of the lost cause of Scotland in its quest for independence. An antebellum South embroiled in a power struggle with the 'churlish Saxons' of Yankeedom could identify with the heroic Ivanhoe." The Confederate battle flag used the design of the Scottish cross of St. Andrew in a highly symbolic tribute to this lingering connection, and the Confederate historians also tried to link Robert E. Lee with the ancestry of Robert the Bruce.[42] Southerners developed a craze for coats of arms and heraldry, a trend that Twain satirized on occasion. More generally, Scott's relevance includes the propagation of the idea that "the Lost Cause is . . . an American legend, an American version of the great sagas like *Beowulf* and the *Song of Roland*. . . . Generally described, the legend tells us that the war was a mawkish and essentially heroic and romantic melodrama, an honorable sectional duel, a time of martial glory on both sides, and triumphant nationalism."[43]

We might compare this view with Twain's own analysis of the Walter Scott disease: "[it] sets the world in love with dreams and phantoms; with decayed and swinish forms of religion; with decayed and degraded systems of government; with the sillinesses and emptinesses, sham grandeurs, sham gauds, and sham chivalries of a brainless and long-vanished society. He did measureless harm; more real and lasting harm, perhaps, than any other individual that ever wrote."[44] Elsewhere Twain added to his list of objects and ideas he associates with Scott, including duels, inflated speech, frilly architecture, "windy humbuggeries," and in general what he calls the "jejune romanticism" of the South. One of his most audacious claims is his statement that "Sir Walter has so large a hand in making southern character, as it existed before the war, that he is in great measure responsible for the war."[45] Such obvious exaggerations are not

---

42. Thomas L. Connelly and Barbara L. Bellows, *God and General Longstreet: The Lost Cause and the Southern Mind* (Baton Rouge: Louisiana State University Press, 1982), p. 2.

43. Gallagher, "Introduction" to Gallagher and Nolan, eds., *The Myth of the Lost Cause,* p. 12.

44. Twain, *Life on the Mississippi,* p. 327.

45. Twain, *Life on the Mississippi,* pp. 327, 285, 328.

to be taken seriously; and yet at least two critics have written articles seriously debating Twain's charges against Walter Scott. But it is more useful to see that Scott has become a handy symbol for something much bigger. Twain enlists Scott as a metonymy for all things southern. He says as much when he most succinctly emphasizes the detrimental effect of Scott on "the character of the Southerner."[46] As such, as one critic puts it, "Mark Twain's indictment of Scott is more than an eccentric, hyperbolic flight of fancy, though it is that too. For all its absurdity it stands as a bold, imaginative, and sweeping criticism of Southerners and of Southern institutions." Another critic states that "Sir Walter Scott is the name of that discourse," the "ongoing dominant discourse" of the South.[47]

Mark Twain took on this "dominant discourse" throughout his postbellum career, particularly in the major writings. Twain commonly portrayed southern culture as being fallen, corrupt, and swinish. The people of the South, typified by many of the characters in *Adventures of Huckleberry Finn* and *Pudd'nhead Wilson,* are lazy, unmotivated, unlearned, and credulous. They are enslaved to superstitious and irrational ways of thinking. As mentioned earlier, in all of *Pudd'nhead Wilson* there are only two freethinkers. Perhaps the most typical attitude of Mark Twain in his 1882 visit to the region, as documented in *Life on the Mississippi,* is grave and solemn disappointment. After his return from that trip, and when taking up the manuscript of *Huck Finn* once more in 1883, it is revealing that Twain began with a crucial critique of southern mob mentality: the shooting of Boggs and Col. Sherburn's stinging invectives against the southern mob that is powerless against him.[48] In his discussion of *Connecticut Yankee,* James Cox has claimed that this book, "seen in a certain light, amounts to fighting the Civil War again."[49] Cox draws upon earlier critics like Henry Nash Smith, who considered the Arthurian kingdom, filled with chivalry, aristocracy, slavery, and superstition, merely "a projection of the benighted

---

46. Twain, *Life on the Mississippi,* p. 327.

47. Quotes from Arthur Pettit, *Mark Twain and the South* (Lexington: University Press of Kentucky, 1974), p. 72; and Schmitz, "Mark Twain's Civil War," p. 86.

48. Tom Quirk, *Coming to Grips with Huckleberry Finn: Essays on a Book, a Boy, and a Man* (Columbia: University of Missouri Press, 1993), p. 54.

49. James Cox, *Mark Twain: The Fate of Humor* (1966; repr. Columbia: University of Missouri Press, 2002), p. 218.

South." Similarly, Smith considered Eseldorf (German for "Assville") from *No. 44: The Mysterious Stranger* to be much the same.[50] The honor and virtue of southerners are constantly indicted by the driven Mark Twain in numerous other stories — so much so that the deconstruction of this idealized southern home front is one of the most prevalent of Twainian themes. Instead, his own eyewitness reaction was, according to one critic, that the South was becoming "one vast pigsty — a region of dirt, grime, and mud."[51] Far from embellishing the Lost Cause version of southern society, Twain became a convert to the northern civil religion as represented by his new homes in Connecticut and New York and his new friends like Twichell and Howells.

Twain's semi-autobiographical tale "A Private History of a Campaign that Failed" is his most sustained reflection on the war's meaning. Although some critics have humorously concluded, like James Cox, that the story itself constitutes "a campaign that failed," there is much to commend in this essay.[52] Stanley Mattson has raised some interesting questions about why the *Century* magazine even asked Twain to contribute the story, given the fact that their famous "Battles and Leaders of the Civil War" series was one of the hallmarks of solemn and serious war reminiscence: "It is precisely this staid and earnest quality of the entire series which lends particular interest in the patently maverick contribution . . . by an even more maverick contributor."[53] Curiously, in the *Century*'s initial issue of the "Battles and Leaders" series in November 1884, Twain had published "An Adventure of Huckleberry Finn: With an Account of the Famous Grangerford-Shepherdson Feud." As Neil Schmitz says, readers of that issue "turned past Huck's account of Buck Grangerford's death . . . to find Warren Lee Goss's mud gritty 'Recollection of a Private'. . . . It put Mark Twain figuratively right in the thick of things, though up a tree, onlooking, *hors de combat*."[54]

50. Henry Nash Smith, "Mark Twain's Images of Hannibal, from St. Petersbury to Eseldorf," *University of Texas Studies in English* 37 (1958): 15.

51. Pettit, *Mark Twain and the South*, p. 70.

52. Cox, *Mark Twain: The Fate of Humor*, p. 197.

53. J. Stanley Mattson, "Mark Twain on War and Peace: The Missouri Rebel and 'The Campaign That Failed,'" *American Quarterly* 20 (1968): 784.

54. Schmitz, "Mark Twain's Civil War," p. 80.

Twain's fictional feud, we learn from Chapter 26 of *Life on the Mississippi*, had a real life basis in the tragic tale of the Darnells and Watsons, two families who faced off for many years, with much bloody violence for both families. As the narrator says, "Nobody don't know now what the first quarrel was about, it's so long ago." Nevertheless, the families "went on shooting each other, year in and year out — making a kind of religion out of it, you see."[55] In *Huckleberry Finn*, the feuding Grangerfords and Shepherdsons attend the same church, guns in tow, and attend to a sermon "about brotherly love, and such-like tiresomeness." Huck notes that "[the] men took their guns along, so did Buck, and kept them between their knees or stood them handy against the wall."[56] Arthur Pettit has documented many other connections between the feud in Twain's masterpiece and the actual feuds along the Mississippi that Twain encountered. In particular, he notes that the Darnell and Watson families, as in the novel, "[attended] the same church services. . . . 'Part of the church,' Clemens wrote in his river notebook, was 'in Tenn., part in Ky.,' with the aisle serving as neutral territory between the two armed camps."[57] The deadly feud of the novel causes the most shocking moment of Huck's journey — the horrific death of his pseudo-twin Buck, discovered face down in the river, shot to death. It is revealing that during the discussion of the feud in *Life on the Mississippi*, both at the chapter's beginning and just as the narrator begins describing the real-life feud, Twain invokes memories of the Civil War. This close association in Twain's mind suggests that the heavy ironies of the feuding "Christian" families can appropriately be extended to a consideration of the Civil War itself. In effect, both sides, as Lincoln noted in his Second Inaugural Address, "read the same Bible" — and yet, ironically, bloodshed and horror were the direct result. Twain's depictions of the feuding families thus relate directly to his critique of heroic renderings of the Civil War — especially those that "make a kind of religion out of it."

Of all the essays commissioned and published by the *Century* in its

55. Twain, *Life on the Mississippi*, p. 194.

56. Mark Twain, *Adventures of Huckleberry Finn: A Case Study in Critical Controversy*, ed. Gerald Graff and James Phelan (Boston: Bedford, 1995), p. 148.

57. Pettit, *Mark Twain and the South*, p. 91.

58. Mattson, "Mark Twain on War and Peace," p. 785.

"Battles and Leaders" series, Twain's sketch "alone was cut from the subsequently published four-volume edition" of the series.[58] One of the chief reasons, according to Mattson, is the fact that Twain's piece has a distinctly pacifistic tone. Twain describes the killing of the apparently Union soldier as "an epitome of war . . . all war must be just that — the killing of strangers against whom you feel no personal animosity; strangers whom, in other circumstances, you would help if you found them in trouble, and who would help you if you needed it."[59] In addition, Mattson suggests that the "conversion in 'The Private History' was immediate and complete."[60] Seeing the story as a sort of religious conversion tends to work against the postwar emphasis on reunion and toward an understanding of the war that celebrates the righteousness of one side over against the wrongheadedness of the other. However, the conversion that Mattson has in mind is more fully blown: it is an utter rejection and denunciation of war in every respect. Of course, this rejection includes a view of war as a children's game, little more than an opportunity for showing off, and an escape from the drudgery of everyday southern life. The fullness of Twain's ire against war is most forcefully represented in such later pieces as "The War Prayer," where the faithful beseech God to "help us to tear their soldiers to bloody shreds with our shells; Help us to cover their smiling fields with the pale forms of their patriot dead."[61] Moreover, in the context of the Lost Cause emphasis on the idealized Confederate soldier, Twain's war memoir counteracts a heroic view by depicting the soldiers, including himself, as "boys" who are on a lark. Curiously, in this way the tale takes on a bit of autobiographical confession: Twain is baring his own soul as well as uncovering the true nature of the vast majority of the boys who were forced into actually fighting the war. As Mattson concludes, the "Private History" "directs an arsenal of grapeshot at the entire concept of the glory of war."[62] But it goes beyond this general view. The "Private History" anticipates Twain's growing critique of the precepts of southern Lost Cause ideology and suggests that his

59. Mark Twain, "A Private History of a Campaign that Failed," in *Great Short Works of Mark Twain*, p. 160.

60. Mattson, "Mark Twain on War and Peace," p. 793.

61. Twain, "A Private History," p. 220.

62. Mattson, "Mark Twain on War and Peace," p. 794.

consideration of the Civil War was much more pervasive than has previously been realized. Finally, its critique of ossified and enslaved war mentalities reflects his growing interests in the themes of freethinking and of Robert Ingersoll.

## The Man of the Border

Ingersoll's more brash and uncouth versions of freethinking, however, do not exemplify the greatest heights of the freethought movement — at least not for the public Mark Twain. His most inspiring discussion of freethought precepts was reserved for another resident of the American middle west — like Ingersoll, an Illinois attorney who became a key national figure. At Carnegie Hall on February 11, 1901, Mark Twain gave a speech entitled "On Lincoln's Birthday." The purpose of this event was the raising of funds for Lincoln Memorial University, denoting the fact that it was an occasion of high civil religion. He appeared on stage with Henry Watterson, a former colonel for the Confederacy, whom he called a "reconstructed rebel." In this speech, Twain is insistent on foregrounding his own southernness along with Watterson's, as he has been in the various versions of his tale of service that were published as narratives or presented as speeches prior to 1901. It is one of Twain's lengthiest renditions of the religious elements of the Civil War itself, echoing passages from Lincoln's key speeches, and invoking directly Lincoln's Gettysburg Address:

> For the hearts of the whole nation, North and South, were in the war. We of the South were not ashamed; for, like the men of the North, we were fighting for flags we loved; and when men fight for these things, and under these convictions, with nothing sordid to tarnish their cause, that cause is holy, the blood spilled for it is sacred, the life that is laid down for it is consecrated. . . .
>
> North and South we put our hearts into that colossal struggle, and out of it came the blessed fulfillment of the prophecy of the immortal Gettysburg speech which said: "We here highly resolve that these dead shall not have died in vain; that this nation, under God, shall have a

new birth of freedom; and that a government of the people, by the people, and for the people shall not perish from the earth."[63]

Twain agrees here with crucial aspects of reunion discourse, as in his equating of all soldiers in terms of commitment and sacrifice, or of putting their "hearts" fully into it. Both sides, he says, loved their "flags" — a comment that sounds patriotic but reminds us of the abstract qualities of nationalism and perhaps even the blind allegiance powerfully symbolized in the carrying of the flag in Stephen Crane's *The Red Badge of Courage.* Religious language is invoked especially at the end of the first section, and is even presented in the threefold manner that Lincoln was so fond of ("that cause is holy, the blood spilled for it is sacred, the life that is laid down for it is consecrated"). And Twain directly quotes Lincoln's call to the entire nation to remember the mission of America and not allow the blood of the war to have been spilled in vain; rather, the war must issue in a "new birth," and the government of the Union must go forth into perpetuity.

In the final passage of the speech, Twain makes clear a desire to showcase his supposed former allegiance with the southern cause, and his reliance on reunion discourse, even more directly: "The old wounds are healed; you and we are brothers again; you testify by honoring two of us, once soldiers of the Lost Cause and foes of your great and good leader — with the privilege of assisting here; and we testify it by laying our honest homage at the feet of Abraham Lincoln and in forgetting that you of the North and we of the South were ever enemies, and remembering only that we are now indistinguishably fused together and namable by one common great name — Americans." Here Twain names directly the Lost Cause as his former allegiance, and draws most obviously on the desire for reunion that marked postwar rhetoric. His identification of himself as a Confederate is playing fast and loose with the historical reality. But again, confessing former ties with the Lost Cause mythos serves the rhetorical purpose of positioning himself as a convert. Indeed, in the terms given here, the entire speech becomes in the closing sentences an elaborate form of testimony. For Twain, the fact that two former southern rebels

63. Fatout, ed., *Mark Twain Speaking,* pp. 229-30, 230-31.

(including Watterson), both of whom were ostensibly Confederate offi-
cers, are honored on this solemn occasion commemorating the greatest
of Union saints testifies to reconciliation and reunion. Furthermore,
Twain states that "we [southerners] testify it" by genuflecting to the memory of Lincoln. The "it" in this case must surely be reunion and reconciliation. "It," says Twain, has been fully achieved — and this occasion is emblematic of that achievement. As Twain put it in an 1887 speech to Union
veterans, "there is no North, no South any more."[64]

Although Twain did not often speak or write about Lincoln, it is
clear from this speech and other extant remarks that he held high praise
for this patron saint of Unionist nationalism. In fact, Twain's remarks
supporting attempts to preserve Lincoln's Kentucky birthplace in 1907
contain a certain autobiographical ring:

> If the Union was to be saved, it had to be a man of such an origin that
> should save it. No wintry New England Brahmin could have done it,
> or any torrid cotton planter, regarding the distant Yankee as a species
> of obnoxious foreigner. It needed a man of the border, where civil war
> meant the grapple of brother and brother and disunion a raw and gap-
> ing wound. It needed one who knew slavery not from books only, but
> as a living thing, knew the good that was mixed with its evil, and knew
> the evil not merely as it affected the negroes, but in its hardly less bane-
> ful influence upon the poor whites. It needed one who knew how hu-
> man all the parties to the quarrel were, how much alike they were at
> bottom, who saw them all reflected in himself, and felt their dissen-
> sions like the tearing apart of his own soul. When the war came Geor-
> gia sent an army in gray and Massachusetts an army in blue, but Ken-
> tucky raised armies for both sides. And this man, sprung from
> Southern poor whites, born on a Kentucky farm and transplanted to
> an Illinois village, this man, in whose heart knowledge and charity had
> left no room for malice, was marked by Providence as the one to "bind
> up the Nation's wounds."[65]

64. Louis Budd, *Mark Twain: Social Philosopher* (Bloomington: Indiana University
Press, 1964), p. 109.

65. Mark Twain, "A Lincoln Memorial: A Plea by Mark Twain for the Setting Apart
of His Birthplace," *New York Times*, January 13, 1907.

Twain shows here a familiarity with Lincoln's phrasing and style, including lines like "when the war came," the single word "malice," and the ending quote, all of which echo the Second Inaugural Address. The statement clearly supports a Unionist view, and brilliantly considers the position of a man like Lincoln as a "man of the border" — very much as Twain himself was. Like Missouri, Kentucky also raised armies for both sides; for people of these states, the war literally often meant "brother grappling with brother." Lincoln is also like Twain himself insofar as both "knew slavery not from books only, but as a living thing." Unfortunately here Twain slips briefly into Lost Cause mode in stating that Lincoln also knew "the good that was mixed with [slavery's] evil." Overall, though, this brief paean displays Twain's sincere regard for the mainstream view of Lincoln as the leader who through Providence was able to save the Union. As such, it was a very predictable theological reflection on the war — especially in the period immediately after the war ended and Lincoln was murdered.

But Twain's speech also shows traces of an ambivalence that he shared with Lincoln as a "man of the border." Indeed, it was just such status as a liminal figure that allowed both Lincoln and Twain to see so deeply into the values and beliefs of both sides so powerfully — and thus to assure the binding of the "Nation's wounds." The phrase "man of the border" is also suggestive of massive changes in belief and epistemology in American religion that were greatly exacerbated by the events of the Civil War. These changes would ultimately mean that the religious meaning of Abraham Lincoln, and of the Civil War, would need to go much deeper than most preachers had taken it in their simple analyses in the weeks and months after the assassination of Lincoln in 1865. Mark Twain, along with many other northern intellectuals, somehow knew this intuitively. And Abraham Lincoln, as it turned out, was the great articulator of a newer, more nuanced version of the religious implications of the war. His meditations contained theological reflections far more subtle and profound than those of practically any other commentator, and they reflected prophetically the massive changes in social belief that would emerge in the war's great wake.

Ideas of a sublime American civil religion were tested to the limits by the sheer horror and irrationality of events like the battle of Fredericksburg, for example. On December 13, 1862, thousands of Union troops were ordered to cross a temporary bridge over the Rappahannock River into the town of Fredericksburg while Confederate troops fired into their ranks. Almost 13,000 Union troops died in that slaughter, which many observers considered a suicide mission undertaken by incompetent leadership. George Whitman, brother of the poet Walt, was injured in the battle and stated that the battle "was lost in my opinion solely through incompetent generalship"; Walt called it "the most complete piece of mismanagement perhaps ever yet known in the earth's wars."[66] Oliver Wendell Holmes, later to become Justice of the U.S. Supreme Court, was a soldier in a regiment that lost forty-eight men: "I firmly believe . . . that the men who ordered the crossing of the river are responsible to God for murder." According to Louis Menand, "The lesson Holmes took from the war can be put in a sentence. It is that certitude leads to violence. . . . 'I detest a man who knows that he knows,' as he wrote, late in life, to his friend." Menand goes on to make important observations about the meaning of the Civil War for Holmes: "In 1932, after he had retired from the Court and was nearing the end, Holmes tried to read aloud [to a woman friend] a poem he liked about the Civil War, but he broke down in tears before he could finish it. They were not tears for the war. They were tears for what the war had destroyed. Holmes had grown up in a highly cultivated, homogeneous world, a world of which he was, in many ways, the consummate product: idealistic, artistic, and socially committed."[67] But that world had somehow been destroyed by the events of the war — and Holmes knew it. Certainty breeds violence — and so certainty must be abandoned. Christian prayers in support of either side, in the context of horrific eyewitness accounts of the butchery at Fredericksburg, Antietam, or Gettysburg, become pagan acts of moral degeneracy — a realization that is captured memorably in Twain's late satire "The War Prayer." The war's ramifications for religion and belief have been staggeringly overlooked ever since.

66. Roy Morris, *The Better Angel: Walt Whitman in the Civil War* (New York: Oxford University Press, 2000), p. 57.

67. Louis Menand, *The Metaphysical Club* (New York: Farrar, 2001), pp. 61-62, 68-69. The entire narrative of Holmes's experiences and changes in his thinking is fascinating; see pp. 3-69.

In this emerging epistemological context, a "man of the border" becomes one who, like William James a few years later, became convinced that "certainty was moral death."[68] The confusion, indecisiveness, and finally the emergent agnosticism of the post–Civil War era is notable in seed form in the almost sublime expressions of Abraham Lincoln in his Second Inaugural Address, although it is not often viewed in this manner. Lincoln makes three main observations there signaling the rapid change in outlook. First, Lincoln repeats a view that was first stated in the Gettysburg Address: the victors must have Christian charity for the defeated foe. This is even more profound given the fact that at the time of the Second Inaugural's delivery, the war had not actually come to its conclusion. Second, Lincoln refrained from claiming the moral high ground for the Union victors alone. He did not take that opportunity to denounce the South and its soldiers or leaders, and he did not openly celebrate the righteousness of the Union. Finally, and perhaps most significantly, Lincoln articulated a progressively modern view of the providence of God as mysterious and obscure. Lincoln emphasized to his listeners his firm belief that the will of God is not easily discerned and is often affected by contingencies and human stupidity. While most commentators in the North spoke confidently about the ways of God in the aftermath of the war, Lincoln injected a strong note of modern uncertainty and, in the end, humility before a great and awesome God who is very difficult for mankind to size up.[69] As such, Lincoln's analysis anticipated major shifts in postbellum thinking. One might say that his brand of agnosticism was decidedly theistic — a notion that in the twenty-first century must sound like a contradiction. Lincoln believed in God, but like many deists of the nineteenth century, he had serious reservations about trying to read God's mind with any confidence. As a result, as Ronald White notes, he "offered little comfort for those who in every crisis or war want to chant, 'God is on our side.'"[70]

Meanwhile, the more popular expositors of the war, like Henry

68. Menand, *The Metaphysical Club*, p. 75.

69. On these three themes in Lincoln's work, see Mark Noll, *America's God: From Jonathan Edwards to Abraham Lincoln* (New York: Oxford University Press, 2002), pp. 426-32.

70. Ronald C. White, *Lincoln's Greatest Speech: The Second Inaugural* (New York: Simon, 2002), p. 202.

Ward Beecher, Horace Bushnell, and Joseph Twichell, drew upon Lincoln when he fit their particular viewpoints of confidence and American exceptionalism. But they somehow missed the more progressive and mystical nuggets of wisdom that Lincoln was offering to them — while the more agnostically inclined picked right up on those themes. Even the great freethinker himself, Robert Ingersoll, premised his speech in 1879, with Mark Twain seated a few feet away, on a strongly transcendental vision of America endorsed and energized by some sublime and perfect will: the Union soldiers "broke the shackles from the limbs of slaves, from the souls of masters, and from the Northern brain. They kept our country on the map of the world and our flag in heaven."

Lincoln never seemed so triumphant or confident as this while the war was drawing to its close. We can never know, of course, what he might have said about the war as late as Ingersoll's speech in 1879. Perhaps that is just as well, since freethinking intellectuals like Mark Twain were drawn powerfully to Lincoln's thought for its nuanced questioning of American exceptionalism and its disavowal of a clear understanding of God's will in the affairs of man. Lincoln's voice was hushed without the benefit (or potential hazards) of long introspection — a fact that ironically adds to its power and its mystery. All of this helps explain why Lincoln was such a hero to both Robert Ingersoll and Walt Whitman, "the two defining voices of the golden age of freethought."[71] They, along with Mark Twain (who might be considered a third "defining voice" of that age), seemed to understand intuitively what the historian Mark Noll has recently stated: "the Civil War proved to be the climax, but also the exhaustion, of the synthesis of common sense, republicanism, and evangelical Christianity" in America, and Lincoln was the prophet signaling its demise. Lincoln was one of the very few clarion voices who recognized how the war had called into question America's brazen confidence in a "clear-eyed moral certainty about God and His will."[72] And Mark Twain's strong affinity with Lincoln was based on more than their shared status of being from the border states of Kentucky and Missouri. Twain perceived cor-

71. Susan Jacoby, *Freethinkers*, p. 225.
72. Noll, *America's God*, pp. 426, 425. My analysis of Lincoln draws heavily on pp. 422-38.

rectly Lincoln's liminal status as both a believer of God and a doubter of man's ability to conceptualize or describe God. It is plausible to claim that this emergent modern agnostic temperament, more than anything, may be what Twain meant by describing Lincoln as a "man of the border." And together, these two men of the border illustrate some of the most crucial epistemological changes in American history.

# The Liberal Saint:
# American Liberalism and the
# Problem of Character

## M. D. Walhout

TRADITIONALLY, liberal political philosophy has been concerned primarily with what Iris Murdoch calls "axioms," general political maxims having to do with rights or utility that are separate both from private morality and from particular political systems.[1] Recently, however, liberal political philosophers have begun to focus on a different problem, one traditionally associated with conservatism: the problem of character. What type of character, what virtues, does liberalism presuppose or require? Is this character adequate to the particular needs of liberal society, or to the general requirements of human well-being? Does it correspond to the type of character liberal societies actually form? The prominence of such questions in contemporary liberal political philosophy reflects an emerging consensus that the traditional axioms of political liberalism need to be supplemented by a model of the liberal character.

This consensus has emerged, by and large, in response to the critique of liberal political philosophy advanced by contemporary virtue ethicists and communitarians. Simply put, the virtue ethicist's objection is that the liberal conception of the person emphasizes *following rules* at the expense of *cultivating virtues,* while the communitarian's objection is that the liberal conception emphasizes *individual autonomy* at the expense of *communal affiliation.* Those who raise these twin objections to liberal political philosophy include both internal and external critics of liberalism.

1. Iris Murdoch, *Metaphysics as a Guide to Morals* (New York: Penguin, 1993), pp. 360-61.

Internal critics of liberalism regard the liberal conception of the person as a misrepresentation of the individuals who live in actual liberal societies; such critics believe that liberal institutions might be improved if liberal political philosophy were to place greater emphasis on virtue and community. External critics of liberalism regard the liberal conception of the person as an all too accurate representation of liberal individuals; such critics believe that liberal political philosophy and institutions must be abandoned before virtue and community can be restored. Hence the political differences between internal and external critics of liberalism may be as great as their philosophical similarities.

The most influential contemporary critique of liberalism from the standpoint of virtue ethics is Alasdair MacIntyre's *After Virtue*. MacIntyre's thesis is that modern moral philosophy has, by abandoning the classical and Christian tradition of the virtues, rendered morality as incoherent in theory as it has become in practice in modern liberal society. For the virtues, whether classical or Christian, presuppose a "teleological view of human nature," that is, a "view of man as having an essence which defines his true end." When applied to ethics, such a view yields "three elements: untutored human nature, man-as-he-could-be-if-he-realised-his-*telos* and the moral precepts which enable him to pass from one state to the other." Beginning with the Enlightenment, however, this coherent ethical scheme fell apart, inasmuch as "the joint effect of the secular rejection of both Protestant and Catholic theology and the scientific and philosophical rejection of Aristotelianism was to eliminate any notion of man-as-he-could-be-if-he-realised-his-*telos*," leaving behind "a moral scheme composed of two elements whose relationship becomes quite unclear." As a result, moral philosophers have been forced to invent "moral fictions," such as the concept of rights and the concept of utility, to replace the traditional concept of a human *telos*. But neither of these concepts, MacIntyre contends, can be deduced from human-nature-as-it-is; both have "a highly specific and socially local character," requiring "the existence of particular types of social institution or practice" for their intelligibility — namely the institutions and practices of liberalism.[2]

2. Alasdair MacIntyre, *After Virtue: A Study in Moral Theory* (Notre Dame: University of Notre Dame Press, 1981), pp. 52-53, 65.

For MacIntyre, then, modern moral philosophy is no more than a reflection of modern liberal society, with its incoherent moral arguments over abortion, affirmative action, and so on — arguments that invoke individual rights as well as social utility, but which never end in moral agreement. Because liberal society lacks the conceptual and institutional resources needed to resolve such moral debates, it must rely on purely political means of conflict management: the rules and procedures of the liberal state. Indeed, liberal institutions are precisely those institutions that, MacIntyre suggests, appear in society once it has lost its moral coherence — institutions designed to replace those practices that once instilled the virtues necessary to achieve the human *telos*. But this substitution means that the classical hero and the Christian saint are no longer the "moral representatives" of society. Instead, modern liberal society is represented by the aesthete, the manager, and the therapist. Such characters, as MacIntyre puts it, are "the masks worn by moral philosophies," inasmuch as moral ideas "assume through them an embodied existence in the social world." Thus the aesthete embodies modern emotivism, the belief that moral statements are nothing more than expressions of preference, while the manager and the therapist embody the techniques by which one's preferences are organized and adjusted to accommodate those of others. But because this technical work of organization and adjustment occurs in the absence of belief in moral truth and falsehood, it results in "the obliteration of any genuine distinction between manipulative and non-manipulative social relations."[3] The manager represents the obliteration of this distinction in public life; the therapist represents the same obliteration in private life. In both spheres, the virtues — those qualities of character that enable us to direct our desires toward a particular end regarded as essentially human — are rendered unintelligible.

On the communitarian side, the most influential contemporary critique of liberal political philosophy is Michael Sandel's *Liberalism and the Limits of Justice*. Unlike MacIntyre, however, Sandel is an internal critic of liberalism; his target is the version of liberal political philosophy advocated by John Rawls — what Sandel calls "deontological liberalism" — rather than liberalism as such. "Deontological liberalism," Sandel ex-

3. MacIntyre, *After Virtue*, pp. 27, 22.

plains, "is above all a theory about justice, and in particular about the primacy of justice among moral and political ideals."

> Its core thesis can be stated as follows: society, being composed of a plurality of persons, each with his own aims, interests, and conceptions of the good, is best arranged when governed by principles that do not *themselves* presuppose any particular conception of the good; what justifies these regulative principles above all is not that they . . . promote the good, but rather that they conform to the concept of right, a moral category given prior to the good and independent of it.[4]

As Sandel notes, this thesis incorporates "two different senses of deontology. In its moral sense, deontology opposes *consequentialism;* it describes a first-order ethic containing certain categorical duties and prohibitions which take unqualified precedence over other moral and practical concerns." It is in this sense that deontological liberalism opposes, for example, utilitarian policies that subordinate individual rights to social welfare. "In its foundational sense," on the other hand, "deontology opposes *teleology;* it describes a form of justification in which first principles are derived in a way that does not presuppose any final human purposes or ends, nor any determinate conception of the human good." It is in this sense that deontological liberalism opposes, for example, Martha Nussbaum's Aristotelian justification for social democracy.[5]

The key to evaluating the claims of deontological liberalism, according to Sandel, is its implicit conception of the moral person as an antecedently individuated subject given prior to its ends. "If the claim for the primacy of justice is to succeed, if the right is to be prior to the good in the interlocking moral and foundational senses we have distinguished," he asserts, "then . . . the claim for the priority of the subject must succeed as well."[6] But since "we cannot coherently regard ourselves as the sort of beings the deontological ethic requires us to be," he concludes, "justice

4. Michael Sandel, *Liberalism and the Limits of Justice* (Cambridge: Cambridge University Press, 1982), p. 1.

5. Sandel, *Liberalism*, p. 3. See Martha C. Nussbaum, "Aristotelian Social Democracy," in *Liberalism and the Good*, ed. R. Bruce Douglass, Gerald M. Mara, and Henry S. Richardson (New York: Routledge, 1990), pp. 203-52.

6. Sandel, *Liberalism*, p. 7.

cannot be primary in the way deontology requires." The reason we cannot regard ourselves as antecedently individuated subjects given prior to our ends, Sandel argues, is that we are partly *constituted* by our community and its conception of the good. We do not simply choose to belong to a community and to embrace its conception of the good; rather, we already belong to a particular community with a determinate conception of the good before we develop the capacity to choose our ends. This means not only that the primacy of justice cannot be justified by appealing to a concept of right given prior to and independent of a conception of the good, but also that the best social arrangement is not necessarily one that puts justice before communal virtues like benevolence. As Hume observed, justice is a "remedial" virtue, one that becomes necessary only in the absence of benevolence.[7]

The liberal response to the critique initiated by MacIntyre and Sandel has been to insist that liberal political philosophy includes an adequate conception of the person, and that the liberal character possesses a distinctive set of moral virtues. In *Political Liberalism,* John Rawls acknowledges Sandel's charge that his theory of justice "may seem to presuppose a particular metaphysical conception of the person; for example, that the essential nature of persons is independent of and prior to their contingent attributes, including their final ends and attachments, and indeed their conception of the good and character as a whole." But he insists that "no particular metaphysical doctrine about the nature of persons . . . appears among its premises, or seems required by its argument." Instead, what is presupposed or required is a "political" conception of the person, one that begins with the "idea of a person implicit in the public political culture" of the stable constitutional democracies: that of a person as a free and equal participant in a fair system of social cooperation by virtue of possessing "the two powers of a moral personality, namely, the capacity for a sense of justice and the capacity for a conception of the good."[8]

A person has the capacity for a conception of the good, according to

---

7. Sandel, *Liberalism,* pp. 65, 150, 32.

8. John Rawls, *Political Liberalism* (New York: Columbia University Press, 1993), pp. 27, 29, 34.

Rawls, by virtue of her rationality alone, whereas the capacity for a sense of justice requires in addition the virtue of "reasonableness," that is, of fairness and toleration. It is not merely the case that a liberal theory of justice presupposes or requires such an idea of the person. It is also the case that "the institutions of the basic structure of a liberal society have deep and long-term social effects and in fundamental ways shape citizens' character and aims, the kinds of persons they are and aspire to be." Thus while political liberalism may be neutral in aim with respect to comprehensive doctrines of the good, it is by no means neutral in effect, insofar as it "affirm[s] the superiority of certain forms of moral character and encourage[s] certain moral virtues," namely the political virtues of fairness and tolerance, as distinct from "the virtues that characterize ways of life belonging to comprehensive religious and philosophical doctrines," as well as the virtues appropriate to associational, family, and personal life.[9]

Rawls's reasonable citizen, then, is a subject who, like Sandel's, has been constituted by a particular community and its conception of the good. It is just that this community is a *political* community, namely a stable constitutional democracy, and its conception of the good a *political* conception, that is, one that can be shared by citizens because it does not presuppose a particular comprehensive doctrine — not even the "comprehensive" (as opposed to strictly political) liberalism of personal autonomy and self-development.[10]

This political conception of the good includes, in addition to the idea of the political virtues, the idea of "primary goods," goods citizens need if they are to be free and equal: basic rights and liberties, freedom of movement and occupation, power and responsibility in the basic structure of society, wealth, and the "social bases of self-respect." Second, it includes the idea of permissible comprehensive doctrines of the good — that is, conceptions of the good that are compatible with liberal principles of justice. In a liberal society, some conceptions of the good will be in conflict with these principles, such as conceptions "requiring the repression or degradation of certain persons on, for example, racial or eth-

---

9. Rawls, *Political Liberalism*, pp. 48, 68, 194-95.
10. Rawls, *Political Liberalism*, p. 176.

nic grounds." Third, the liberal political conception of the good includes the idea of the good of political society itself, "the good that citizens realize both as persons and as a corporate body in maintaining a just constitutional regime and in conducting its affairs."[11] Together, these ideas constitute the liberal political conception of the good — one that, Rawls insists, complements the conception of the right.

If Rawls's *Political Liberalism* represents the liberal response to communitarianism, Judith Shklar's *Ordinary Vices* represents the liberal response to virtue ethics. But whereas Rawls bases his definition of the liberal character on the mature political culture of the stable constitutional democracies, Shklar traces the development of that culture back to its most primitive and enduring emotion: the fear of cruelty. The "liberalism of fear," she observes, "was born out of the cruelties of the religious civil wars" of early modern Europe, and thus predates the liberalism of natural rights that emerged during the Enlightenment. This most basic form of liberalism, she hastens to add, is not incompatible with the liberalism of rights; on the contrary, "it underwrites rights as the politically indispensable dispersion of power, which alone checks the reign of fear and cruelty." But it "does not begin with rights, natural or other."[12] Instead, it begins with the cruelty practiced in the name of religion and its modern successor, ideology. As a result, Shklar's definition of the liberal character is based not on the virtues liberals admire, like Rawls's, but rather on the vices they abhor: in addition to cruelty itself, hypocrisy, snobbery, and treachery, all of which can lead to cruelty.

Because of its obsession with the vices that lead to cruelty, the liberal character is tempted by a special vice of its own: misanthropy, which must also be restrained if cruelty is to be prevented. All of these illiberal vices, Shklar notes, "share a special quality: they have both personal and public dimensions," a quality that refutes the traditional conservative criticism of liberalism. "Since the eighteenth century," Shklar reminds us, "clerical and military critics of liberalism have pictured it as a doctrine that achieves its public goods . . . by encouraging private vice." But the

---

11. Rawls, *Political Liberalism*, pp. 181, 196, 201.

12. Judith N. Shklar, *Ordinary Vices* (Cambridge: Belknap Press of Harvard University Press, 1984), pp. 7, 238.

double nature of the illiberal vices makes it clear that "nothing could be farther from the truth. The very refusal to use public coercion to impose creedal unanimity and uniform standards of behavior demands an enormous degree of self-control. Tolerance consistently applied is more difficult and morally more demanding than repression."[13]

Shklar's history of the liberal character reminds us of the heroic moral struggle that lies behind Rawls's conception of the reasonable citizen. In response to MacIntyre's story about the decline of morality and the rise of liberalism in its place, Shklar tells a different story about the moral achievement of liberalism itself, one whose hero is not the aesthete who believes that morality is a matter of taste, but the near-misanthrope whose hatred of cruelty makes his moral character "profoundly negative." "All our virtues," Shklar suggests, "are, in fact, avoidances of vices."[14] This implies that the liberal virtues must be sharply distinguished from the "positive" virtues that define the classical and Christian conceptions of the human *telos.*

For the liberal virtues presuppose no particular *telos;* all they assume is that cruelty is our worst vice. This assumption, Shklar declares, "place[s] one irrevocably outside the sphere of revealed religion." Cruelty, she notes, "is not one of the seven deadly sins, of which pride is by far the worst." Cruelty may have been regarded as one of the offspring of pride, and "to hate cruelty . . . is perfectly consistent with Biblical religiosity."[15] But "putting cruelty first," Shklar insists, "is an altogether different matter. It is a turning away from sin entirely, and from divine punishment as well. It has only two figures and one place: victimizers and victims here and now." Thus while "pride may be a deadly sin for those who preach faith and meekness, . . . it recommends itself to those who put cruelty first," inasmuch as pride is a virtue in a victim. The difficulty is that putting cruelty first in this way "dooms one to a life of skepticism," not only toward religion, but toward any ideology that legitimizes cruelty.[16]

Shklar's portrait of the liberal character, then, deliberately omits the distinctively religious virtues, inasmuch as the political liberalism it em-

13. Shklar, *Ordinary Vices,* pp. 2, 4-5.
14. Shklar, *Ordinary Vices,* p. 234.
15. Shklar, *Ordinary Vices,* pp. 9, 7.
16. Shklar, *Ordinary Vices,* pp. 241, 15, 8-9.

bodies is represented as distinctively secular in nature. "It is only if we step outside the divinely ruled universe," Shklar contends, "that we can really put our minds to the common ills we inflict upon one another every day."[17] Rawls is more circumspect, but just as firm: "For the moderns the good was known in their religion; with their profound divisions, the essential conditions of a viable and just society were not." At most, there is a causal link between Christianity and liberalism. "The historical origin of political liberalism," Rawls grants, "is the Reformation and its aftermath," although religious liberty was "certainly not Luther's or Calvin's intention."[18] Shklar is somewhat more generous. The historical answer to the question "Why put cruelty first?" she suggests,

> lies within the dynamics of Christianity. That part of Christian morality that demands unconditional charity was bound sooner or later to [undermine] faith, and above all . . . institutional religion. For it was the latter that seemed to express itself in fanaticism, violence, and the most devastating cruelties.[19]

Thus neither Rawls nor Shklar denies a historical connection between Christianity and liberalism. What they assume is simply that contemporary liberalism has, out of historical and philosophical necessity, left its religious origins behind.

## The Liberal Saint

Nevertheless, Shklar's passing nod to Christian charity raises some interesting questions. Is avoiding cruelty a sufficient basis for liberal society, or is something like benevolence needed? Can liberal society survive without a comprehensive doctrine of the good, or would it become a manipulative society of aesthetes, managers, and therapists? Is the relation between Christianity and liberalism merely historic, or does liberal society continue to depend on, or benefit from, the cultivation of the Christian

17. Shklar, *Ordinary Vices*, p. 1.
18. Rawls, *Political Liberalism*, pp. xxiv-xxv.
19. Shklar, *Ordinary Vices*, pp. 239-40.

virtues? Because I am proposing to address these questions in terms of character, let me now introduce an alternative portrait of the liberal character: Timothy P. Jackson's sketch of the "civic agapist." *Agape* or charity, on Jackson's account, is admittedly a "supernatural" virtue, one which is made possible only by the grace of God. At the same time, it is a civic virtue, issuing in a "civic agapism" that "remains both distinctively Christian and recognizably liberal." "*Agape* is typified," Jackson explains, "first, by unconditional commitment to the good of others; second, by equal regard for the worth of others; and, third, by service even unto self-sacrifice for the upbuilding of others."[20] Civic agapism thus accomplishes the same goals as the political liberalism of Rawls and Shklar: it includes the basic requirements of justice conceived as fairness and toleration, even as it transcends them; it avoids cruelty, even as it puts charity first.

But Jackson's claim is not simply that civic agapism is *compatible* with political liberalism; it is that liberal society *needs* the virtue of charity. Given the reality of modern secularism, of course, liberal political philosophers tend to resist the suggestion that charity is necessary in a liberal society. The virtue of reasonableness, Rawls insists, is not to be confused with altruism, "the impartial acting solely for the interests of others. If we cannot trust others to act on fair terms of social cooperation, he warns, "then it may be irrational or self-sacrificial to act from those principles" ourselves. "The reasonable society," he concludes, "is [not] a society of saints. . . ."[21] Jackson's response to this liberal renunciation of charity is to argue that the liberalism espoused by Rawls and Shklar — what Jackson call "pragmatic" liberalism — is an inadequate basis for a liberal society. What defines pragmatic liberalism, he notes, is its aspiration to "a high degree of moral and metaphysical neutrality." But this aspiration leads pragmatic liberals, he claims, "to reduce the good to identity with the right," thereby "overdo[ing] the individual means to freedom" and "opening the door to . . . alienation." What liberal society needs in order to prevent such alienation is the "marriage of justice and *eros* in *agape*," a sacrament only the civic agapist can consecrate.[22]

20. Timothy P. Jackson, "Liberalism and *Agape*: The Priority of Charity to Democracy and Philosophy," *The Annual of the Society of Christian Ethics* 13 (1993): 49.

21. Rawls, *Political Liberalism*, p. 54.

22. Jackson, "Liberalism and *Agape*," pp. 47, 70-71.

Before seeking support for Jackson's claim in the classic texts of liberalism, it may help to consider the relationship between the civic agapist and the figure of the saint dismissed by Rawls. One type of saint is what Susan Wolf calls the "moral saint," the person whose life is "dominated by a commitment to improving the welfare of others or of society as a whole." The moral saint may be a "rational saint," one who acts out of duty, sacrificing his own happiness for that of others; or a "loving saint," one who acts out of love, finding his own happiness in the happiness of others. But whether he acts out of duty or love, the moral saint "must cultivate those qualities which are apt to allow him to treat others as justly and kindly as possible. . . . He will be patient, considerate, even-tempered, hospitable, charitable," and so on. Yet there is a problem:

> There comes a point in the listing of the virtues that a moral saint is likely to have where one might naturally begin to wonder whether the moral saint isn't, after all, too good — if not too good for his own good, at least too good for his own well-being. For the moral virtues . . . are apt to crowd out the nonmoral virtues, as well as many of the interests and personal characteristics that we think generally contribute to a healthy, well-rounded, richly developed character.[23]

The ideal of moral sainthood, however, hardly does justice to sainthood itself as a historical phenomenon. As Robert M. Adams points out, "there *are* saints — people like St. Francis of Assisi and Gandhi and Mother Teresa — and they are quite different from what Wolf thinks a moral saint would be." In the case of such actual saints, Adams observes, "it would be misleading to say that their lives have been 'dominated by a commitment to improving the welfare of others or of society as a whole.' For sainthood is an essentially religious phenomenon, and even so political a saint as Gandhi saw his powerful humanitarian concern in the context of a more comprehensive devotion to God."[24] Likewise, John A. Coleman insists that "sainthood is not primarily about ethics. Religion always deals with a tension between the mystical and the ethical, and with sainthood the mystical dimension is the controlling one." In

---

23. Susan Wolf, "Moral Saints," *Journal of Philosophy* 79 (1982): 421.
24. Robert M. Adams, "Saints," *Journal of Philosophy* 81 (1984): 239, 395.

fact, saints "resist being described as models of individual behavior. Instead [they] are mediators of the transcendentally holy" whose "ethical status . . . carries an ambiguity that is hard for modern society to accept." That is why, in the modern world, "the cultural work of saints" must "of necessity be counter-cultural," pointing to "the hiddenness of God in modern secular society." Coleman's list of modern saints includes such figures as Simone Weil, Dietrich Bonhoeffer, Dorothy Day, Thomas Merton, and Dag Hammarskjöld.[25]

Here, then, are two types of saints: the moral saint and the religious saint. Is Jackson's civic agapist a moral saint, in Wolf's sense? "Charity," he admits, "is neither identical with nor a sufficient replacement for all other goods. As important as love is, it is not sufficient for full human flourishing."[26] This implies that the civic agapist need not be a moral saint. Is the civic agapist, then, a religious saint? Not, perhaps, on Coleman's definition. Jackson's description of the civic agapist leaves no room for ethical ambiguity, for the tension between the ethical and the religious that makes Coleman's saint an uncertain model of individual behavior. "But," as Adams suggests, "perhaps some of us assume too easily that we could not be a Gandhi. In all probability there could be more Gandhis than there are, and it would be a very good thing if there were." Moreover, he continues, even "if it is right to conclude that not everyone should aspire to be a Gandhi or a Martin Luther King or a St. Francis, it may still be too hasty to infer that not everyone should aspire to sainthood. Perhaps there are other ways of being a saint," ways that "may be compatible with quite different human excellences."[27] For our purposes, however, it is the virtues exemplified by such political saints as Gandhi and Martin Luther King, Jr., that are the relevant human excellences, insofar as they contribute to the building of a genuinely liberal society. Indeed, Martin Luther King, Jr., is, together with Abraham Lincoln, Jackson's own model of civic agapism.[28]

25. John A. Coleman, S.J., "Conclusion: After Sainthood?" in *Saints and Virtues,* ed. John Stratton Hawley (Berkeley: University of California Press, 1987), pp. 207, 211, 212.

26. Timothy P. Jackson, "The Disconsolation of Theology: Irony, Cruelty, and Putting Charity First," *Journal of Religious Ethics* 20 (1992): 12-13.

27. Adams, "Saints," pp. 470-71.

28. Jackson, "Liberalism and *Agape*," p. 71.

It would seem, then, that Jackson's civic agapist is a type of religious saint. There are, however, two reasons why civic agapism should not be divorced from secular liberalism altogether. The first is that, as Jackson himself implies, the two traditions have developed in dialectical relation to each other. On the one hand, Jackson claims, "liberal theorists . . . take a commitment to justice, freedom, and equality originally at home in a religious community (the Judeo-Christian) and either incorporate it into or read it out of a secular framework."[29] On the other hand, Jackson insists that the Christian "understanding of *agape* cannot be oblivious to the positive and negative political lessons of the Enlightenment." The second reason is the possibility of a secular counterpart to the Christian virtue of charity. "Is the equivalent of civic agapism possible without God and a religious description of the good?" Jackson asks. His answer is not encouraging: "Possible but not likely."[30] But surely this is also the answer to the question of whether it is possible to become a saint at all; the improbability belongs to the phenomenon of sainthood itself. What we need is a category of sainthood that makes room for the improbable possibility of a secular counterpart to the civic agapist: the category of the "liberal saint," a figure who appears in two turn-of-the-century liberal classics: William James's *The Varieties of Religious Experience* and Henry James's *The Wings of the Dove*. Both affirm the need for saintliness in liberal society.[31]

## Liberal Saintliness in William and Henry James

William James devoted no less than five of his famous Gifford Lectures on religious experience to the phenomenon of saintliness, which he defined as "the collective name for the ripe fruits of religion in a character." In Lectures 11-13, James investigates his subject from the standpoint of

29. Timothy P. Jackson, "To Bedlam and Back: John Rawls and Christian Justice," *Faith and Philosophy* 8 (1991): 424.

30. Jackson, "Liberalism and *Agape*," p. 72.

31. William James, *The Varieties of Religious Experience* (1902; repr. New York: Macmillan, 1961); hereafter cited in the text as *Varieties*. Henry James, *The Wings of the Dove* (1902; repr. New York: Dell, 1958); hereafter cited in the text as *Wings*.

what he calls "natural history," offering an empirical account of "universal saintliness," which is "the same in all religions." "One can never fathom an emotion or divine its dictates by standing outside of it," he insists. "Each emotion obeys a logic of its own, and makes deductions which no other logic can draw." In the case of the saintly character, James identifies four such emotions or "inner conditions," which derive from the prior experience of conversion: first, "a conviction . . . of the existence of an Ideal Power" wider than "this world's selfish little interests," whether that power be "personified as God" or identified with "abstract moral ideals, civic or patriotic utopias, or inner versions of holiness or right"; second, "a willing self-surrender to its control"; third, "an immense elation and freedom, as the outlines of the confining selfhood melt down"; and fourth, "a shifting of the emotional centre toward loving and harmonious affections . . . where the claims of the non-ego are concerned." These fundamental inner conditions, in turn, have four "characteristic practical consequences": asceticism; purity; "strength of soul," including patience, fortitude, and equanimity; and charity (*Varieties* 220-21).

In Lectures 14 and 15, James attempts to calculate the value of saintliness "economically," in terms of its contribution to "the world's welfare" (*Varieties* 297). To the objection that "it would seem illogical to try to measure the worth of a religion's fruits in merely human terms of value," without considering "whether the God really exists who is supposed to inspire them," James replies that our commonsense conception of God is itself "the fruit of an empirical evolution. Nothing is more striking than the secular alteration that goes on in the moral and religious tone of men, as their insight into nature and social arrangements progressively develop" (*Varieties* 262). To "test saintliness by common sense," therefore, is but another instance of "the elimination of the humanly unfit, and the survival of the humanly fittest, applied to religious beliefs" (*Varieties* 265). Specifically, what needs to be eliminated in the saintly character is the "error by excess . . . exemplified by every saintly virtue." Devoutness, for example, can lead, in aggressive characters, to fanaticism, intolerance, and persecution. "A saintly temper is a moral temper," James notes, "and a moral temper has often to be cruel" (*Varieties* 271-72). Similarly, the desire for purity can result in narrowness: "The lives of the saints," James comments, "are a history of successive renunciations of complication" (*Varieties* 277). In the case of charity, "saintliness has to face the charge of preserving the unfit," and asceticism can degenerate into "mortification for mortification's sake" (*Varieties* 281, 287).

Behind James's critique of the excesses of the saints looms the antipathetic (and, for James, pathological) figure of Nietzsche, "the most inimical critic of the saintly impulses." For Nietzsche, "the saint represents . . . slavishness," and "his prevalence would put the human type in danger." Such "dislike of the saintly nature," James suggests, "seems to be a negative result of the biologically useful instinct of welcoming leadership, and glorifying the chief of the tribe." The "positive" result of this instinct is Nietzsche's idealization of the "strong man," who combines "inward freedom" from the scruples of conscience with "outward power" over the consciences of others. Ultimately, then, it is against Nietzsche's glorification of the "strong man" that James feels he must vindicate the saintly character — vindicate it, moreover, in evolutionary terms. "The whole feud," he observes, "revolves essentially upon two pivots: Shall the seen world or the unseen world be our chief sphere of adaptation? and must our means of adaptation in this seen world be aggressiveness or non-resistance?" (*Varieties* 293-95). At this point, James turns to Herbert Spencer's theory of the evolution of human society, which takes both worlds and both types of human conduct into account. On the one hand, there is the actual world in which, because some are aggressive, others must be non-resistant, and to which "the individual saint may be well or ill adapted, according to particular circumstances." On the other hand, there is the ideal world in which aggressiveness would no longer exist, and to which "the saint would be entirely adapted." The saint's "economical" value lies in her function as an evolutionary link between these two worlds. "So far as any saint's example . . . draws [the world] in the direction of more prevalent habits of saintliness," James concludes, she is "magnificently adapted to the larger environment of history" (*Varieties* 296-97).

It is, then, only the excesses of the saintly virtues that James finds "humanly unfit." The saintly virtues themselves, when "subject to the law of the golden mean," prove to be "indispensable to the world's welfare" (*Varieties* 270, 297). But what is James's conception of the world's welfare, in terms of which he measures the value of saintliness? The answer can be inferred from his critique of the saintly virtues. For purity, James has little use. "Purity," he concludes, "is not the one thing needful; and it is better that a life should contract many a dirt-mark, than forfeit usefulness in its efforts to remain unspotted" (*Varieties* 281). As for devoutness, everything depends on "the intellectual conceptions which might guide it towards bearing useful human fruit" (*Varieties* 277).

"So long as the religious person's intellect is on the stage which the despotic kind of God satisfies," fanaticism will destroy the value of devoutness; on the other hand, "the vision of social righteousness" gives rise to a democratic conception of God which, possessing "an essential element of largeness," promotes toleration (*Varieties* 275). In short, the value of devoutness depends on the value of its object. The value of charity, on the other hand, depends on the point of view of the judge. "Momentarily considered," James admits, "the saint may waste his tenderness and be the dupe and victim of his charitable fever." From the perspective of social evolution, however, charity is "a genuinely creative social force tending to make real a degree of virtue which it alone is ready to assume as possible," a force that "expresses itself to-day in all sorts of humane customs and reformatory institutions" (*Varieties* 281-84).

Finally, James comes to asceticism. Insofar as the traditional saintly practice of corporeal mortification is repugnant to "the general optimism and healthy-mindedness of liberal Protestant circles to-day," asceticism might seem to be as humanly unfit as obsessive purity. But "in its spiritual meaning," James continues, "[asceticism] symbolizes the belief that there is an element of real wrongness in this world . . . which must be squarely met and overcome by an appeal to the soul's heroic resources, and neutralized and cleansed away by suffering." It is precisely this spiritual symbolism, long forgotten by liberal Protestantism, that "ought to rehabilitate [asceticism] in our esteem" (*Varieties* 287). For it is only a revival of saintly asceticism, James suggests, that is capable of offering a moral alternative to "the worship of material luxury and wealth, which constitutes so large a portion of the 'spirit' of our age" and makes for "effeminacy and unmanliness" among the citizenry. In the absence of such an alternative, those who recognize the dangers of prosperity turn instead to "athletics, militarism, and individual and national enterprise and adventure as the remedies." (James was writing, it must be remembered, in the wake of the Spanish-American War.) What is needed, therefore, is a "moral equivalent to war," a version of "the old monkish poverty-worship" suitable to modern times. "May not voluntarily accepted poverty be 'the strenuous life,'" James asks, "without the need of crushing weaker peoples?" (*Varieties* 289-90).

Asceticism, then, ranks highest in James's implicit hierarchy of the saintly virtues, if only because it counteracts the habits of luxury that make charity necessary in the first place. The high value James places on voluntary poverty reflects his commitment to freedom (inasmuch as the life of poverty remains an individual choice) and equality (inasmuch as the consequence of such a life is the renunciation of social privilege), the two fundamental values of political liberalism. The same is true of James's defense of charity. Other liberal values motivate his critique of devoutness and purity, notably tolerance and openness to experience. It would seem, then, that the conception of the world's welfare by which James tests the saintly virtues is a distinctively liberal conception, and that his ultimate purpose is to justify the saints of the world in terms of their prophetic role in the evolution of a genuinely liberal society. It is for this reason that James compares "the saint's belief in an existent kingdom of heaven" to "the Utopian dreams of social justice in which many contemporary socialists and anarchists indulge . . . , in spite of their impracticability and non-adaptation to present environmental conditions" (*Varieties* 285). To be sure, James's case histories are, by and large, those of traditionally religious saints. But he insists that, just as primitive religion evolves into more "humanly fit" beliefs and rituals, so too is the phenomenon of saintliness transformed by the social consciousness of modernity. Thus it becomes possible to envision the evolution of "liberal saints" in a more exclusive sense: not just religious saints whose virtues happen to be useful to liberal society, but saints whose primary object of devotion is liberalism itself.

The same year that William James delivered the Gifford Lectures in Edinburgh, his brother Henry wrote a novel that might well have been added to William's collection of saintly case histories. As Edith Wyschogrod has noted, *The Wings of the Dove* lends itself to hagiographic retelling insofar as Milly Theale, the dove of James's biblical title, is "a radical altruist, one who is dedicated to the alleviation of the suffering of others irrespective of the cost to herself/himself."[32] This, of course, is Wolf's definition of a "moral" saint, but it would seem to apply perfectly to Milly, who embodies all of the saintly virtues enumerated by William in *Varieties*. She is as pure as she is inexperienced, yet her soul proves strong enough to bear the burden not only of her own suffering, but of others' as well. She is as charitable as she can possibly be, especially toward those who attempt to deceive her about the secret relationship between Merton Densher, with whom Milly has apparently fallen in love, and Kate Croy. Finally, once she learns the truth, she voluntarily renounces not only her fortune but her will to live. No doubt these virtues serve to make Milly, in Wolf's words, "too good for her own wellbeing." But they also make her a canonical example of a liberal saint.

The London society into which Milly is introduced resembles nothing so much as the world of manipulative social relations denounced by Alasdair MacIntyre as the logical outcome of liberalism. As Kate explains to Milly, "the working and the worked were in London . . . the parties to every relation. . . . The worker in one connection was the worked in another" (*Wings* 143). Kate even warns Milly, "We're of no use to you — it's decent to tell you. You'd be of use to us, but that's a different matter. My honest advice to you would be . . . to drop us while you can" (*Wings* 214). Significantly, this warning comes soon after Kate begins to suspect that Milly is as ill as she is wealthy. Eventually, on the occasion of Lord Mark's first suit to her in Venice, the light dawns on Milly: "wouldn't her value, for the man who should marry her, be precisely in the ravage of her disease? *She* mightn't last, but her money would" (*Wings* 334). This, of course, is precisely Kate's plan for Merton Densher, as he slowly begins to understand. "Since she's to die," he asks at the party where Milly appears in white for the first and only time, "I'm to marry her?" "I don't like it," Kate replies, "but I'm a person, thank goodness, who can do what I don't like" (*Wings* 387-88). It is this "strategic" behavior on Kate's part that has caused Frederick Olafson to assert that "she is in some profound sense outside the whole set of considerations and perceptions and feel-

---

32. Edith Wyschogrod, *Saints and Postmodernism: Revisioning Moral Philosophy* (Chicago: University of Chicago Press, 1990), p. 58.

ings that constitute the moral" and Edith Wyschogrod to classify her as a "postmodern cynic."[33]

In order to appreciate Milly's generosity in the midst of this cynical strategizing, it is important to understand the nature of her love for Merton Densher. James hints that she had already begun to fall in love with him in New York, just prior to her departure for Europe with Susan Stringham. In Switzerland, for example, Milly suddenly announces, "I want to go straight to London," bringing "it out in truth as she might have brought a huge confession" (*Wings* 113). When Mrs. Stringham reminds her of her vague promise to visit Densher there, however, Milly insists that "in fact she might very well not have thought of London at all if she hadn't been sure he wasn't yet near coming back," adding that "the last thing she desired was the air of running after him" (*Wings* 116). She reacts in much the same way when Mrs. Stringham first informs her that Kate Croy is acquainted with Densher: "Milly had at first a little air of not knowing whom she meant; and the girl really kept, as well, a certain control of herself while she remarked that the case was surprising, the chance one in a thousand" (*Wings* 147). The next time she sees Kate, however, she finds herself "fixing her in the light of the knowledge that it was a face on which Mr. Densher's eyes had more or less familiarly rested and which, by the same token, had looked, rather *more* beautifully than less, into his own" (*Wings* 151).

But it is not until Mrs. Condrip, Kate's sister, warns her that Densher is in love with Kate and begs her to intervene that Milly's love begins to blossom. Repeating her conversation with Mrs. Condrip to Mrs. Stringham, Milly speaks "with an almost unprecedented approach to sharpness; as if Mrs. Condrip had been rather specially disconcerting. Yet never so much as just of late had Mrs. Stringham seen her companion as exalted, and by the very play of something within, into a vague golden air that left irritation below." When Mrs. Stringham asks what Mrs. Condrip has against Densher, Milly replies romantically, "It's the state of his fortunes. . . . He's as poor, she calls it, as 'poverty'" (*Wings* 154). At this point, Milly's earlier romantic interest in Densher is heightened by the activation

---

33. Frederick A. Olafson, "Moral Relationships in the Fiction of Henry James," *Ethics* 98 (1988): 303; Wyschogrod, *Saints and Postmodernism*, p. 42.

of her sympathetic imagination. She begins to think of Densher not simply as the handsome, clever journalist she met in New York, but as a fellow sufferer, a victim not only of limited means, but of unrequited love — precisely the two needs that she herself might provide for. Her image of the suffering Densher presupposes, of course, that Kate does not return his love, a pretense that Milly refuses to doubt, or at least to admit that she doubts, for the better part of the novel. "I don't think Mrs. Condrip imagines *she's* in love," Milly insists to Mrs. Stringham. "If she did care Mrs. Condrip would have told me" (*Wings* 160). Even when Lord Mark finally tells her that she is mistaken — which is, significantly, the last time James lets us enter Milly's consciousness — she responds by defending Kate's veracity and welcoming Densher in his presence.

In the last three books of the novel, the focus shifts to Densher's guilty conscience and gradual moral transformation. The latter begins with his decision, after Milly refuses to see him following Lord Mark's second visit, to remain in Venice as "proof of his not having stayed for the thing Kate had named" — that is, marrying Milly for her money (*Wings* 416). Later, Kate informs Densher that Milly had convinced Lord Mark "that it was *her* you loved," thereby preserving the secret of their engagement (*Wings* 496). But Densher does not yet know this when Milly asks to see him once more before sending him away forever. While James never reveals what took place at this last interview before Milly's death — as though the central scene of the novel were too sacred for representation — he later observes that Densher "had been, to his recovered sense, forgiven, dedicated, blessed" (*Wings* 469). But he recovers this sense only in retrospect, after Kate has, with her usual shrewd grasp of Milly's character, explained to him that "she never wanted the truth [about our engagement]. . . . She wanted *you*. She would have taken from you what you could give her, and been glad of it even if she had known it false" (*Wings* 457). What Milly wanted, in fact, was Densher's *happiness*, as well as Kate's, and Aunt Maud's, and even Lord Mark's. That is why she leaves him a bequest that will enable him to marry Kate with her aunt's approval — and also, perhaps, why she dies.

Densher's moral transformation is completed on Christmas, the day of his decision, "consecrated" by his attending mass, to surrender to Kate the unopened letter in which Milly has announced her posthumous gift.

As it happens, Kate is spending Christmas not at her aunt's mansion, where Lord Mark is waiting for her, but at Mrs. Condrip's tenement, where her spendthrift father has taken refuge — a vivid reminder of the equally unpleasant alternatives that dominate Kate's life. When Kate responds by tossing the still unopened letter into the fire with the words, "You'll have it all from New York," Densher knows what he must do: set her free from her obligation to him (*Wings* 500). On the one hand, he has witnessed firsthand the domestic tragedy that has led her to covet Milly's fortune. On the other hand, he has concluded that he can no longer marry her on the basis of such ill-gotten gain. What he offers Kate, therefore, is a choice: either to marry him and renounce the money, or to accept it from him as a parting sacrifice. When she tells him that the only thing that can save him from her choice of Milly's money is "your word of honour that you're not in love with her memory," he is unable to give it (*Wings* 512). With the nurture of his spiritual love for Milly, his carnal love for Kate has grown impotent.

How does James intend for us to respond to Milly's canonization? For his brother William, it was the social fruits of saintliness — its contribution to liberal society — that constituted its human value. If the social fruits of Milly's life and death are a fair indication, the same was true for Henry. Admittedly, *Wings* is not a generic social novel in the sense that *The Bostonians* and *The Princess Cassamassima* are. But it is a novel in which, as Edith Wyschogrod observes, "the effects of saintly action" are "socially manifested," inasmuch as it "illustrates the influence of altruistic action on moral self-interpretation and practice."[34] Wyschogrod is referring, of course, to Milly's effect on Densher, who is morally redeemed by her exemplary love for him. But her love for Kate, who is not redeemed, is just as important, if less effective. It is thanks to Milly's generosity, after all, that Kate receives the money that will enable her to escape the manipulation of her aunt and Lord Mark, and to satisfy the demands of her equally manipulative family. Of course "the arena of action" in *Wings*, Wyschogrod acknowledges, is "the sphere of life designated as private," and she rejects the view "that the spheres of individual and social morality are homologous." Milly is not to be classified with "political saints" like Gandhi, Mar-

---

34. Wyschograd, *Saints and Postmodernism*, p. 33.

tin Luther King, Jr., and Nelson Mandela, whose arena of action is "the political sphere." But Wyschogrod does grant that "the public and private spheres are bound up with each other sociologically and culturally," an assumption that, presumably, makes the "interpersonal context" of the action in *Wings* relevant to social as well as individual morality.[35]

If *The Wings of the Dove* is indeed a canonical narrative of liberal saintliness, we should expect to find in it expressions of liberal social values as well as implications for liberal society. One such implication, clearly, is the danger of manipulative relations that social mobility and freethinking entail. By turning the other cheek to her London "friends," Milly stands as a reminder that money and personal liberty need not entail cynicism and "strategic" action. As for Densher, his veneration of Milly might seem a purely personal act of atonement with no social significance. But it is important to see that the choice he feels obliged to offer Kate — either to marry him or to take Milly's money — is predicated on two of the central values of liberal society: freedom of conscience and material well-being. On the one hand, Densher must be free to act according to the dictates of his conscience, namely, by renouncing Milly's money. On the other hand, he knows that Kate cannot help her family, let alone live the beautiful life to which she is so perfectly suited, without the means to do so.

This, for James, is a tragic choice; it is not what Milly intended, any more than she meant Densher to fall in love with her memory. But tragic choices are, as Martha Nussbaum has insisted, as inevitable in the moral life as they are in James's fiction.[36] This conclusion may not sit well with Nussbaum's own social democratic perfectionism, but it certainly accords with the experience of liberal society, whose saints, from Abraham Lincoln to Martin Luther King, Jr., tend to be marked by tragedy. That, in fact, may be the primary reason why liberalism needs its saints: to remind us of the moral limits of society even as they point beyond them.

---

35. Wyschograd, *Saints and Postmodernism*, pp. 150-55, 42-43.

36. Martha Nussbaum, *Love's Knowledge: Essays in Literature and Philosophy* (New York: Oxford University Press, 1990), pp. 134-38.

# A Homemade Heaven:
# Modernist Poetry and the Social Gospel

*Gail McDonald*

"'With a tear for the dark past, turn we then to the dazzling future, and, veiling our eyes, press forward. The long and weary winter of the race is ended, Its summer has begun. Humanity has burst the chrysalis. The heavens are before it.'"

"Mister Barton's Sermon,"
in Edward Bellamy's *Looking Backward*

Le paradis n'est pas artificiel,
L'enfer non plus.

Ezra Pound, Canto 76

*we know no rule*
*of procedure,*
*we are voyagers, discoverers*
*of the not-known,*
*the unrecorded;*
*we have no map;*
*possibly we will reach haven,*
*heaven.*

H. D., section 43, *The Walls Do Not Fall*

Where is the wisdom we have lost in knowledge?
Where is the knowledge we have lost in information?
The cycles of heaven in twenty centuries
Bring us farther from GOD and nearer to the Dust.

T. S. Eliot, Chorus I, "The Rock"

THE TITLE of this essay, "A Homemade Heaven," alludes to Hugh Kenner's book *A Homemade World*, my revision acknowledging my debt to and divergence from Kenner's assessment of the peculiarly American elements of American modernism. Kenner creates a portrait of the American artist as craftsman, inventor, and tinkerer in the medium of language at a time when "the very question gets raised, what the written word may be good for."[1] No essay on modernism will ever stray far from that question, I suspect, no matter how thoroughly continuing scholarship complicates our understanding of what modernism was. But I want here to shift the emphasis in Kenner's statement slightly — off the word "word" and onto the word "good," to ask what the *good* was and what and whom it might be *good for*. Inevitably, that question too will lead back to the word or Word.[2]

The American social gospel movement of the late nineteenth and early twentieth centuries was a renovation project with important links to that other project of "making it new" — literary modernism. In both undertakings, what was at stake was nothing less than the world, imagined as it could be and might become. After a review of the social gospel and its aims, I will turn to the poetry of Ezra Pound, H. D., and T. S. Eliot to consider how the tenets and practices of the social gospel are made manifest in their writings and, additionally, how their poetry may be seen as a critique of the movement. Pound was born in 1885, H. D. in 1886, Eliot in 1888. All were the children of decent, dutiful citizens who were churchgoers and "do-gooders." Homer and Isabel Pound, Presbyterians, left their suburban home to work in the slums of Philadelphia. H. D.

1. Hugh Kenner, *A Homemade World: The American Modernist Writers* (New York: Knopf, 1974), p. xviii.

2. That the two may be connected in the minds of the modern poet is evidenced in, for example, W. B. Yeats's line, "Words alone are certain good."

spent her childhood in Bethlehem, Pennsylvania, a Moravian community. Eliot's paternal grandfather was a Unitarian minister crucial to the development of St. Louis's spiritual and educational life; his accomplishments were celebrated by the poet's mother, Charlotte, who impressed upon her children the exemplary life led by their grandfather by writing his biography, and who herself engaged in considerable community service. The childhoods and young adulthoods of the poets coincided with the flourishing of the social gospel in America. Because all three came from religious families and all three were schooled in the doctrine of service to the less privileged, the ideology of the social gospel provides an illuminating context for their ideas of the sacred, the religious attitudes of their poetry, and their faith in art as a means of social reform.

American culture of the 1880s and 1890s is a crucial and inadequately investigated component of what made the high modernists modern. These years comprise the childhoods of major American modernists and thus the era is, at minimum, of biographical interest. But there are other compelling reasons to consider the turn of the last century as an entryway to the American literary works normally labeled "modernist." To consider the topics of public discourse in the so-called Gilded Age is to encounter a table of contents for the discontents of modernism: the redefinition of workmanship in Taylorized factories; corruption, waste, and greed in high places that undermined the reliability of authority figures; the vacuity of mass culture; movement to reform education, penal systems, and urban housing; New Women seeking suffrage and other liberties; the professionalization of previously unregulated occupations; nativist fear and loathing of the immigrant "other"; anxiety and illness surrounding the integrity of the self — everywhere a sense that change, big change, was imminent.

Religious belief was not exempt from this ferment and change. Nor was it, however, inconsequential or merely "lost," as standard narratives of modernity often suggest. The bromide many of us picked up in a first introduction to Victorian literature, usually via Matthew Arnold's "Dover Beach" — i.e., people lost their faith because of Darwin's findings, and science created the crisis of belief — oversimplifies the cultural shift. Precisely because such clichés still govern our thinking, the loss of religious belief is too often taken for granted when we speak of modernism.

But just as feminist scholarship has amply illustrated how much we miss when we accept what goes without saying about gender, so too can scholarly attention to religious cultures expose the inadequacy of the phrase "loss of belief" for describing the varieties of faith that writers in the modern period experienced or sought or wrote about.

## The Social Gospel

What then was the social gospel and what does it have to do with American modernism? Robert T. Handy notes that the phrase "social gospel" was not in common use until after 1900, the label more widely used prior to that being "social Christianity."[3] By the time the term did come into frequent use, it was primarily associated with "Progressive Social Christianity," a movement that occupied a middle position between conservative and radical Christian reform movements. These distinctions mattered very much to Protestant congregations: this was a period of progressive reform, to be sure, but also an era of labor riots, anarchists carrying dynamite, and other forms of violent protest that made the comfortable uncomfortable.[4] Religious conservatives continued to emphasize individualism, free will, and personal responsibility, and to distance themselves from social determinism. Radicals believed change would come not through the repentance of individuals but through the rejection or dramatic revision of existing social and economic institutions. These distinctions, though vital to the Protestant debate, are less important for my purposes than the larger principles that united church-based reform across this fifty-year period. First, the social gospel was a set of commitments originating in the Protestant churches and seminaries. Second, the movement was both a product of, and a contributor to, the larger socio-political projects of American Progressivism. Third, like Progressivism, the social gospel was a response to

3. Robert T. Handy, ed., introduction to *The Social Gospel in America, 1870-1920* (New York: Oxford University Press, 1966), p. 5.

4. "The 1880s witnessed almost ten thousand strikes and lockouts; close to 700,000 workers went out in 1886 alone, the year of the 'Great Upheaval.'" Alan Trachtenberg, *The Incorporation of America: Culture and Society in the Gilded Age* (New York: Hill and Wang, 1982), p. 89.

urbanization and industrialization, a recognition that earlier models of self-reliance were deficient as character templates for the factory worker or the urban slum-dweller. Christian activism focused on assisting impoverished and otherwise disenfranchised city residents and supporting safer working conditions and reasonable pay for blue-collar workers, many of them recent immigrants. Handy summarizes the main emphases of the movement as follows: 1) "a conviction that the social principles of the historical Jesus could serve as reliable guides for both individual and social life in any age"; 2) "stress on the immanence of God, the goodness and worth of man, and the coming kingdom of God on earth."[5]

This "coming kingdom of God on earth" warrants special note, for it was understood that this "coming" need not await Christ's Second Coming. The kingdom could exist *on earth,* and possibly quite soon. Faith in human reason and the efficacy of education, confidence in humanity's ability to act in an enlightened manner, and optimism that material progress presaged spiritual progress meant that, as Handy comments, "the whole movement had something of a utopian cast."

Though similar schools of thought in England also motivated reform, this utopianism has an American stamp. Embedded in social gospel doctrine are convictions certainly traceable to the American Transcendentalists and, to a certain degree, even to the Puritans. Nowhere in Jonathan Edwards will we find reference to the fundamental goodness of man, to be sure, but we will find in John Winthrop and elsewhere the notion that America shall be the city on a hill or New Jerusalem, a beacon to the nations.[6] The sense of being charged with the special task of creating God's earthly kingdom pervades Puritan historiography. This is the newness of the New World, the errand into the wilderness. The Gilded Age seems to have been particularly enamored of the notion of model cities. The most famous example is perhaps the one least real: the immense plaster-construction called the White City at the Columbian Exposition of 1893. One might also point to corporation-sponsored cities like Pull-

5. Handy, *Social Gospel,* p. 10.

6. See "A Model of Christian Charity": "For we must consider that we shall be as a city upon a hill, the eyes of all people are upon us." Reprinted in *Pragmatism and Religion: Classical Sources and Original Essays,* ed. Stuart Rosenbaum (Urbana, Ill.: University of Illinois Press, 2003), p. 23.

man, Illinois, or to camp-style cities set up for Chautauqua programs in the summertime.[7]

A second principle of the social gospel, the fundamental goodness of man, was also a tenet of Transcendentalism, a foundation of Emerson's exhortation to self-reliance. Social gospelers could no longer conceive of self-reliance in strictly Emersonian terms, as I have indicated, but they could and did hold as an article of faith that humanity, because of its inner divinity, could be educated to recognize the good.[8] Such recognition would enable individuals to see that their personal interests were served by the good of the whole, thereby preparing the believer to embrace what Edward Bellamy, the author of the widely influential utopian novel *Looking Backward* (1888), called "the religion of solidarity."[9] Finally, the optimism and enthusiasm that pervades the rhetoric of social gospelers has a decidedly Yankee accent: *Let's roll up our sleeves and pull together. Can do!* The speech of a character in another utopian novel of the era is typical of the optimistic mood. In Bradford Peck's amusingly titled *The World a Department Store* (1900), Mr. Browning explains to Mr. Brantford how admirably the system formerly used to organize department stores has been adapted to society as a whole: "From this high grade of cooperative commercial life was the department-store system extended to all by the simple removal of the roof and the walls. In . . . our present Cooperative Association, we have what you now see, 'the World's Department Store' . . . so that we now enjoy a true 'heavenly' existence in the most beautiful world that has ever been made known to any of us."[10] In these and other

---

7. For treatment of the symbolic and real cities of this era, see James B. Gilbert, *Perfect Cities: Chicago's Utopias of 1893* (Chicago: University of Chicago Press, 1991); Carl S. Smith, *Urban Disorder and the Shape of Belief* (Chicago: University of Chicago Press, 1991); Robert Wiebe, *The Search for Order, 1877-1920* (New York: Hill and Wang, 1967); and Dolores Hayden, *Seven American Utopias: Landscape, Dwellings, and Towns, 1790-1940* (Cambridge: MIT Press, 1976).

8. I treat Pound's and Eliot's attitudes toward human educability at length in *Learning to Be Modern: Pound, Eliot, and the Modern University* (Oxford: Clarendon Press, 1993).

9. For a succinct analysis of Bellamy's thought, see Cecilia Tichi's introduction to *Looking Backward: 2000-1887* (New York: Penguin, 1982), pp. 7-27.

10. Bradford Peck, *The World a Department Store* (1900; repr. New York: Arno, 1971), pp. 242-43.

novels espousing social gospel philosophy, humanity's perfectibility is neither theoretical nor deferred until some misty future.

The social gospel movement attained its greatest influence in the 1890s, diminishing after the First World War. One indication of its effect on Americans (even those not specifically declared as affiliates of the movement) was the popularity of novels like Bellamy's *Looking Backward* and Charles Sheldon's *In His Steps* (1896), both of which were best sellers. In 1890, there were 162 Bellamy clubs in 27 states. Sheldon's famous phrase "What would Jesus do?" has proved so sturdy that "WWJD" now appears as a logo on t-shirts and bracelets worn by evangelical teenagers. Inspired by fiction and one another's fervor, Christians banded together to take action in groups: the Men and Religion Forward Movement, the Sunday Schools Movement, the Student Volunteer Movement, and the Laymen's Missionary Movement attest to the vitality of the social gospel. The consensus among historians of the movement is that the popularity of social gospel activity waned during the twenties and thirties and by the 1940s the social gospel was no longer a notable force in American culture. But the residual effects on American culture were long-lived. In 1935 the philosopher John Dewey and the historian Charles Beard, asked for the most influential books of the previous half-century, both named *Looking Backward* second only to *Das Kapital*.[11]

After the heyday had ended, the Protestant churches, especially those in urban areas of the Northeast, did not cease to attend to the physical and social needs of their neighborhoods. Nor did the churchmen retreat to their studies and refuse to speak of matters outside the confines of church walls. The ideological impress of the social gospel remained visible in the broader culture, too, as the religious historian Susan Curtis demonstrates in *A Consuming Faith: The Social Gospel and Modern American Culture*. Viewing the social gospel in relation to progressive politics, war, and the emergence of consumer culture, Curtis argues that by 1920 its effects were evident in several domains outside the church: 1) a redefined work ethic; 2) a redefined model of the family; 3) progressive politics; and 4) adoption of commercial idiom and images

11. Paul T. Phillips, *A Kingdom on Earth: Anglo-American Social Christianity 1880-1940* (University Park: Pennsylvania State University Press, 1996), p. 126.

by the churches.[12] These transformations, which I will first consider individually, also made a difference in modernist poetics.

The artisan who fashions a product from start to finish and then signs it has a different relationship to work and a different self-image than an assembly-line laborer whose movements have been measured and calibrated for efficiency and who remains either nameless or is designated Inspector 372. In the early twentieth century, the satisfaction of a job well done and of labor joyfully dedicated to God came to seem entirely unconvincing as outcomes of such labor. A worker's sense of dignity is further compromised by filthy surroundings and the recognition that, if profit margins are the sole determinant of quality, the product cannot be other than shoddy. As Walter Rauschenbusch, a leading spokesman for the social gospel, noted in *Christianity and the Social Crisis,* "The making of such cotton or wooden lies must react on the morals of every man that handles them."[13] Social gospel strategies devised to alter this grim scenario included shorter workdays, improved working conditions, and a redefinition of the relationship between individual and occupation.[14] This last aim required convincing workers that their jobs, no matter how menial, were essential to the Big Picture; they must see themselves as team-carpenters in the building of heaven on earth. Just as the ground of salvation had been shifted from the personal to the social, so too was one's work now to be understood as part of a larger and more glorious scheme. We may compare this notion to the "industrial army" that runs Bellamy's utopia. How the assignments are made, who decides what the projects shall be — these are left unexplained. But we are to understand that every person accepts happily the job designated as suitable.

Ann Douglas argues in *The Feminization of American Culture* that in the course of the early to mid-nineteenth century, the world of morals, high culture, and education, in and outside the churches, increasingly be-

12. Susan Curtis, *A Consuming Faith: The Social Gospel and Modern American Culture* (Baltimore: Johns Hopkins University Press, 1991).

13. Walter Rauschenbusch, *Christianity and the Social Crisis* (New York: Macmillan, 1907), p. 234.

14. The many rhetorical and melodic similarities between labor movement songs and hymns are matters of some interest but would form too long a digression here.

came the responsibility of women.[15] In one sense, of course, this is a predictable outcome of the "separate spheres" arrangement that left the worlds of business and politics to men (who were permitted to get their hands dirty) and the worlds of home, children, and the softer arts (the white-gloved pursuits of religion and poetry included) to the women. Curtis's description of the companionate family picks up where Douglas leaves off.[16] In her analysis of post–Civil War culture, she asserts that the increasing emphasis on social cooperation also permits a less hierarchical model for family life. The image of the tyrannical Victorian paterfamilias is gradually replaced by the image of the Father as Friend to his children. Clearly, such a redefinition of authority has implications outside family life, not least in the understanding of the relationship between God and the child of God. By analogy, an angry and unappeasable Old Testament God metamorphoses into a benevolent parent who trusts his children to know and do what is good. If God as Angry Parent emphasizes the divine at the expense of the human, the gentler God poses an opposite risk: that the divine will be seen as merely human — or worse, so gentle as to be effeminate. Not surprisingly, then, as the skies became friendlier (to adapt Wallace Stevens's phrase), there emerged a complementary insistence on the strength and virility of God's son, lest Jesus be viewed merely, in the words of Gregory Wolfe, as a "superior social worker."[17] Hence we have in the first decades of the twentieth century a rash of novels portraying Jesus as a courageous reformer and muscular working man.[18] What lies beneath these negotiations of family and gender roles is an emerging sense that the standard hierarchies of father-child, boss-worker, teacher-student, and master-apprentice were inadequate to the increasingly corporate and managerial structures it took to organize American life.

15. Ann Douglas, *The Feminization of American Culture* (New York: Knopf, 1977).

16. Curtis, *Consuming Faith*, pp. 87-88.

17. The line appears in Stevens's "Sunday Morning": "The sky will be much friendlier then than now / A part of labor and a part of pain, / And next in glory to enduring love, / Not this dividing and indifferent blue." Gregory Wolfe discusses this social worker Jesus in "Religious Humanism: A Manifesto," *Image: A Journal of the Arts and Religion* 16 (Summer 1997): 1-5.

18. Examples of the revised Jesus appear in Thomas DeWitt Talmage's *From Manger to Throne* (1890), Bouck White's *The Call of the Carpenter* (1911), and Harry Emerson Fosdick's *The Manhood of the Master* (1913).

There is not space in an essay of this length to trace the manifold ways that liberal Christian thought and reform activity coincided with progressive politics. I want to emphasize only one point of intersection. The social gospel led Christians to expect more from their churches — more social services, more intervention in family life, a more vocal public presence. Contemporary commentators noted that, whereas twenty years earlier the topic of a church's social responsibility would have been a rare subject for a sermon, by the 1890s it had become customary for social issues to be discussed from the pulpit, analyzed in Christian magazines, and debated in regional and national meetings of various denominations. Similarly, progressive politics led American citizens to expect more from their government: enforcement of safer working conditions, protection of children from exploitation, inspection of food and drugs. Social life was increasingly viewed as too complex to be managed at any but the highest levels. Americans looked to a managerial class and to "experts" for aid and advice. As church and state pursued similar reforms, the boundary between the sacred and the secular blurred.

The cooperation of the two is strikingly evident in the ways that social gospel ministers, especially after the initial excitement of the movement had passed, employed popular culture and the language of advertising to "sell" the faith. Curtis cites the example of a Methodist Episcopal Church in Iowa that boasted a "full lineup" of programs and services, its minister assuring potential members of the best "sermon, music, athletics, social services, education and a deep spirituality that money can buy."[19] Like the more sophisticated of the settlement houses (Hull House in Chicago, for example), the biggest and most ambitious churches sought to be full-service operations, small "cities" with schools, restaurants, arts, and sports. The Iowa church even offered free embalming for funerals. The pitch for the spiritual life had to be made loudly, even vulgarly, to be heard above the carnival of choices in popular culture. It was as if ministers had to become barkers for the White City in order to lure customers away from the exotic delights of the Midway.

19. Curtis, *Consuming Faith*, p. 237.

*Gail McDonald*

## Three Modernist Poets

Imagine the poet who has assimilated the works and plans of the social gospel in discussion around her parents' dinner table or in a bull session in his dormitory room or over a tea table in Boston. The conversation might include questions about the efficacy of activism on behalf of social justice, debate about the inherent goodness or sinfulness of humanity, the evidence or lack thereof of God's presence in an increasingly demystified physical world. Someone would assert the exceptionalism of the United States, its special role as beacon to the nations, and another might curl a lip at such innocence or arrogance. Others might offer excited declarations about the possibility of real change happening in their own lifetime. In talk of careers, a young person might wonder how to distinguish herself as an individual nowadays. The assembled would recognize the youthful desire to flout authority, and yet the young would express their uncertainty about what authority needed most to be flouted. Is one's self the final arbiter? Who is it one works to please now? Is life to be merely the exercise of duty? And duty to whom? What would one have to do to go to hell? And if we are inherently good, what need is there for hell? In any case, is anyone ever solely to blame? Isn't all sin finally society's sin? And, conversely, supposing the kingdom of God were now here on earth, what would it be like? Would we place the same emphasis on money and creature comforts? Would people want to read poetry?

These imaginary scenarios are offered as a synopsis of the manifestos, editorial policy statements, essays, and letters in which "les jeunes," as Ezra Pound liked to call them, expressed their hope and their trepidation about the world they had inherited, the world they must either accept or try to change. Curtis nicely summarizes the contradictory features of that legacy:

> Much of the admirable strength of twentieth-century American culture — its commitments to activism in behalf of freedom, egalitarianism, social justice, and social unity — can be traced to the influence of the social gospel. But it can also be argued that the same social and moral movement furthered less welcome qualities of twentieth-century American culture — a vacuous mass culture; extreme fears of

cultural, intellectual, and political decline in the international arena; . . . and pervasive materialism.[20]

Such welcome and unwelcome things at once. Not every modern American poet would attempt to reconcile them but many of the greatest did. Stevens's cure for the "malady of the quotidian" would be poetry itself: "Exceeding music must take the place / of empty heaven and its hymns." For Stevens there were compensations, albeit bittersweet ones, in the knowledge that mankind is "unsponsored, free" and that poetry "is the only possible heaven."[21] But for other poets this demystification of the sacred was unsatisfactory: "To explain grace requires," as Marianne Moore writes in "The Pangolin," "a curious hand."[22]

For Pound, H. D., and Eliot, such explanation would sustain their poetic careers, as they strove to know and articulate what is, as Georges Bataille writes, "situated at the boundary of that which escapes cohesion."[23] Pound would declare, even at the last, that "it coheres all right / even if my notes do not cohere" (Canto 116).[24] What is the antecedent of "it"? He ostensibly refers to the refractory disorder of the *Cantos,* but I would argue that he has a larger failure in view. What coheres is a vision of the light, a vision of what might be; his notes are the sometimes-incoherent attempts to ground that vision. Of the three poets, Pound most nearly resembles the utopian novelists in his faith that a terrestrial paradise need not be artificial, a painted scene. Of the three poets, only Pound could be described as an activist in the way that a social gospeler would understand the term. He was an activist on behalf of poetry, creating slogans, raising money, bullying editors, promoting careers, and expressing his often-belligerent opinion that *usura* was the destroyer of

20. Curtis, *Consuming Faith*, p. 13.

21. Quotations are from "The Man Whose Pharynx Was Bad," "The Man with the Blue Guitar," "Sunday Morning." All poems from *The Collected Poems of Wallace Stevens* (New York: Penguin, 1981), pp. 96, 165, 66.

22. Marianne Moore, *The Complete Poems of Marianne Moore* (New York: Penguin Books, 1981).

23. Georges Bataille, *Theory of Religion,* trans. Robert Hurley (New York: Zone, 1989), p. 10.

24. All references are to Ezra Pound, *The Cantos* (1970; repr. New York: New Directions, 1986); hereafter cited by canto number within the text.

beauty. From the thirties until the end of the Second World War, his activism took the form of radio broadcasts, broadsides, and generalized, grotesquely misguided attacks on bankers, Jews, the American educational system, and other "enemies" of his conceptions of the good, true, and beautiful. His targets may appear to be far different from those of the social gospel faithful. Yet he shared their fervor to make things new, their concern for just government, their sense that the gifted had an obligation to serve mankind. Further, he shared the view that inequities traceable to greed were observable throughout human history. The job of the enlightened was to study these "luminous details" and moral exempla and to promulgate their findings.

H. D.'s social conscience and her inheritance of social gospel ideals are best expressed through her agonized inquiries into the causes of war. She confessed a disinclination to roll bandages or to perform the other sort of good works expected of a woman of her class in wartime. But she was indefatigable in pursuing the causes of evil. These took the form of psychoanalysis with Freud, visions and dreams revisited obsessively in her writing, occult studies of many sorts (from astrology to the Eleusinian mysteries), and the reading and rewriting of myth and ancient histories, particularly those of Greece and Egypt. At once Transcendentalist and Progressive, H. D.'s inclination was to look within for both the causes of and the solutions to violence and tyranny. As Margaret Fuller had demanded, she knew she must be a unit before she could enter a union, must be herself before she could be a citizen of the world. The personal costs of war — a brother killed in France, a stillborn child, breakdowns of physical and mental health, a failed marriage — were significant for H. D. not only as personal sufferings but also as signs of a fallen world. Her contribution to a terrestrial paradise must therefore be measured in abstract terms, not in projects achieved. She sought to understand in her own body and in the imagined bodies of Helen, Isis, the Bona Dea, and other mythical women how the causes of war might be understood as a problem of gender: her attempt, as she put it, to reconcile "my father's science and my mother's art."[25]

T. S. Eliot, a more elusive and reticent figure than either Pound or

25. H. D., *Tribute to Freud,* rev. ed. (1974; repr. Manchester: Carcanet, 1985), p. 145.

H. D., is predictably harder to categorize. Certainly as drawn to mysticism as H. D., he would nevertheless have seen most of her studies as unorthodox and therefore either risible (think of Madame Sosostris) or dangerous (think of his view of Blake's mysticism).[26] Throughout his editorship of the *Criterion* and especially after his public conversion to Anglicanism in 1927, he took an active interest in public affairs and published frequently on the subject of religion. Notable examples include *Christianity and Culture* and the controversial *After Strange Gods*. He was an influential editor at Faber and Faber, a sought-after speaker on both literary and social topics, and an air raid warden during the Second World War. Though the evidence suggests that he was as busy as and more effective in social action than Pound, he remained uncertain of the value of such activity. He did not share Pound's assurance that he could, to borrow Henry Adams's phrase, "solve the universe."[27] Quite early in his career, well before his public embrace of Christianity, he wryly observed, "Certain saints found the following of Christ very hard but modern methods have facilitated everything."[28] Eliot's skepticism about progress made him a reluctant Progressive.

If belief in the social gospel means working in a soup kitchen or teaching English to immigrants, the three poets were poor disciples. Only Eliot seemed inclined toward such duties; he is also the only one to embrace orthodox Christianity. However, if we understand social gospel reform as a desire not just to revise the role of the church in society but to revise society itself, Pound and H. D. begin to look more like the true inheritors. "Do I wish myself, in the deepest unconscious or subconscious layers of my being, to be the founder of a new religion?" H. D. wrote in *Tribute to Freud*.[29] And Pound joked (seriously) that he had "a curious letch to start a new civilization."[30] Even the more decorous Eliot al-

26. References here are to *The Waste Land* in *The Complete Poems and Plays, 1909-1950* (New York: Harcourt, 1952) and to "William Blake," in *Selected Essays* (1932; repr. New York: Harcourt, 1950); references to the poems hereafter cited in the text as *Complete*.

27. "Boston had solved the universe." Henry Adams, *The Education of Henry Adams* (1918; repr. Boston: Houghton, 1961), p. 34.

28. T. S. Eliot, review of *Conscience and Christ: Six Lectures on Christian Ethics*, by Hastings Rashdall, *International Journal of Ethics* 27 (1916): 112.

29. H. D., *Tribute to Freud*, p. 43.

30. Ezra Pound to Katsue Kitasono, *The Selected Letters of Ezra Pound, 1909-1965*, ed. D. D. Paige (New York: New Directions, 1971), p. 346.

lowed himself to envisage "a new type of intellectual, combining the intellectual and the devotional," but he found it hard to imagine any earthly system that would be ideal and was drawn to no plan that might have eliminated moral struggle.[31]

Of the three, Eliot, the most conventionally religious, is paradoxically the least endowed with missionary zeal. But all three writers are inclined to think in cosmic terms and to see their poetry as contributing to a worthy cause, however differently articulated. In this regard, they inherit the Gilded Age ideology that Martha Banta has described as "the culture of management, densely populated by intelligent, determined individuals who wished to explain everything that had to be explained in order to achieve a . . . useful universe and society." "There is," she writes, "something about being the person charged with uncovering 'the one true theory' that excites the imaginations of the best and the worst of us."[32] This desire for an ordered whole, for aesthetic harmony that reflects spiritual and ethical harmony, is the vision uniting the social gospelers and the modern poets. All three poets were driven by what Stevens called the "blessed rage for order" ("The Idea of Order at Key West"). We should note in this quotation not only "rage" and "order," words used disparagingly about the politics of Pound and Eliot particularly, but also the word "blessed," a word rarely associated with high modernism.

In their earliest writings H. D. and Pound were both drawn to the myth of Isis and Osiris. One of Pound's lengthiest statements of his attitudes toward history, literature, and the role of the artist is the early serialized essay "I Gather the Limbs of Osiris" published in 1911-12. And H. D. turned repeatedly to the figure of Isis. In repeating this story, the two poets expressed a powerful longing not just for order but for fusion, wholeness, and synthesis, figured in the reunification of the limbs of the male body and in the reunion of brother/sister and husband/wife. From H. D.'s *The Walls Do Not Fall:*

31. Eliot made this remark in a letter to Paul Elmer More (unpublished). On the development of Eliot's religious belief, see Ronald Schuchard, *Eliot's Dark Angel: Intersections of Life and Art* (New York: Oxford University Press, 1999).

32. Martha Banta, *Taylored Lives: Narrative Productions in the Age of Taylor, Veblen, and Ford* (Chicago: University of Chicago Press, 1993), p. 29. The impulse toward the unified field, we might say, found its literary-critical expression in the New Criticism.

. . . my thought
would cover deplorable gaps

in time, reveal the regrettable chasm
bridge that before-and-after schism

recover the secret of Isis
which is: there was One
in the beginning, Creator,
Fosterer, Begetter, the Same-forever. (section 40)

Eliot famously employed other versions of the fertility-myths in *The Waste Land*. Once past this poem of "fragments . . . shored against my ruins," however, he would increasingly invoke specifically Christian iconography to express the yearning for union with something larger and more glorious: "And the fire and the rose are one" (*Complete* 145).

The imaginary heavens or glimpses of heaven treated in Pound's, H. D.'s, and Eliot's poetry, like all pictures of paradise, reflect earthly desires. As William McClung explains in *The Architecture of Paradise*, the patterns are linked to the dimension of time:

> As a general pattern, it may be said that to the extent that Paradise is of the past, it is arcadian and open . . . ; to the extent that it is imagined to survive into the present (but in some obscure or inaccessible or forbidden spot), it is a secret garden walled or otherwise barred against man; to the extent that Paradise signifies the Paradise to come, it is urban and conspicuously fortified.[33]

McClung's exposition of paradisical designs is a lesson in both aesthetics and social planning, a reminder of the myriad ways that moral and physical beauty have historically seemed inextricable. The properties of imaginary heavens McClung outlines, such as ideal shape, hardness and brilliance of surface, great mass, and multiplication of units, unite the making of ideal cities with the making of art. Consider how easily these same terms might also be applied to the structure of long modern-

---

33. William A. McClung, *The Architecture of Paradise: Survivals of Eden and Jerusalem* (Berkeley: University of California Press, 1983), p. 19.

ist poems. And, of course, pastoral nostalgia, the walled garden, and the fortified city all make appearances in modernist poetry.

If we abstract Pound's design from the *Cantos,* his heaven on earth would be the terraced city of Ecbatana, overseen by multiple gods floating in an azure sky, lit at all times by stars or sunlight. The word "light" appears 144 times in the *Cantos.* The denizens of the terrestrial paradise would speak simply and frankly, observing always the method of "right naming," *le mot juste.* Such speech would be the unwobbling pivot, the axis of sincerity. A man would feel connected to his work in this world: he would sign it *Adamo me fecit,* as carvers once did their stonework in churches like St. Trophime (Canto 44). The populace would be well educated, particularly in principles of government, including self-government, culled from the wisest examples in world culture from Confucius to John Adams. Children would be taught the "luminous details" of history, those events, facts, and exemplary lives that enhance life in the present moment and contribute to a just society now. Aspiring artists would learn the arts by practicing them. Poets would be honored and recognized as "antennae of the race," tellers of the tale of the tribe, and preservers of cultural value, including that most treasurable commodity, the language.[34] Pound's heaven-on-earth would be founded on a Social Credit economy. Usury would be forbidden: "The temple is not for sale" (Canto 91). Both animals and people would enjoy excellent health. Fertility in all forms, agrarian, human, artistic, would be of highest value. The architecture would not be rococco; the bread would not be "of stale rags" (Canto 45). We gather from his earlier poem *Hugh Selwyn Mauberley* that plaster molds, pianolas, and other mechanized arts would be frowned upon. War would be unthinkable, there being "no / righteous / wars" (Canto 78). For those unwelcome in the kingdom, look to the Hell Cantos. For the beloved and desirable — "what thou lov'st well" — look to the Pisan Cantos.

H. D. would be welcome and, to a considerable extent, at home in Pound's pagan paradise, but her own blueprint for heaven included a more generous allowance for privacy, contemplation, time to "rededicate

---

34. A formulation Pound employed on many occasions. For one example, see "Murder by Capital," *Selected Prose, 1909-1965,* ed. William Cookson (New York: New Directions, 1973), p. 229.

our gifts to spiritual realism," and to recognize "sterile logic, trivial reason" for the limited instruments they are.[35] She is less inclined than Pound to enumerate undesirables, but like him she mines history for the exemplary lives and images that speak most emphatically of truth. Her history takes the form of the palimpsest, his the form of the "repeat," but they share the view that the repeats and layers will lead eventually to the final "bust thru from quotidien into 'divine or permanent world.'"[36] They believe in a kind of progress that Eliot doubts. H. D. recognizes that the scribe or writer is undervalued, even "pathetic" to a positivist culture, and she would alter the poet's status in her heaven of "jasper, beryl, and sapphire" (*Trilogy* 15, 33).

Like Pound, H. D. thinks of the poet as a mage, one initiated to the mysteries. The character of Kaspar, one of the magi, figures large in the final section of *Trilogy*, "The Flowering of the Rod." Because language commands more powerful magic, the Sword is inferior to the Word. On two counts, H. D.'s imagination of paradise, however, is far less "realistic" than Pound's. First, she is at home with, even delights in, the notion that reality is hieroglyphic. She desires to understand — but is not in the hurry that marks Pound's quest. Indeed she would reserve always some mystery to engage our wonder. While she happily mixes religious traditions, seeing in them all universal spiritual truths, her favored biblical text is, tellingly, "Revelation." For H. D. the most vital mode of activism is interpretation and re-interpretation. And this re-interpretation is the source of her other significant difference from Pound: in her paradise, terrestrial or otherwise, the spiritual status of the Bona Dea, the Lady, the Magdalene, will equal that of any male god. Indeed, in her view (as in her Moravian upbringing), the soul is *anima*, female. This shift is significant, so disorienting that she seems herself to be at a loss for words as she describes the appearance of the Lady, emphasizing what she is not: "but she wasn't hieratic, she wasn't frozen, / she wasn't very tall" (*Trilogy* 103). As she strives to unravel centuries of gendered speech and imagery, diffused as it is through the English language, she finds herself straining for

35. All references to the three poems of *Trilogy* are from H. D., *Trilogy* (New York: New Directions, 1998); hereafter cited in the text as *Trilogy*. These phrases appear on pp. 48, 40.

36. In a letter from Pound to his father, 1927. *Selected Letters*, p. 210.

the vocabulary to get at "the meaning that words hide" (*Trilogy* 53). Finally, while suffering is virtually absent from Pound's *Cantos* (with the exception of the Pisan Cantos), in H. D.'s work suffering is revelatory and redemptive. Suffering herself as she visits the bombsites of London, the speaker of *The Walls Do Not Fall* comes upon the charred tree that is nonetheless flowering. This image becomes central to H. D.'s sense of spiritual realism (*Trilogy* 82-87).

This insistence on the redemptive power of suffering is the point at which H. D.'s imagined paradise lightly touches the even more elusive paradise in Eliot's poetry. The few depictions of joy, brief and ephemeral, occur most often in a flower garden, walled, usually in the presence of a nameless but beloved woman. Beyond the garden is the intermittent laughter of children, the tinkling of a street piano, the sound of church bells. In other settings the odor of hyacinths, the smell of "wild thyme unseen" attest to something other than "the butt ends of my days and ways" that demoralize the speakers of Eliot's poems (*Complete* 136, 5). As his career proceeds, Eliot's poems grow more compassionate, his speakers more forgiving of their own absurdities and flaws, and the fellow feeling toward others more generous. The humility he strives for in both life and work is strikingly expressed in the third section of *Four Quartets:*

> For most of us, there is only the unattended
> Moment, the moment in and out of time,
> The distraction fit, lost in a shaft of sunlight,
> The wild thyme unseen, or the winter lightning
> Or the waterfall, or music heard so deeply
> That it is not heard at all, but you are the music
> While the music lasts. These are only hints and guesses,
> Hints followed by guesses; and the rest
> Is prayer, observance, discipline, thought, and action.
> The hint half guessed, the gift half understood, is Incarnation. (136)

The terms of difference between Pound's and Eliot's notions of heaven and hell are audible in Eliot's response to Pound's Hell Cantos: "Mr. Pound's Hell, for all its horrors, is a perfectly comfortable one for the modern mind to contemplate, and disturbing to no one's complacency: it is a Hell for the *other people.*"[37] A banker, an editor, a standard-setting literary critic, Eliot appears to be an active participant in the modern culture of management. But he was an uneasy manager. His chief disagreement with Pound in this regard — and it is a difference that prevented his imagining fully any form of utopia — is that he could not embrace meliorism. The optimistic view of progress and of mankind's essential goodness, tenets of the social gospel, were fundamental to what Eliot here disparagingly calls "the modern mind." I would argue that the refusal of a homemade heaven is apparent even in texts where he attempts to imagine a "Christian culture." The most passionate denial of the possibility of a terrestrial paradise appears in one of the choruses for "The Rock":

> The Word of the Lord came unto me, saying:
> O miserable cities of designing men,
> O wretched generation of enlightened men,
> Betrayed in the mazes of your ingenuities
>
> . . . . . . . . . . . . . . . . . . . . . . . . . . . . . .
>
> Though you have shelters and institutions . . .
> Or a house a little better than your neighbour's:
> When the Stranger says: "What is the meaning of this city?
> Do you huddle close together because you love each other?"
> What will you answer? "We all dwell together
> To make money from each other"? Or "This is a community"?
> And the Stranger will depart and return to the desert.
>
> (*Complete* 102, 103)

Unlike the "onward and upward" progressions that mark the most sanguine passages of Pound's and H. D.'s work, the circular patterns of Eliot's poetry are either futile (and thus despairing) or, particularly after his conversion, circular in such a way that the place returned to is now known "for the first time" (*Complete* 145). What differs most significantly in Eliot's conception of this life and the afterlife is the overwhelming presence of a powerful God — without whom, nothing. Jesus as social worker is not for him.

37. T. S. Eliot, *After Strange Gods: A Primer of Modern Heresy* (New York: Harcourt, Brace and Co., 1934), pp. 45-46.

I have sketched out ways that the two domains — social gospel reform and modern poetry — intersect beyond chronological coincidence. Both recognized and responded to a culture in which authority, self, work, professionalism, and the meanings of gender were shifting their foundations. Both suspected that the old, hierarchical modes of organization were growing obsolete. Both thought it not naïve to imagine that progress toward something better was achievable. Both found it hard to retain most people's attention without resort to the methods of consumer culture. Both are susceptible to accusations of superiority and smugness — the hazards of thinking one knows what's best for others. Paul Giles has studied the proposals for better worlds in the work of a number of high modernists (and he includes in this list both Pound and Eliot); "All of these fictive utopias," he argues, "were driven by a desire for social and religious replenishment, the urge to invent a secularized modernist *logos,* which would have the power of 'recreating God in the artists' image.'"[38]

Giles's description of the goals of high modernism seems consistent with much that was said and done in the name of the social gospel as well. The friendly church-woman visiting the newly arrived Italian mother in the slums intended to help the newcomer by making her more like her own middle-class and well-intentioned self; she also sought to strengthen her own faith through purposeful action. But was the intent always to recreate God in one's own image? This diagnosis of narcissism disallows a seeking *outside* the self that would not so smack of self-congratulation. For the social gospel faithful, the goal was *imitatio* — the modeling of their actions on Christ's. While we cannot attribute to the poets (excepting Eliot) so Christocentric a perspective, we can see a parallel form of *imitatio* in their focus on other great teachers, sages, artists, and artistic traditions of the past. The effort to make God (or the gods) new is an effort to retain the category of divinity in human thought, to keep the sacred alive and meaningful, to posit a world not utterly divorced from heaven, to make a heaven on earth according to exemplary models. Inevitably, in such an undertaking, energies were sometimes

38. Paul Giles, *American Catholic Arts and Fictions: Culture, Ideology, Aesthetics* (Cambridge: Cambridge University Press, 1992), pp. 122-23.

mischanneled and jobs botched. To focus solely on the errors is, however, to miss a crucial point: works for good and words for good assist the imagination of perfection. As Pound expresses it,

> This is not vanity.
>     Here error is all in the not done,
> all in the diffidence that faltered. (Canto 81)

# Religion and the Environmental Imagination in American Literature

*Lawrence Buell*

L ITERATURE, Religion, Environment, America.[1] Viewed one way, these terms interlock. Viewed another way, they wobble and pull apart. That doubleness is my central theme — especially the internal tensions. Full examination of the latter has been inhibited even while being partially enabled by the American Studies movement's critique of nature discourse as national ideology. That critique, briefly reviewed in Section 1, directs us, as Section 2 indicates, beyond its own limited agenda toward a more nuanced and cosmopolitan skepticism about the assumed convergence of the four domains. That in turn will set the stage for a fresh look, in Section 3, at the state and prospect of the relation between religious and environmental imagination in the United States today.

1. General Note: I am grateful to Robert Richardson, Jr., Grant Wacker, fellow members of the Pew Charitable Trusts–funded American Literature and Religion Seminar, the 2002-2003 fellows of the National Humanities Center, and the faculty and students of Wheaton College for their thoughtful comments on a previous version of this essay given in lecture form.

 This essay uses "religion" in a highly elastic sense, to comprehend civil religion and personal spirituality (both in life practice and in expressions of religious imagination) as well as religion in the sense of the history and theology of organized religious groups. "Environment" comprehends both the natural and the human-constructed — not that the two domains can be pried apart in practice. "American" is generally used here as a convenient and familiar synonym for "U.S.," though I call attention to the distinction and question the adequacy of conceiving environmental imagination in nation-bounded terms.

## National Destiny and the Mystique of Nature

All Americanists are familiar with the long tradition of linking national to natural, with religion as a ligature. The first Puritan colonists justified settlement on the authority of Genesis 1:28: "the whole earth is the lords Garden" lying in wait for "the sonnes of men" — the settlers rather than the aborigines, of course — to "replenish" and "subdue."[2] This was the start of the myth of the U.S. as a "virgin land" of infinite bounty and possibility, a myth that reached its peak in the mid-nineteenth century with the expansion of national territory to include the whole lower forty-eight states, coast to coast, and in the mid-twentieth century became a defining theme of first-wave American Studies from Henry Nash Smith to Leo Marx. Revision of their account from a more assertively anti-nationalist perspective, the seeds for which had already been sown in first-stage statements like Perry Miller's "Nature and the National Ego," then became a major theme of next-wave American Studies from Richard Slotkin to Myra Jehlen and Amy Kaplan, which crystallized what today stands as the orthodox grand narrative of U.S. settler culture history: from genocidal conquest to manifest destiny to post–Cold War imperium. According to this revisionary reading, the distinction between simple pastoral and complex contrarian pastoral for which Marx argued tended to get overridden and Virgin-Landism aggressively demystified as a settler-culture ideology of conquest.[3]

Common to both readings of British American settlement history, however, is recognition of the dream of U.S. national destiny as under-

2. John Winthrop, *Conclusions for the Plantation in New England* (1629), quoted in Roderick Nash, *Wilderness and the American Mind,* 3rd ed. (New Haven: Yale University Press, 1982), p. 31.

3. Henry Nash Smith, *Virgin Land: The American West as Symbol and Myth* (Cambridge: Harvard University Press, 1950); Leo Marx, *The Machine in the Garden: Technology and the Pastoral Ideal in America* (New York: Oxford University Press, 1964); Perry Miller, "Nature and the National Ego" (1955), in *Errand into the Wilderness* (Cambridge: Harvard University Press, 1956), pp. 204-16; Richard Slotkin, *Regeneration Through Violence* (Middletown: Wesleyan University Press, 1973); Myra Jehlen, *American Incarnation* (Cambridge: Harvard University Press, 1985); Amy Kaplan, "'Left Alone with America': The Absence of Empire in the Study of American Culture," in Kaplan and Donald Pease, eds., *The Cultures of U.S. Imperialism* (Durham: Duke University Press, 1993), pp. 3-21.

written by a mystique of American nature. As Miller long ago summed up, with a characteristically mordant irony that anticipates later revisionists more closely than New Americanists usually grant: "America can progress indefinitely into an expanding future without acquiring sinful delusions of grandeur simply because it is nestled in Nature, is instructed and guided by mountains, is chastened by waters."[4]

As this pronouncement suggests, no less significant than the emphasis American Studies scholarship has traditionally placed on the convergence of religion and environment in the national imagination is its alienated, disaffected reading of that synergy, especially since Slotkin. This prevailing and by no means groundless suspicion of the bad faith of nature discourse as a cover for settler expansionism has too often tempted the American Studies tradition to reduce religious and environmentalist motives to politics of culture, short-shrifting the possibility that they might be autonomous concerns, legitimate in their own right. On the other hand, American Studies' embedded skepticism also has the value of putting one on notice that our four signifiers do not line up as neatly as the stereotypes of nature's nation-talk have made it seem — indeed, in some respects even less well than has been recognized, as Section 2 will show in more detail.[5]

Americanist accounts of nature's nation discourse like Miller's draw heavily on the testimony of national literature, which to a marked extent has tended historically to associate its literary distinctiveness with U.S. landscapes of certain kinds and indeed even now to a considerable extent still does. The landmarks are familiar, including such particular natural "wonders" as Niagara Falls and the Grand Canyon and such characteristic landscape forms as the "wide open" spaces of the plains states. Popular culture as well as high culture, even today, is marked by a tendency to mysticize the "heartland" as the locus of national essence in defiance of the demographic facts — as if to identify essential U.S.-ness with some

---

4. Perry Miller, "The Romantic Dilemma in American Naturalism and the Concept of Nature" (1955), in *Nature's Nation* (Cambridge: Harvard University Press, 1967), p. 202.

5. I can imagine resistance to my lumping references to "the tradition," as if to conflate Marx and Slotkin, Miller and Kaplan, etc. Obviously the disagreements are at least as strong as the resemblances. My point is simply to underscore a shared skepticism toward mainstream nature discourse as self-justifying settler rhetoric.

imagined backcountry *omphalos* somewhere in the central plains, portions of which actually happen to be depopulating to the extent that a sizeable portion of the upper midwestern tier threatens to revert to a frontier condition in point of population density. Of course Americanist criticism recognizes variant emphases within the repertoire of environmental representation, such as the Jeffersonian-style agrarian vision of Willa Cather, Wendell Berry, and others; the more countercultural idealization of wilderness or wildness in such figures as Henry Thoreau, John Muir, and Robinson Jeffers; equivocating balancings of the two, as in James Fenimore Cooper and Ralph Waldo Emerson; and the representation of hinterland areas as a contact zone perceived differently according to gender and race, as again in Cooper's fiction, or as represented by the differences between (say) the writing of John Muir and Mary Austin or Edward Abbey and Terry Tempest Williams or Leslie Silko. Cutting across divergences in aesthetic practice and doctrinal orientation, however, is a tendency for land, nature, wilderness in the work of all these writers to get more or less invested with a certain mystique that partakes of the religious in a minimal, borderline sense (as in Cather and Jeffers and Abbey) if not in a more emphatically creedal or denominational sense (as in Berry). Of course for numerous other American environmental writers, religion is a side issue or a non-issue. One might easily discuss (say) the scene of clashing race and gender perspectives on natural environment during the mid-nineteenth century by focusing on Francis Parkman, Caroline Kirkland, and John Rollin Ridge without once mentioning the subject. But the sampling of names above is far from haphazard. Whether or not you grant religious concerns autonomous force or whether you read them as a stalking horse for something else, the pervasiveness of religious tropes and rhetoric in U.S. environmental writing is conspicuous and remarkable. The extent to which this pervasive religio-environmentalism can validly be considered a constructive cultural resource rather than as a source of cultural blindness or arrogance I shall take up in Section 3.

What I've indicated so far implies that essentialization of U.S.-ness as physical environment boils down only to identification of iconic or paradigmatic landscapes. That is often but by no means always true. To name just one alternative mode of thinking to which I shall return later on: various individual life forms have also been drafted into service as national symbols. Franklin proposed the wild turkey as the national icon. The revolutionary patriots brandished the rattlesnake. The republic opted for the bald eagle. The Treasury Department has promoted the bison as well as the eagle. Wetlands writers often prefer the beaver. Every state designates a state bird and a state flower, if not also a state animal.

Obviously not all of these hypostatizations bear a sense of the religious — or even of the literary. The choice of the chickadee as the state bird of Massachusetts was probably not arrived at by prayer or conjuration, nor has it inspired great spiritual or poetic flights. But broadly speaking such emblematic practices must be deemed ritual acts of collective imagination — or individual imagination in the case of Franklin's turkey and Melville's white whale. Always there is the potential for the emblems to get invested with a sense of sacred awe — as with the white whale, or the white pine, Henry Thoreau's favorite tree, which he saw both as a regional signifier and as a spiritual symbol. Hence his complaint when *Atlantic Monthly* editor James Russell Lowell suppressed his neopagan assertion that the white pine "is as immortal as I am, and perchance will go to as high a heaven, there to tower above me still."[6]

Perhaps Thoreau deserved what he got for so pugnaciously resisting mid-nineteenth-century consensus about the place of nonhumans in the great chain of being. But less polemical forms of literary pantheism were and remain mainstream. Faulkner's development of Old Ben in his novella "The Bear" as a symbol of the mystique of "the vanishing wilderness" of the Mississippi Delta region taps into an older and widespread national folkloric tradition that goes back at least a century.[7]

## Questioning the Connections

As I have already hinted, the synergy of religion, literature, environment, America as treated in critical and creative writing starts to fall apart the

6. Henry David Thoreau, "Chesuncook," in *The Maine Woods*, ed. Joseph Moldenhauer (Princeton: Princeton University Press, 1972), p. 122.

7. William Faulkner, quoted in *Faulkner in the University*, ed. Frederick L. Gwynn and Joseph L. Blotner (Charlottesville: University of Virginia Press, 1959), p. 280.

more closely one examines its underlying complications, of which I shall discuss six.

1. Literary representations of material nature, of nationness, of religious experience are not transparent windows onto these domains, but at most simulacra: artifacts of linguistic craft and intertextuality that form their own domains even when they bridge from image to history or from image to actual landscape. The epiphany that Henry Thoreau reports having had at the top of Mount Katahdin in *The Maine Woods* may reflect an actual mystical experience, but we are justified in reading it as such only if we also understand the experiential element as having been filtered through the vocabulary of the romantic sublime.

2. U.S. environmental imagination is hardly homogeneous. Shift focus, for example, from Euro-American settler culture to contention among different subcultures, and innumerable lines of division open up. From a traditional indigenous perspective, "wilderness" and "America" are factitious categories. Traditional native spirituality is monistic, Euro-settler cultures' traditions of spirituality predominantly dualistic. For native cultures, sacred space tends to be both more territorialized and more comprehensively spread out within the home range. Places held sacred by Native Americans have often been settler targets of exploitation. What looks like an empty landscape to settlers may seem symbolically dense and meaningful to indigenes, as anthropologist Keith Basso shows with respect to the rich tangle of place-specific stories underlying the toponymy of the western Apache.[8] Creatures held sacred by native peoples have often seemed varmints to settlers: crow, raven, coyote, wolf.

Cutting across such dichotomies is much criss-crossing and hybridization. In her novel *Ceremony,* which concerns the return of a World War II–traumatized Native American veteran to his home Pueblo in west-central New Mexico, Laguna writer Leslie Silko borrows from T. S.

---

8. Keith Basso, *Wisdom Sits in Places: Landscape and Language among the Western Apache* (Albuquerque: University of New Mexico Press, 1996). In reciting these broad-brushstoke distinctions between "settler" and "native" perspectives I do not mean to deny the force of such critiques of romantic otherization of natives by settlers as Shepard Krech III's *The Ecological Indian: Myth and History* (New York: Norton, 1999), particularly — as noted below — the history of intercultural contact and hybridization.

Eliot's *The Waste Land* and its anthropological pre-text, Jessie Weston's *From Ritual to Romance,* to develop her own postwar narrative of redemption of land from a drought to a fertility that is spiritual as well as literal. Her protagonist Tayo is named after a minor figure in Laguna legend, but he is also the Fisher King of Eliot and Weston.[9] Conversely, anthropologist-turned-nature-writer Richard Nelson draws on his twenty years of field ethnography among the Koyukon in the Alaska panhandle for the personal narrative of *The Island Within,* a quest to nativize himself insofar as possible.[10] Without the dream of hybridization operating from the settler side, James Fenimore Cooper could never have invented the most original fictive character in all of U.S. settler culture history: Natty Bumppo, the Leatherstocking, who has a foot in each world. And if we believe anthropologist of religion Sam K. Gill, without a process of strategic adaptation operating from the native side, the figure of a personified Mother Earth would never have loomed so large in Native American imagination and cosmography since the mid-nineteenth century, when by Gill's account Native leaders began to realize that this personification had charismatic appeal for whites.[11]

So the claims of radical cultural difference can be as tendentious as claims of a unitary sort about American religio-environmental imagination. But the point still holds that right perception of American sacred space and sacred figures must start from the assumption of cultural contestedness playing against and/or within whatever seeming consensus. Thoughtful contemporary literary treatments of U.S. religio-environmental experience grasp that fact: for example, Gary Snyder's *The Practice of the Wild,* the most extended of his several attempts to imagine a bioregional ethic faithful to northern California multiculture; Barry Lopez's *Of Wolves and Men,* a meditation on comparative mythography and cultural valuation of wolves; and Chickasaw writer Linda Hogan's novel *Power,* about white and Indian confusion over what to do about a Native woman's freelance ritual mercy-killing of a sick Florida panther,

---

9. Leslie Marmon Silko, *Ceremony* (New York: Viking, 1977); Jessie Laidlay Weston, *From Ritual to Romance* (Cambridge: Cambridge University Press, 1920).

10. Richard Nelson, *The Island Within* (San Francisco: North Point, 1989).

11. Sam K. Gill, *Mother Earth: An American Story* (Chicago: University of Chicago Press, 1987).

which is protected both by Taiga law as a tribal totem and by national law as an endangered species.[12]

3. Whether we think of American culture holistically, or of differences arising from plurality of multicultures, we must recognize that our models of environmental imagination are less culture-specific and more transnational than we tend to suppose. Jurisdictional borders do not neatly correspond to environmental borders. Sometimes they do, as with the island nation of Iceland, where indeed the human gene pool has stayed remarkably constant for centuries. But much more often they do not. There is no defensible *ecological* reason for the border between the U.S. and Mexico, or for most of the U.S.-Canada border, either.

Granted, official borders can also become environmental borders. Difference in prosperity and in environmental regulation make the U.S.-Mexico border look much more distinct from the air today than it did when the airplane was invented a century ago. But such produced contrasts have been largely offset by cross-border migration. Joseph Nye, international politics expert and long-time Dean of Harvard's Kennedy School of Government, rightly remarks that "the oldest form of globalization is environmental interdependence," and that such interdependencies have dramatically accelerated in modern times.[13] Nye refers specifically to epidemics, and how their spread has accelerated. Smallpox took three thousand years to spread worldwide, but AIDS has taken less than half a century; and it has only taken a decade for something like a global discourse of AIDS awareness to override widespread nationalist denials. The dissemination of food crops and domestic animals is another striking case. The importation of the horse to the Americas from the Iberian Peninsula in the 1500s has created analogous transnational cowboy cul-

12. Gary Snyder, *The Practice of the Wild: Essays* (San Francisco: North Point, 1990); Barry Lopez, *Of Wolves and Men* (New York: Scribner, 1978); Linda Hogan, *Power* (New York: Norton, 1998). This point about cultural contestedness could be ramified much further by taking note of such things as the array of different religiocentric persuasions among Euro-settler groups more or less identified with specific territories, like the Amish; the full range of disparate U.S. minority cultures, some much more territorially based than others; and the disparity, central to Hogan's novel, for instance, between individual faith position and one's cultural or group position.

13. Joseph Nye, Jr., *The Paradox of American Power: Why the World's Only Superpower Can't Go It Alone* (New York: Oxford University Press, 2002), p. 82.

tures — and cowboy lore — that stretches from Patagonia to southern Alberta. So too with dissemination of environmental values. Parallel practices of wilderness protection loosely unite the various Anglophone settler countries, as historian Thomas Dunlap shows.[14]

Whenever I teach Willa Cather's novel *O Pioneers!* I make a point of trying to get students to think about the paradox that land-wisdom here ironically correlates with cultural maladaptiveness. The book's most landwise character, the heroine's sometime-mentor old Ivar, is such because he is more attuned than anyone else in this prairie enclave to the rhythms of Norwegian peasant life and folk spirituality. It is easy and understandable to fault Cather for sounding as if she shared the immigrants' disregard for the very recent presence of the Native American dispensation, for the mistake of assuming a still-living culture was dead and indeed sometimes (in other works especially) positively seeming to prefer it that way, as by making the extinct cliff-dwellers of Mesa Verde her preferred reference point for fictionalizing the indigenous dispensation of North America. But it is also important to credit Cather's insight that "native" elements cannot be cleanly separated from imported elements in American mystiques of the land. Immigrant groups from Winthrop's Puritans to Cather's Scandinavians on down to the present have brought such traditions with them. Native American writers, conversely, also regularly draw on imported traditions of religio-environmental imagination, as in Silko's *Ceremony*.

It is a strange and unnecessary irony, therefore, that the seminal precontemporary accounts of American and British pastoral, Leo Marx's *Machine in the Garden* and Raymond Williams's *The Country and the City*, are so rarely paired. Williams seemingly had no interest at all in American imagination of environment, as Marx found to his disappointment during a residency at the University of Cambridge, even though Williams's last chapter develops the thesis that England's colonies have been regularly imaged as a sort of pastoral locale from the standpoint of the

---

14. Jared Diamond, *Guns, Germs, and Steel: The Fates of Human Societies* (New York: Norton, 1997); Richard Slatta, *Cowboys of the Americas* (New Haven: Yale University Press, 1994); Thomas Dunlap, *Nature and the English Diaspora: Environment and History in the United States, Canada, Australia, and New Zealand* (Cambridge: Cambridge University Press, 1999).

imperial center.[15] Marx, for his part, despite — or perhaps in part because of — his exegesis of Shakespeare's *The Tempest* as a New World pastoral fable, seems not to have cared about the ways in which U.S. pastoral imagination reinvented British identification of Englishness with ruralness. Yet the fact is that pastoral nationalism is distinctly *multinational*. To generalize still more broadly, England, Scotland, Germany, Russia, Japan, China; the major Anglophone settler cultures; a number of Latin American creole cultures and sub-Saharan African cultures — all manifest tendencies of one sort or other to essentialize culture and/or nation with countrified exurban space.[16] Nor is this practice confined to literature alone. Music is an equally striking case: Grieg, Sibelius, Smetana, Dvorak, Copland.

So the challenge of specifying what makes cultural practice in the U.S. distinctive — pastoral tradition, mystique of land or nature or wilderness — is tricky if not quixotic. Almost always it can be shown about this or that claim that one is really talking about variation on a widely manifested trope. Likewise, in order to understand how creative writing about environment might be understood as religious experience, it often if not always makes best sense to think in terms of broad patterns of western or nonwestern theology rather than simply in terms of national units.[17]

4. Up to this point I've been referring to environment as if the term

15. Raymond Williams, *The Country and the City* (New York: Oxford University Press, 1973).

16. This point I develop further — although it deserves further development than I have given it — in *The Environmental Imagination: Thoreau, Nature Writing, and the Formation of American Culture* (Cambridge: Belknap Press of Harvard University Press, 1995), pp. 53-68. Obviously, as both Marx and (especially) Williams point out, urban space can also be thought of as nationally quintessential, as in identifications of Britain with London or the U.S. with New York, Chicago, and Los Angeles.

17. For example, Douglas Burton-Christie's essays on the spirituality in nature writing focus wholly on American texts but wholly as theological rather than as national or cultural acts of imagination: "'A Feeling for the Natural World': Spirituality and Contemporary Nature Writing," *Continuum* 2 (1993): 154-80; "Mapping the Sacred Landscape: Spirituality and the Contemporary Literature of Nature," *Horizon* 21 (1994): 22-47; "Living between Two Worlds: Home, Journey and the Quest for Sacred Place," *Anglican Theological Review* 79 (1997): 413-32.

simply referred to the nonhuman domain. That's far too reductive. Even if you believe that certain natural environments are physiographically better candidates for sacred space than built environments (a contested point thoughtfully adjudicated by Belden Lane in his *Landscapes of the Sacred*), there is always an element of cultural construction involved in designating them as such.[18] Mount Taylor in western New Mexico is a sacred mountain not just because certain kinds of vertically protuberant land forms worldwide tend to be sacralized, but also — and more decisively — because Pueblo, Navajo, Hopi, and Zuni ethnoreligious imagination made it so. Much if not most sacred space in the U.S. and elsewhere is reckoned such because of events of human history. Such is most obviously the case with formally consecrated space like church buildings and cemeteries. But it holds also for secular monuments like the Statue of Liberty, Revolutionary and Civil War battle grounds, and even for such technological marvels as the Brooklyn Bridge — which Hart Crane sanctifies in his epic poem, *The Bridge:* "Unto us lowliest sometime sweep, descend / And of the curveship lend a myth to God."[19] For many, Thoreau's Walden cabin-site, Aldo Leopold's Wisconsin shack, Jefferson's Monticello, even Frank Lloyd Wright's signature houses, such as Fallingwater, also count as sacred space. Even some intensely unaesthetic urban places: just off the Grand Concourse of the Bronx, a grotto was built in the mid-twentieth century to sanctify the apparition of the Virgin Mary to a nine-year-old Italian-American boy.[20]

At least as early as the rural cemetery movement of the early nineteenth century there has been a tendency to "naturalize" the sacred spaces of human engineering: the Mall in Washington, D.C.; the Revolutionary park at Valley Forge, Pennsylvania, that extends for acres upon acres of gently rolling countryside; Civil War cannonball parks like Gettysburg. In mini-form, we see this in many if not most of the thousands

18. Belden C. Lane, *Landscapes of the Sacred,* expanded ed. (Baltimore: Johns Hopkins University Press, 2001), pp. 42-61, thoughtfully adjudicates the underlying issue of whether the luminosity of places is at least sometimes inherent, or whether it is always only humanly ascribed, and by what cultural or phenomenological processes.

19. Hart Crane, "Proem: To Brooklyn Bridge," *The Bridge,* in *The Compete Poems of Hart Crane* (Garden City, N.Y.: Doubleday, 1958), p. 4.

20. John McGreevy, "Bronx Miracle," *American Quarterly* 52 (September 2000): 423-24.

of small-town monuments — north and south — to the Union or Confederate soldier, often located on or by a central square with a green space of some sort. Quiet spaciousness with greensward and tasteful planting makes for reverent meditation but also, increasingly it seems, for irony. Kent Gramm's autobiographical anti-pastoral meditation *Gettysburg*, for example, invokes the memory of Thoreau's *Walden* (with chapter titles like "Where They Fought, and What They Fought For"), but then turns pastoral against itself, repeatedly disowning its usual comforts and castigating it as an anesthetic playground for touristical consumerism: a protective buffer between present-day remembrance and the actual sweat and horror of war, and its heroism too.[21] Gramm's sense that pastoral charm can make for dubiously euphemized sacred space was obviously shared by Maya Lin when she designed the Vietnam Memorial, as well as by those today who want the site of the World Trade Center's fallen twin towers preserved in a stark way rather than neatened up.

Whether the American public at large will in the future opt increasingly for stark memorials of tragic events as against prettily landscaped ones I do not know. This much is sure, however. As the country becomes more populous and urbanized, and as the landmarks of both folk and canonical history proliferate, an increasingly greater proportion of sacred space is becoming artifactual space, even as wilderness protection and national park efforts have also moved ahead, however falteringly.

Not long ago I found myself in a small town about an hour north of my home, on Massachusetts' northeastern tip, not far from Plum Island, a coastal island that 300 years ago Samuel Sewall immortalized in one of the most gorgeous passages in all of Puritan rhetoric, in *Phaenomena Quaedam Apocalyptica* (1697):

> As long as Plum Island shall faithfully keep the commanded post, notwithstanding all the hectoring words and hard blows of the proud and boisterous ocean; as long as any salmon or sturgeon shall swim in the streams of the Merrimack; or any perch or pickerel in Crane Pond; as long as the sea-fowl shall know the time of their coming, and not neglect seasonably to visit the places of their acquaintance; as long as any

21. Kent Gramm, *Gettysburg: A Meditation on War and Values* (Bloomington: Indiana University Press, 1994).

cattle shall be fed with the grass growing in the meadows, which so humbly bow down themselves before Turkey Hill . . . as long as nature shall not grow old and dote, but shall constantly remember to give the rows of Indian corn their education, by pairs: So long shall Christians be born there; and being first made meet, shall from thence be translated, to be made partakers of the inheritance of the saints in light.[22]

As I recalled this enchanting paean to Puritan agrarian fulfillment in the Lord's garden, I thought also of T. S. Eliot's early twentieth-century image in "The Dry Salvages" of "the sound of the sea bell's / Perpetual angelus," which sacralizes the bell-buoys of Cape Ann in a naturalizing way that mingles the mechanical sound with the roll of the waters.[23] The immediate cause of my remembering these things, however, was the jolting effect of the quite different image, right in front of me, in the most banal-looking strip mall one could imagine, of a sign that read "Bible Church." Dry cleaners on the one-hand, real estate office on the other. Yet this too was American sacred space, space staked out by some homegrown Protestant splinter sect ten generations removed from seventeenth-century Puritanism.

Such is the way U.S. history will surely continue to tend. More and more of our poets who feel moved to sacralize physical environment will be moved to imagine big secular urban public buildings as Langston Hughes did Penn Station in New York, "like some vast basilica of old / That towers above the terror of the dark / As bulwark and protection to the soul," or an obscure random lamppost in Harlem with its light burned out as "the Cross — / The Cross itself / A lonely arm / Whose light is lost."[24]

Nor is this unequivocally a bad thing, whatever seems to be the loss of beauty in a recognizably traditional sense. Arguably everyone has an

22. Samuel Sewall, *Phaenomena Quaedam Apocalyptica*, in *The Puritans in America: A Narrative Anthology*, ed. Alan Heimert and Andrew Delbanco (Cambridge: Harvard University Press, 1985), pp. 292-93.

23. T. S. Eliot, *The Four Quartets*, in *The Complete Poems and Plays, 1909-1950* (New York: Harcourt, 1952), p. 135.

24. Langston Hughes, "Pennsylvania Station" and "Late Corner," in *The Collected Poems of Langston Hughes*, ed. Arnold Rampersad and David Roessel (New York: Knopf, 1994), pp. 159, 454.

interest in the reclamation of abused and despised landscapes as precious, even if not sacred. As environmentalist Wes Jackson puts it, "Harlem and East Saint Louis . . . and the rest of the world where wilderness has been destroyed must come to be loved by enough of us, or wilderness is doomed."[25] A counterpart vision is key to the environmental justice movement, which seeks to activate a sense of protective care for the inhabitants of abused, neglected, disadvantaged places: first of all, among the residents themselves, but then (no less crucially) among outside actors in a position to determine these communities' fates. Jackson rightly sees caring for place as a link across the urban-wilderness divide. One of the strategies on which environmental justice activism relies, in the tradition of Rachel Carson's introduction to *Silent Spring,* is neo-pastoral appeal to an iconic peaceable-kingdom type image of the quiet, clean, safe, and pleasant small rural or suburban community that the now-endangered community (so it is argued) once was, inherently is, and by all rights should be allowed to be.[26] Not that there was in fact anything very pristine about the Love Canal subdivision of the city of Niagara Falls, originally built on an incompletely remediated waste dump — to name the case perhaps most often cited as the environmental justice movement's takeoff point around 1980. But the underlying cultural logic is not unique or strange. The appeal to a sense of pastoral betrayal is a contemporary update and activist mobilization of the pastoral "escalator" effect Raymond Williams sees at work in British cultural memory: each age conceiving itself as a declension from an earlier generation that was somehow closer to nature.[27]

5. The foregoing remarks about environmental sacralization or desecration have focused on certain points or areas of space. This is *prima facie* the most logical way of thinking about religious imagination *vis-à-vis* the national, insofar as the national in the first instance is a territorial

25. Wes Jackson, *Becoming Native to This Place* (Lexington: University Press of Kentucky, 1994), p. 67.

26. Rachel Carson, *Silent Spring* (Boston: Houghton Mifflin, 1962).

27. Williams, *The Country and the City,* pp. 9-12. For more on the place of pastoralism in environmentalist rhetoric of toxification, see Lawrence Buell, *Writing for an Endangered World: Literature, Culture, and Environment in the U.S. and Beyond* (Cambridge: Belknap Press of Harvard University Press, 2001), pp. 35-45.

category.[28] Yet place is not the only aspect of environment about which religiously serious creative writers care, as I suggested earlier with regard to the practice of symbolizing regional or national identity through animals or other nonhumans. Take this pair of contemporary writers: Wendell Berry and Barry Lopez — one intensely lococentric, the other migratory. Berry perfectly fits the correlation between American religio-environmentalism and sacred space, while Lopez does not, as we see from a glimpse at Berry's essay "The Making of a Marginal Farm" and Lopez's essay "Renegotiating the Contracts."[29]

Berry recalls the personal commitment that has inspired his life's work as a writer: he and his wife's return to his Kentucky home ground to buy and restore a down-at-the-heel farm. Like Thoreau, the Berrys move into their homestead on Independence Day; unlike Thoreau, they stay there in order to dedicate themselves to a lifelong reclamation project that Berry deems both a culturally representative act and a sacred duty. "Land like ours," he writes, "and there are many such acres of land in this country," requires "a devotion more particular and disciplined than patriotism, and by ceaseless watchfulness and care."[30] Never in our time has there been a more dramatic example of a creative writer basing his whole vocation both as a writer and a citizen on pious reenactment, within the context of a strong and explicit Protestant faith commitment, of the side of Jeffersonianism that fits within the broader, longer tradition of voluntary simplicity that historian David Shi traces within U.S. settler culture from early Puritan and Quaker origins down to the present.[31]

Not so Lopez. The country of his imagination is almost always else-

---

28. This point is not uncontested, however. See Homi Bhabha's critique of Benedict Anderson's insistence on borders as key to imagined nationness, "DissemiNation: Time, Narrative, and the Margins of the Modern Nation," in *Nation and Narration,* ed. Bhabha (London: Routledge, 1990), pp. 308-11.

29. Wendell Berry, "The Making of a Marginal Farm," in *Recollected Essays, 1965-1980* (Berkeley: North Point, 1981); Barry Lopez, "Renegotiating the Contracts," in *Parabola* 8 (Spring 1983), both conveniently reprinted in Thomas J. Lyon, ed., *This Incomperable Lande: A Book of American Nature Writing* (Boston: Houghton, 1989), pp. 356-65 and 381-88 respectively.

30. Berry, "The Making of a Marginal Farm," p. 363.

31. David Shi, *The Simple Life: Plain Living and Right Thinking in American Culture* (New York: Oxford University Press, 1985).

where. Perhaps his Catholic spirituality, less overt than Berry's religiosity but no less pervasive, helps explain his partiality to sojourning as against dwelling. One of Lopez's most persistent ethico-spiritual environmental commitments is succinctly framed in his essay "Renegotiating the Contracts": North American settler culture's disrespect for nonhumans. "Our relationships with wild animals," he writes, "were once contractual — principled agreements, established and maintained in a spirit of reciprocity and mythic in their pervasiveness."[32] We have lost our understanding of how other animals have their own independent cultures, too; and of how basic human needs include the ability to interact with animals as more than varmints, prey, or data-yielding machines. For Lopez, the environmental values gap most in need of address is not between stewardship and commodification of land, but instead between aggressive anthropocentricism and the species relativism that he associates, however romantically, with indigenous thought and its greater ethos, as he takes it, of interspecies respect.

In teaching American environmental writing, which always involves discussing ethics and spirituality too, I often pose the question of which should be one's first task: to commit yourself to a place, or to wean yourself from anthropocentric centripetalism? Most students immediately grasp that this needn't be an either/or, nor need the answer be the same for everyone — but also that the two priorities can easily clash. Berry the sturdy farmer-poet and conservative Protestant Christian has no time for species egalitarianism, whereas Lopez the lapsed Catholic sojourner generally wants to keep roaming, respectful though he is of land-based peoples' wisdom. For Berry the American environmental icon is place-centered, whereas for Lopez it is a life form: a seal, a whale, a polar bear, a wolf.

6. The contrast I have just drawn points toward a more fundamental and intractable fissiparousness within U.S. religio-environmental aestheticism, owing to the sheer diversity of environmental(ist) orientations that U.S. literary history offers up. Come what may, even if we grant literature (as some would not) the capacity for accomplishing at least a mediated mimesis of environment, even if we posit (as some would not) that

---

32. Barry Lopez, "Renegotiating the Contracts," p. 383.

a remarkable number of U.S. writers drawn to environmental representation manifest an incipiently religious bent, the four signifiers — religion, literature, environment, America — can never converge if only because works of literary imagination are by definition more or less idiosyncratic. This holds even for relatively stereotyped genres, like captivity and slave narratives. Among (for example) the narratives of Frederick Douglass, Harriet Jacobs, and Solomon Northup the engagement of the human with physical environment varies enormously. For example, Northup (through his amanuensis) evokes the presence of southern landscape — its challenges, terrors, and occasional consolations — with much greater fullness than the other two. The further we probe, especially into the intricacies of our subtlest writers like Henry James and William Faulkner, the more remote we seem to get from unitary generalizations about the relation between our four signifiers.

Consider the climactic scene in Book 11 of James's *The Ambassadors,* when Lambert Strether takes his fateful excursion into the French countryside, where by a complete accident he finds Chad Newsome and Madame de Vionnet in the middle of a tryst that finally forces upon him the traumatic realization that their relation must have been sexual all along — as everybody else close to him has long known. Strether has sallied forth in search of the model French landscape pictured in his mind's eye from the memory "of a certain small Lambinet that had charmed him, long before" at the "sky-lighted inner shrine" of a Boston art dealer's.[33] What he finds when he immerses himself in the real thing first indulges, then shatters, his penchant for investing his environment with an old-fashioned holistic idealizing Barbizon-school haze. His experience of awakening from Elysium would have been traumatic in any case, given his willful blindness to the affair; but it is made all the more so by the prior activation of religio-aesthetic hypersensitivity by a particular kind of landscape felt to be culturally iconic according to Strether's quaint Yankee view of the case. It has been activated by the peculiar convergence of our four domains of signification: physical environment (the sense of being in physical contact with a particular rustic physiography);

---

33. Henry James, *The Ambassadors: An Authoritative Text, the Author on the Novel, Criticism,* ed. S. P. Rosenbaum (New York: Norton, 1994), p. 303.

religion (the religion of art, at any rate, conducive of an incipient sense of the holy inherent in both the sites visited and the experience of relating to them); imagination (Lambinet's nostalgic luminosity augmented by Strether's own aesthetic sensibility, his proto-Jamesian impressionism), America (the cultural logic of his genteel-provincial vision that in itself — to this would-be man of culture — suffuses French landscape with a sense of the iconic). But the convergence is so peculiarly, so distinctly Jamesean that it is hard to imagine another writer, except possibly Edith Wharton, having the wit or good fortune to concoct it.

## The Open Question of Hope

Fortunately we are not left with nothing more than a morass of particularities. At least two conclusions can be drawn that bring our signifiers back toward alignment, at least to a degree.

First, American environmental concern not only has been but also, I think, will likely continue to be energized by religious insights and commitment, however discrepantly and with whatever degree of post-religious secularizing torque, as in James's *The Ambassadors*. Strategic reasons alone suggest the likelihood of the persistence of strong imaginative appeals more overtly "religious" than James's. In *Caring for Creation*, environmental philosopher Max Oelschlaeger argues that religion is the single likeliest venue for generating an environmental counterculture in the U.S. today because it is "the only form of discourse widely available to Americans (through the institution of the church) that expresses social interests going beyond the private interests articulated through economic discourse and institutionalized in the market."[34] Although limiting the field of vision to "the institution of the church" seems far too restrictive to me, Oelschlaeger's basic point is well taken, and not just for the United States. The arena of religious thought and practice, however one defines "the religious," *is* certainly an arena where individuals are likely to try, at least during those times they feel

34. Max Oelschlaeger, *Caring for Creation: An Ecumenical Approach to the Environmental Crisis* (New Haven: Yale University Press, 1994), p. 11.

the spirit, to step aside from narrow self-interest, measure that against some ideal standard, and — at least sometimes — adjust their behavior accordingly. Even the most repulsive and frightening examples of religious zealotry, such as the carnage of September 11, 2001, suggest that this is so. Contemporary secularized academics, which comprise a high fraction of literary scholars, chronically underestimate the life-changing potential of the religious in individual lives.

Neither coincidence nor fashion, then, begin to explain the fact that within all the world's major religious traditions today we find green reform movements in theology, scriptural exegesis, and critical interpretation that seek to retrieve lost templates — and in some instances, even to invent new ones. In contemporary American Catholicism, the creation spirituality of Father Thomas Berry is an example of the first kind. An instance of the second is the ecofeminist Protestantism of Sallie McFague, who has argued for remetaphorization of the divine in terms like Mother, Lover, Friend that recognize God as "physical as well as spiritual" and "God's body" as "the entire organic complex of which we are a part."[35] A goodly sample of such revisionary work appears in the ten-volume Harvard Religion and Ecology series edited by Mary Evelyn Tucker and John Grim, based on a series of conferences at the Divinity School, that includes volumes on all the world's "great" religions as well as on indigenous and neopagan spirituality.

Eco-theological revisionism is not just a matter of environmentalist strategy. Underlying it is the recognition that environmentalism itself is, or at least entails, a faith commitment — a commitment, furthermore, that presupposes a challenge of reenvisioning, to which end the work of creative imagination is no less central than the work of exegesis or formal argument. Hence the importance McFague attaches to metaphor. Hence, too, the frequency with which contemporary environmental writing of a wholly secular kind has felt moved to resort to religious or quasi-religious modes of appeal.

Take for example Aldo Leopold's concepts of "biotic right" and "eco-

---

35. Thomas Berry, *The Dream of the Earth* (San Francisco: Sierra, 1988); Sallie McFague, *Models of God: Theology for an Ecological, Nuclear Age* (Philadelphia: Fortress, 1987), p. 112.

logical conscience," which enlist scientific ecology in the service of an environmental ethics that amounts to a secularized extension of Judeo-Christian stewardship tradition, holding up the survival of individual life forms and of ecosystems as its ideal.[36] Likewise Rachel Carson's attempt, concurrent with *Silent Spring,* to argue for the importance of a "sense of wonder" toward the natural world. "Those who contemplate the beauty of the earth," Carson writes, "find reserves of strength that will endure as long as life exists." This is because the "affinity of the human spirit for the earth and its beauties is deeply rooted," rooted mystically *because* also rooted biologically. "Our origins are of the earth"; human "protoplasm is built of the same elements as air, water, and rock." According to this logic, it is actually as well as metaphorically true that destruction of natural beauty is spiritual suicide.[37] Carson here looks forward both to the deep ecology movement of the 1970s and after, in which the spiritual dimension of this evolutionary bio-logic is more outspokenly stressed, and to the biophilia theory of E. O. Wilson and others, which defines the religious in entirely material, evolutionary-genetic terms but nonetheless feels compelled to draw on religion to make its case. "People need a sacred narrative," Wilson candidly declares in *Consilience.*[38] Even self-professed atheist Edward Abbey likens himself in *Desert Solitaire* to the desert fathers of the early Christian era and holds up the transformative power of peak experiences during his wilderness sojourn as key to its meaning for him.

Cases like these suggest that however much religion is repressed or theorized out of existence by western intellectual discourse, its resources will still be needed and called upon not just to dramatize but also to conceptualize humankind's relation to the nonhuman.

---

36. Aldo Leopold, *A Sand County Almanac* (New York: Oxford University Press, 1949), pp. 209-26; Leopold, "The Ecological Conscience" (1947), in *The River of the Mother of God and Other Essays,* ed. Susan L. Flader and J. Baird Callicott (Madison: University of Wisconsin Press, 1991), pp. 338-46.

37. Rachel Carson, *The Sense of Wonder* (New York: Harper, 1956), p. 88; Carson, "The Real World around Us," in *Lost Woods: The Discovered Writings of Rachel Carson* (Boston: Beacon, 1998), p. 160.

38. Edward O. Wilson, *Consilience: The Unity of Knowledge* (New York: Knopf, 1998), p. 289.

But is the converse also true? Does religion need environment? Here the situation seems considerably less clear. In some traditions, religion yearns for emplacement and embodiment, but in others it yearns at least as much for *dis*embodiment. As ecotheologian Douglas Burton-Christie remarks, biblical tradition recognizes the possibility of places becoming suffused and sanctified as sites of a community's "experience with God," but it also "expresses an indifference or even hostility toward place."[39] The Protestant Christianity that in its manifold forms so far has exercised the greatest influence within U.S. settler culture traditions has a strong anagogic thrust that sets life to come over life that is, sets spirit above body. In the event of rapture, this car will be unoccupied. That is probably not how most contemporary Protestants, evangelicals included, think and behave on a daily basis for the most part. Still, in-principle devaluation of the earthly cannot help but attenuate an environmentalist commitment to the here and now in proportion to the degree one turns one's sights to the new heaven and the new earth to come.[40]

I recall deriving immense comfort as a boy from the King James version of the 121st Psalm: "I lift mine eyes unto the hills, from whence cometh my help. My help cometh from the Lord," and so forth. It felt immensely comforting to imagine a pantheistic God speaking to me in and through the landscape God had made. How disillusioning it was to be told this was a mistranslation: that those hills were meant to signify the very opposite, that they were pagan altar-places the true believer was supposed to shun. Know that thy help comes from the unseen transcendent, not from the earth that felt much more my own proper home, despite my also knowing full well how fickle and frightening physical nature sometimes was. The premillennialist warnings of Jehovah's Witnesses, which take environmental apocalypse as an inevitable part of the divine plan, express this mentality in its starkest form.

I question, then, whether contemporary green theology is likely in and of itself to close the gap between the core concerns of environmentalists and the core religious beliefs of average Americans, who according

39. Burton-Christie, "Living between Two Worlds," p. 422.

40. Certainly there are exceptions to this paragraph's generalizations, such as Martin Luther's assertion that if he knew the world was to end the next day he would plant a tree (Grant Wacker, commentary to the lecture version of this paper).

to all the polls have a much more supernatural and theocentric cast than is true for any other modernized country in the world today. Perhaps this is a point at which the country's believers of whatever stripe, liberal or evangelical, might do well to take instruction from its creative writers. Backsliders and reprobates though they usually seem from an orthodox religious standpoint, their styles of environmental imagination are so often suffused and animated to a remarkable degree by a sense of the religious. Berry, Lopez, Snyder, Hogan, Silko; Annie Dillard, Mary Oliver, Robert Hass, Jorie Graham, Karen Tei Yamashita, Terry Tempest Williams, Gretel Ehrlich, W. S. Merwin, Octavia Butler, Ursula Le Guin — hardly a complete list, but enough to make the point. Since the romantic movement if not before, and certainly still today, the fate of the earth has ironically been a more conspicuous animating spiritual concern for American writers than for American religion.

This disparity is perhaps diagnosable historically as an after-effect of the intellectual embrace of nature in the post-Enlightenment as a corrective to or substitute for theocentric religion. Emerson the minister becomes Emerson the poet. "The priest departs, the divine literatus comes," as Walt Whitman grandly put it.[41] That was admittedly pouring it on a bit thick. Literati are too wayward to be trusted as spiritual lawgivers. But by taking that turn toward free-lance religio-environmental questing, early national writers showed better prophetic intuition than the churches did — and mostly still do — of what may well become the most intractable crisis of religious and ethical values in the twenty-first century. In stating this, I do not mean to gloss over other pressing issues — the deplorable state of human rights, global economic inequality, internecine world conflict. But in those arenas the doctrines and secular institutional structures seem to be evolving to a degree less true — so it seems to me — of the great questions of environmental value, such as the responsibilities of individuals and societies for the earth's future, the requirements of environmental justice, the moral standing and rights of nonhuman beings, the degree to which environmental stewardship is indispensable to a theology or religious commitment worthy of the name. That such issues have been more earnestly and

<hr />

41. Walt Whitman, *Democratic Vistas, Prose Works 1892*, ed. Floyd Stovall (New York: New York University Press, 1964), 2:365.

longstandingly addressed by creative writers than by moral philosophers and the religious intelligentsia is symptomatic and disquieting. Since the space of encounter with the other creative arts also potentially fits Oelschlaeger's description of an arena where narrow self-interestedness can get suspended, the pervasiveness of religio-environmental themes in U.S. creative writing may be cause for hope. But just how much hope remains an open question.

# Afterword

*Andrew Delbanco*

"THE CHALLENGE of specifying what makes cultural practice in the
U.S. distinctive," writes Lawrence Buell in his contribution to
the present volume, ". . . is tricky if not quixotic." So it seems — especially now that international capital treats borders and nations as merely
bothersome checkpoints or taxing agencies to be evaded or ignored. In
our brave new "McWorld," as the sociologist Benjamin Barber calls it,
where linguistic, ethnic, and creedal differences conform less and less to
the territorial entities we call nations, it is fair to question the rationale
for singling out the literary culture of one nation — more precisely, that
segment of English-settled North America that became a nation some
two hundred thirty years ago — for yet another critical study.

The contributors to the present volume have an answer. They believe that a singular force helps to account for the special character of literary creation in America — namely, the force of religion. At least since
Tocqueville traveled to the United States in 1831, foreign visitors have
been struck by the extraordinary vitality of religion in a nation where, as
the legal scholar Noah Feldman puts it, "for the first time in history," a
government was "designed . . . with no established religion at all."
Tocqueville was amazed not only by the novelty of this arrangement but
by its paradoxical effect. Attributing the "peaceful ascendancy of religion" to the "complete separation of church and state," he recognized
that under the New World rule of established disestablishment, religion
had sprouted and taken root, while in the Old World state religion with-

ered on the vine. And since Tocqueville's day, the contrast has only grown sharper. I recall giving a talk not long ago on religion in the United States, after which an eminent Scottish historian remarked, with a quizzical cock of his head, that in his "country the churches are mostly bingo halls," drawing out the "ing" in bingo until it settled somewhere between a growl and a hiss. Here, I think, was a clue to the "tricky if not quixotic" search for American distinctiveness.

A second clue may be found in the variety of ways in which words such as "sacred" are used in this book. In his essay on Thoreau, John Gatta describes how Thoreau created a sense of the sacred by recovering a "spiritually archaic" relation to the universe. Buell, in his essay on environmentalist thought, employs the word "sacred" in what he calls a "highly elastic sense" to describe Aldo Leopold's shack in Wisconsin, Frank Lloyd Wright's "signature houses," Thomas Jefferson's neoclassical home in Virginia, as well as a memorial marking the spot where the Virgin Mary putatively appeared to a child near the Grand Concourse in the Bronx. These are broad definitions. Their breadth is all the more striking if one considers that in other parts of the world the category of the sacred is reserved for a few highly charged sites such as the Yasukuni shrine or the Dome of the Rock or the Temple Mount — places where the solvent of collective memory dissolves all distinctions between history and myth, where sectarian passion attaches itself to symbols on which depend the worshippers' sense of identity and, sometimes, the very possibility of meaning in life or death. If we consider the Shiite mosques in Iraq that have lately been turned into killing zones by suicide bombers, against, say, the gift shop at Graceland where tourists buy dolls manufactured in the image of King Elvis, one glimpses the difference between what "sacred" means in America and what it means elsewhere in the world. Americans have lost intensity, and, perhaps, integrity, in their relation to the sacred. But surely there is gain as well as loss, since piety rarely furnishes a motive in America for slaughtering the impious. Exceptions such as the Salem witchhunters or the abolitionist John Brown have tended to become admonitory symbols of fanaticism.

The present book amounts nevertheless to a collective portrait of some classic American writers who have struggled against attenuation in their sense of the sacred. These writers are individualistic, experimental, skeptical of institutional authority — in short, emphatically Protestant. Consider Gatta's description (he is paraphrasing Mircea Eliade) of the sacred according to Thoreau: any place "auspicious for experiencing some opening toward the transcendent." There is in this definition no hint of dogma, or of priestly mediation, or of the past as a chain of precedents that constitutes a tradition. Anyone who takes this definition seriously is left on her own to seek an "opening" into transcendence. The task of finding it is, moreover, indistinguishable from the act of making it. It is to be found or made in solitude or, at most, with the tutelary help of a master who leads by example. Yet for Thoreau, as for so many American writers (think of Emerson's remark that "nothing is at last sacred but the integrity of your own mind") there can finally be no master above or beyond one's own inner self.

In one way or another, each writer discussed in this book is contending with what Roger Lundin, in his essay on Emily Dickinson, calls the "historicity" of faith. He or she is living in the wake of Enlightenment rationalism, the higher criticism, and Darwinian science, and trying to come to terms with the depredations visited by human beings upon themselves (the carnage of the Civil War) and upon non-human nature (the industrial assault on the environment). To be sure, this buffeted protagonist recurs in different guise from essay to essay. But with the notable exception of Katherine Clay Bassard's essay on biblical authority in African American thought, relatively little attention is paid in this book to the process of "edification" in the root sense of that word — to church-building, that is, or, more broadly, to community-building through collective consent to divine authority as evinced in a divinely inspired text. To read through the essays assembled here is, instead, to keep company with solitary seekers in search of some metaphysical, or aesthetic or political, insight that promises a transformative experience comparable to what earlier theologians had called grace. In this sense, this is a book about post-religious writing. It is about writers who feel radically alone until and unless they apprehend an intimation of the consoling presence of the divine.

The scholars represented here are not without their divergences. But they have in common an almost devotional quality of critical sympathy. From Barbara Packer's account of how Emerson renewed his fading faith by making a new political commitment, to Gail McDonald's unexpected affiliation of Social Gospel reform with the modernist poetic project, there is great scrupulosity here in telling the experience of individuals under existential stress. Harold Bush's inquiry into Mark Twain's evolving sense of his own southernness gives us new insight into a man reckoning with a certain moral casualness by which he has become embarrassed and of which he is ultimately ashamed. Michael Colacurcio's account of Herman Melville amounts to a spiritual biography of a tormented soul for whom the fact of evil remains an outrage long after the hypothesis of a benevolent god has been abandoned or, at least, set aside. Mark Walhout's essay, organized around the problem of reconciling charity with sincerity, proposes a post-Christian model of the saint — a figure who is given a name (Milly Theale) by Henry James in his great novel of moral heroism, *The Wings of the Dove*. All these essays are about the pursuit of religious experience in a culture that makes the pursuit both possible and arduous. It is possible because there is no limiting prescription for how it may be achieved, and it is arduous because there is no authoritative doctrine to explain when, or if, the sought has been found.

This book is timely, if not overdue. As Lundin notes in his introduction, the past quarter century of American literary studies has been generally indifferent toward the subject of religion. Religion has become an "invisible domain" — a phrase he quotes from the late Jenny Franchot, a young scholar who wrote insightfully during her short career about both Protestant and Catholic themes in American literature. Perhaps the slide into invisibility that Franchot and a few others tried to reverse was an inevitable reaction to earlier scholars such as Perry Miller and Sacvan Bercovitch, who insisted that religious ideas were formative and even dispositive, and whose powerful paradigms (declension in the case of Miller; the secularization of millenarian ideas in the case of Bercovitch) virtually controlled American literary studies for several generations. Whatever the reasons, it is a conspicuous irony of contemporary academic life that at a time when religion has reasserted itself as the most consequential human phenomenon in the world, it has been largely dropped from serious inquiry in American English departments, where it tends to be treated as just another superseded ideology.

The present book can hardly be expected to redress the failure. Still, it is a salutary reminder of the centrality to our literature of a strong religious current that runs from the Puritan founders to such contemporary writers as John Updike and Marilynne Robinson. Lundin's title — *There Before Us* — is aptly borrowed from the contemporary poet Richard Wilbur, another writer who belongs squarely to the tradition expounded here. Wilbur's phrase conveys not quite a belief but a yearning to believe that the things of this world exist "before we look / Or fail to look; there to be seen or not / By us" — not in inert indifference to human sight, but in enduring self-sufficiency, awaiting recognition from human beings who may, if blessed with the spirit of discernment, recognize in them intimations of eternity.

There is much left unsaid and even untouched in the foregoing essays, especially concerning writers whose heritage or chosen commitments keep them or take them outside the Protestant fold. Yet it would be consonant with the spirit of these essays, and with the distinctive religious pluralism that evolved out of early American sectarianism, if this book were to serve as an overture to studies of Native American, Catholic, Jewish, Muslim, and other writers whose search for spiritual fulfillment diverges from yet carries forward the story adumbrated here. *There Before Us* is a welcome reminder of what Tocqueville asserted after completing his American tour, that "incredulity is an accident; faith is the only permanent state of mankind." With that insight in mind, there is reason to hope that the cumulative force of these essays — if properly received as partial in both senses of that word — may contribute to the recovery of a coherent if not exhaustive sense of the Americanness of American literature.

*New York City*
*August 2006*

# Index

# Index